Chasin' the Bird

Chasin' the Bird
The Life and Legacy of Charlie Parker

Brian Priestley

OXFORD
UNIVERSITY PRESS
2006

OXFORD
UNIVERSITY PRESS

Oxford University Press, Inc., publishes works that
further Oxford University's objective of excellence
in research, scholarship, and education.

Oxford New York
Auckland Cape Town Dar es Salaam Hong Kong Karachi
Kuala Lumpur Madrid Melbourne Mexico City Nairobi
New Delhi Shanghai Taipei Toronto

With offices in
Argentina Austria Brazil Chile Czech Republic France Greece
Guatemala Hungary Italy Japan Poland Portugal Singapore
South Korea Switzerland Thailand Turkey Ukraine Vietnam

First edition published under the title Charlie Parker in 1984 by Spellmount in
the UK and by Hippocrene Books in the USA. This revised and expanded edition
published by arrangement with Equinox Publishing Ltd., London, 2005.

Published by Oxford University Press, Inc.
198 Madison Avenue, New York, NY 10016
www.oup.com

Library of Congress Cataloging-in-Publication Data is available

Priestley, Brian, 1946–
Chasin' the bird: the life and legacy of Charlie Parker / Brian Priestley.
p. cm.
Includes bibliographical references and indexes.
ISBN-13: 978-0-19-530464-0
ISBN-10: 0-19-530464-0 (alk. paper)
1. Parker, Charlie, 1920-1955.
2. Jazz musicians--United States--Biography. I. Title.

ML419.P4P72 2006
788.7'3165092—dc22
[B}

2005054703

3 5 7 9 8 6 4 2
Typesetting by CA Typesetting, www.sheffieldtypesetting.com
Printed in the United States of America
on acid-free paper

contents

preface

It is always stimulating to write about a major artist such as Charlie Parker. That it is also challenging, and sometimes depressing, perhaps goes without saying. But this book has been a unique experience for me, initially because much of the work was done in new surroundings in a friendly but foreign land. The main claim to uniqueness, however, was that this project necessitated revisiting and expanding an earlier work, written at a very different time of my life.

The challenge seemed to be one of preserving whatever qualities the original had, notably concision, while adding incidental information (some of which has only come to light since the first version) and hopefully some increased insight. Other writers in such a situation might want to start from scratch, to improvise a new take, but might end up repeating themselves. My own leanings towards composition and arrangement (and the consequent quirk of not wanting to throw away anything) led me to preserve virtually all of my first text — except where it has since turned out to be inaccurate — and add new layers, more akin to overdubbing than improvising.

Whereas I thought this would prove difficult, it seemed surprisingly easy, once the typescript of my previously published text had been located. The real headache turned out to be that my notes were not retrievable, and that the original brief was for a short book, with no space allowed for notes or sources. So some of the quotations used the first time around seemed very unfamiliar, except in the context of my own publication. Help in tracing these has come from several individuals and, in addition, I have had the support and assistance of many people, some of whom I didn't even know personally back in 1984.

Without going on at length about their various kindnesses and efficiencies, I am grateful to: Chris Albertson, George Avakian, Philippe Baudouin, Roger Boyes, Frank Büchmann-Møller, Alan Cohen, Chris DeVito, Krin Gabbard, Mark Gardner, Dave Gelly, Gary Giddins, Ira Gitler, Maxine Gordon, Dennis Harrison (Wendover Bookshop), Geoffrey Haydon, Nat Hentoff, David Hill, Orrin Keepnews, Wolfram Krauer, Joan Malin,

David Meeker, Dan Morgenstern (Institute of Jazz Studies), David Nathan (National Jazz Archive), Lewis Porter, Peter Pullman, Peter Symes, Alain Tercinet, Thierry Trombert, Ken Vail, Malcolm Walker, Tony Williams, Val Wilmer and Carl Woideck. I am also indebted to Janet Joyce and Valerie Hall of Equinox Publishing, my editor Sarah Norman, my agent Barbara Levy and especially to Alyn Shipton, who first suggested the project. The whole thing would have proved impossible without the spirit of adventure and the supportiveness of my wife Yvette Shea.

A further source of stimulus over the last few years has been the teaching of groups of jazz history students. This not only made it mandatory for me to listen again to classic recordings (no great hardship, to be sure, yet often allowed insufficient time when journalism requires assessing the new rather than the old), and to focus on details worth highlighting and ways to describe them. All the above have been significant in bringing this book to the state in which you now find it, although any errors remain my own responsibility.

Brian Priestley
London, January 2005

acknowledgements

Another Hair-Do
Music by Charlie Parker
©1948, 1976 Atlantic Music Corp./Screen Gems-EMI Music Inc., USA
Screen Gems-EMI Music Ltd, London WC2H 0QY
Reproduced with permission of Atlantic Music Corp./International Music Publications
Ltd. All rights reserved.

Anthropology
Music by John Dizzy Gillespie and Charlie Parker
©1946, 1948 (Renewed) by Music Sales Corp. (ASCAP) and Atlantic Music Corp.
Reprinted with permission of Music Sales Limited and Atlantic Music Corp.
International copyright secured. All rights reserved.

Billie's Bounce
Music by Charlie Parker
©1945, 1973 Atlantic Music Corp./Screen Gems-EMI Music Inc., USA
Screen Gems-EMI Music Ltd, London WC2H 0QY
Reproduced with permission of Atlantic Music Corp./International Music Publications
Ltd. All rights reserved.

Cherokee (Indian Love Song)
Words and music by Ray Noble
©1938 Peter Maurice Music Co. Ltd, London WC2H 0QY
Reproduced with permission of International Music Publications Ltd. All rights reserved.
Copyright renewed and assigned to Shapiro, Bernstein & Co., Inc., New York for USA
and Canada
International copyright secured. All rights reserved.
Used with permission.

Embraceable You
Music and lyrics by George Gershwin and Ira Gershwin
©1930 Chappell & Co. Inc., USA
Warner Chappell Music Ltd, London W6 8BS
Reproduced with permission of International Music Publications Ltd. All rights reserved.

Hootie Blues
Words and music by Charlie Parker, Jay McShann and Walter Brown
©1941, 1963 MCA Music (a division of MCA Incorporated, USA)

introduction

Like the great majority of people who will read this book, I first became aware of Charlie Parker after his death. In my case, it was through his death that I gained my first awareness of his name. As a comparative novice, I had no idea of the connotations of either word in the title *Cool Blues*. But the sound of the record on the radio, and the surprising information that its creator had died at the age of thirty-four, made enough of an impact to outweigh my lack of understanding. Naturally, although the memory of that first hearing is still strong, any such encounter depends on the listener's previous listening (and reading), and it was an awfully long time before I was really able to appreciate Parker's importance as one of the most significant jazzmen ever.

These days, the diversity and the sheer amount of jazz has increased to such an extent that it is much more common to hear about the man before hearing any of his music. Perhaps a liking for a musical descendant of Parker such as saxophonists Dave Sanborn or Greg Osby, themselves now almost senior statesmen, will have been the vehicle for bringing Charlie's name to the attention, or the fact that later influential figures such as John Coltrane or Ornette Coleman are often discussed in terms of the enormous influence that Parker had on them. Equally, it may be that the iconography of musicians who died as a partial result of drug abuse – whether it be Jimi Hendrix or Jaco Pastorius, both hugely important in terms of their music rather than their lifestyle – is often linked to a list that begins in an earlier generation, with the names of Billie Holiday and Parker. Or it could just be the knowledge that the Weather Report tune *Birdland*, and its laudatory lyrics added later by Manhattan Transfer, was dedicated to the New York nightclub called after Charlie's nickname "Bird."

Whatever it is that sparks a listener's initial interest, the sad truth is that it may arouse expectations which are not entirely satisfied, or in some respects even deflated, by listening to his records. One reason for this is the sound quality of even his best studio recordings, which is often indifferent by today's audio standards. Another important factor is that, because of the fanatical interest of his contemporary fans, a far greater percentage of the surviving documentation has been taken from in-person recordings than with any other musician ever. And sadly, from a standpoint of the impact on potential new listeners, there are no efficient marketing regulations that insist on low-fidelity sound being identified as such. Though there are consumers rightly disillusioned by surface aspects of much of what is available, it's a fact that in any case they need to be sensitized to sound for its own sake in order to be impressed by Charlie Parker. It is also true that today's Western culture is more and more a visually oriented culture and, unfortunately, next to nothing is available of Bird on video, for the simple reason that African-American music had not entered the visual mainstream by the time of his death. There is precious little of Billie Holiday even, whereas another unique musician who died in the 1950s, Art Tatum, survives in just a few minutes' material where he can be seen as well as heard. So it is with Parker.

A final problem, which often stands in the way of appreciating what it is that he brought to the music, can easily be that so much of Parker's sound and style has entered the present-day language as to make the original seem old-hat, at least initially. To some extent, this mistaken perception is exacerbated by reverential treatment of the man and his music as a historic phenomenon. But it's striking that the changes in the music world and in society generally, while putting a distance between us and the first half of the twentieth century, in practice do little to detract from the impact of Parker. For some listeners, the dynamism and conviction of his recorded playing – even seen through the distorting prism of poor sound and the different values of today's society – can cut to the heart of the matter and evoke an immediate emotional recognition. For others, it has to be a gradual process of acquaintance with more recent figures such as Coltrane or Coleman, before the dawning awareness that Parker's music contained the seeds of so much that followed it. This, however, becomes blindingly obvious after such a listener has spent sufficient study on the altoist's own recordings to realize that he was light-years ahead of all but a handful of his contemporaries.

The purpose of this book is to make that fact clear, and also to relate his musical development to his private life. Such a relationship is never straightforward – not for any artist who produces anything memorable, that is. In the time when music was folk music, no one worried about the life of individual musicians. They were valued by their society because they dealt with the needs and thoughts of the society, rather than their own needs and thoughts. But the growth of individualism required artists who could express the demands and emotions of the individual. It is appropriate therefore and somehow inevitable that, already by the time of Mozart and Beethoven (with whom Parker is comparable in stature and influence), the process of creating music was being subtly distorted by the difficulties of earning a living thereby. At least in the mind of the artists themselves, the ability to concentrate only on the creation, while sailing unconcerned through life, is sometimes replaced by worries about financial survival with a consequent drain on the energy available for music. This in turn requires artists to pay at least a certain amount of attention to the state of their reputation, and whether it will be sufficient to justify the next commission, in the case of European composers, or to be hired for the next gig as a performer.

Of course, the circumstances under which creation takes place are normally masked by the sublime nature of music itself, and the dramatic contrast between the two is even more striking in the case of Parker, since he was an improviser by profession rather than a composer. The contrast is also marked in so far as many of Parker's difficulties were ones he brought on himself – indeed, although he came to resent the fact that his name was often associated with widespread notoriety rather than any positive reputation, there was clearly a side of him that loved to court danger. How far one can draw a parallel between this tendency and the taking of musical risks is debatable, but it is clear that he had a great curiosity about causes and effects. Some of the endlessly fascinating contradictions in his personality, of the kind that filled the first biographical book devoted to him (assembled by Robert Reisner), seem less like contradictions when viewed in this light. He was said to have told bandleader Jay McShann, "If you come on a band tense, you're going to play tense. If you come a little bit foolish, act just a little bit foolish, and let yourself go, better ideas will come." Various acts of self-centredness, often involving high-handedness towards others, can be seen as part of an ongoing research project into which acts produce which results. To suggest this is not to condone the effects on others or on himself, but to look for the motivational wellsprings of both personal interaction and musical investigation.

Music, even of an innovative nature, is not merely a matter of taking risks. In such a collective mode of expression as creating jazz, there are restraints and conventions that have to be acknowledged (by the listener as well as the performer) in order to appreciate what can be added. To this extent, it's crucial to recall that Parker spent so much time – once his interest was aroused – in learning to master his instrument and then, when that proved insufficient for acceptable improvised performance, learning all he could about the mechanics of harmonic and melodic development. The fact that more was probably absorbed through the ear than from the written page should not obscure the meticulous learning process, and the fact that much of this was done under his own steam (with occasional mentors) is sufficient testament to his determination and focus. Despite the debate as to how verbally articulate Parker was about musical details in discussing them with fellow players, the mere fact of listening to what he produced makes it crystal clear that he knew what he was doing – and, indeed, what everyone else in a band was doing simultaneously. The risk-taking occurred within a framework of absolute certainty as to the overall parameters of performance, and as to its moment-by-moment minutiae.

A further debate is sometimes heard, concerning Parker's intellectual grasp of the non-musical world. Although his mother claimed he was fond of reading, referring to his early teens, maybe she too described a brief period of intense absorption. His later consorts Doris and Chan clearly knew him during a period when reading was no longer necessary. But they and a host of other witnesses were impressed by Charlie's ability to converse in a coherent and thoughtful manner (without coming across as a mere magpie) on a huge variety of subjects. Therefore, in the same way that musicians attested to him possessing a photographic memory and omnivorous appetite for music (in addition to a phenomenal ear), he doubtless had a similar recall for things he read and heard, of a more factual or philosophical nature. The mental filing-system to access them at will may perhaps be compared to a library of harmonic relationships and melodic possibilities yet, as with the music, this was no mere archive but an active and dynamic resource that could be deployed and expanded in live interaction.

Of particular interest in assessing his comportment in the everyday world is the comment by Chan that "He studied the workings of people's minds and emotions, and was well aware of the feelings that others were experiencing. He realized that most people were concerned only with the impression they were making, and he capitalized on this." This clearly suggests that Parker, as well as possessing the intuition necessary for any such responsiveness and/or exploitation, had put in the study needed to become consciously aware of how he perceived others and how he might manipulate them. Doubtless, if asked, Doris too would have expressed herself in similar terms about this aspect of Charlie's behaviour – and indeed about the other side of the coin, as noted by Chan: "But Bird was always able to keep his personal self private. The displays he put on were always because of the circumstances and not because of his feelings or thoughts." This observation, in turn, underlines the defensive nature of such an attitude to others, and reminds us that, in addition to possible justifications connected to his family and upbringing, there were clear reasons why Parker would have shared many experiences and reactions common to most African-Americans who grew up during the Depression.

Over and above this, he was also a thinker. The testimony in Reisner's book from Julie McDonald, a sculptor to whom Charlie opened his heart on more than one occasion, includes the following statements: "He rejected the Church. At one time, around 1953, he tried Yoga. He was interested in extrasensory perception, the theory of past lives, mysticism... I think he had a grand disregard of law and courts, most probably stemming from the miscarriages of justice towards the Negro." The last phrase is not hard to believe, but he also attempted to disregard the musicians' union and certainly had a great ambivalence concerning the business side of music. This feeling was only partly caused by injustice towards blacks, or even towards the totality of musicians (of whatever colour) who played this historically black music. There is a pervading sense in several of the anecdotes about Parker that he was concerned for the underdog generally and, though he may have made some exceptions, he was likely to have less sympathy for managements than for employees. He was initially impressed by his producers, such as Ross Russell or Norman Granz, but it didn't take long for him to feel that they were acting against his interests. When, near the end of his career, he was under contract to a booking agency he described as his "judges," he referred not only to a foreign-language movie that he had seen but to the perverted exercise of justice in society generally.

The last part of his career was, of course, the period that put him most directly in touch with feelings of failure and injustice. It is instructive that another visual artist, Harvey Cropper, introduced a Parker anecdote from this period with the words "Poverty and want angered him." Given that his own statements were totally apolitical, one might question whether Parker's anger was caused by the feeling that society should make a better job of looking after its citizens, or whether he bought into the American myth that anyone could raise themselves up by the bootstraps. Certainly, by this time, he was aware and open about the fact that such success as he had experienced was totally compromised by his own actions. In January 1955 he said of an audience waiting to hear him, "They just came to see the world's most famous junky," identifying the same prurient interest that was felt at times by Billie Holiday (and by Judy Garland, Edith Piaf and others). However, as well as the damage to his reputation, he was also aware of the effect upon his actual playing – and the comparative effects on it of chemicals and liquor. Five years after Parker's death, Dizzy Gillespie referred to this disparity as follows:

> I've seen a well-known musician under the influence of narcotics – I know he was high because he was nodding, and you'd wake him up and he'd start playing and just play, play, play, play, play – and I've seen the same musician under the influence of alcohol and I had to call him off, and say, "Look, think about all your fans out there."

One may ask if there is such a thing as an addictive personality type, and what its relationship would be to the artistic temperament. But, if psychological speculation is the name of the game, it would be just as pertinent to point to the socio-historic factors that made twentieth-century African-American society so matriarchal, and to query the effect of Parker's idealization by his mother on the potentially addictive-artistic male offspring.

It is hard to overestimate the long-term effects of drug abuse, including of course its debilitating financial consequences. And yet this was so prevalent at one time in the jazz world that, as well as a number of fatal victims, we can also find numerous examples of individuals (Miles Davis, Stan Getz, Sonny Rollins and John Coltrane among them) sufficiently strong-minded to have decided after a period of addiction to shun any further involvement. What is noticeable, though, is that all the musicians in the latter category took up hard drugs knowingly in their early twenties or even later, whereas Charlie (like so many youngsters today) became a user while still a teenager and without a knowledge of its eventual effects. The fact that he was an addict waiting to happen was noted by Doris Parker, undoubtedly quoting the saxophonist himself: "Charlie had no childhood whatsoever... His kind of fun at fourteen was going on benzedrine parties with his friends." It is worth noting in passing that both Doris and Chan referred to periods in his adulthood when – whether because of financial or societal pressures – Charlie was able to wean himself off his preferred substances without any other substitute than alcohol. Granted that both of them may have been deluding themselves at times, a physical constitution that was strong enough to withstand the amount of stuff he did take could also have been strong enough to take the shock of withdrawal. However, the mental control required was not only colossal but, unfortunately, very intermittent.

As to why he should have been such a willing victim, the same egotistical drive which enabled him to master the basics of his playing style so rapidly was merely the reverse side of a coin inscribed: "I am the great Charlie Parker, and I can do anything I want and get away with it." Because he appeared to do just that for a while, he became a hero to many white intellectuals and, of course, to fellow blacks who would have loved to beat the "system." He himself, however, was too aware intellectually to be other than pessimistic about American society, as Kenny Dorham among others pointed out: "His thing was like he'd just get high and blank that other part out. I guess he saw it wasn't going to get together in his lifetime." On the other hand, like so many Americans before and since, he also hoped that the "star" system would work to his benefit. His work with a string section brought him more widespread popularity yet, when the limitations of the format became clear, he blamed others. "He had a great resentment of white management and dictatorship," said Mercer Ellington, although interestingly Parker seldom spoke in that vein to whites. Even with those he trusted, he preferred to brush the subject aside, which is in strong contrast to the approach of some other musicians of his generation such as Max Roach and Charles Mingus. They, however, only became fairly vocal because of the gradual change of climate from the mid-1950s onwards, whereas Parker died in 1955.

Whether the idea of thinking in terms of solidarity with others would have come easily is open to doubt. He knew it was his own personality – rather than the responsibility towards his art which he also felt – that condemned him to be a loner, saying to a friend, "I don't let anyone get close to me. Even you. Or my wife." And he justified the expenditure required by his extravagant needs, with the words: "If I saved my money, the wives would take it away from me." The inevitable, cynical, but also painful conclusion was drawn in the comment to his subsequent biographer Robert Reisner, "Bread is your only friend." Yet the same people who recognized the perversity of his personality also realized what a positive force his music was. Mingus, for instance, once said memorably: "Life has many changes. Tomorrow it may rain, and it's supposed to be sunshine 'cause it's summertime. But God's got a funny soul, he plays like Charlie Parker." Yet Mingus also emphasized that the message in the music both predicted and underscored the solidarity necessary for the African-American civil rights movement to gather pace and strength in the second half of the 1950s. "[Bird] put something else in there that had another kind of expression – more than just, say, the blues or the pain that the black people have been through. And in fact he brought hope in. As Max Roach was saying, we played like this, 'It's hopeless'; now it's like 'Everything gonna be alright'."

1 body and soul

The Charlie Parker who made such an impact on the world of music was in every way a child of Kansas City, in the state of Missouri. But the Charlie Parker who came into the world on August 29, 1920 was brought up, for the first several years of his life, in Kansas City, Kansas at 852 Freeman Street. This suburb was not only beyond the state-line but, during the 1920s at least, quite countrified and relaxed, compared to its big-city sister. At this early period in his life, Charlie enjoyed a relatively stable family background and attended a local Catholic school, where he even sang in the school choir.

There are several areas of confusion about the most elementary information concerning Charlie's background. Partly this is a consequence of the fact that, during his brief career, entertainers generally – and especially African-American instrumentalists – were not extensively interviewed. Biographical information on jazz musicians of Parker's generation has either been researched after their death (sometimes decades after their death, in the cases of Art Tatum and Charlie Christian) or has to be pieced together from the sometimes conflicting nuggets that emerged during their lifetime. His mother Adelaide was known as Addie to her contemporaries and allowed herself to be called "Parky" by younger family members. She has been variously described as having the maiden name of Bailey (as on a copy of Charlie's birth certificate) or Bayley or Boyley (a mock-up of his passport is unclear on this point) or Boxley (according to her first daughter-in-law). But, although she herself was interviewed after Charlie's demise, the details were not clarified.

Her family was originally from Muskogee, Oklahoma, incidentally the birthplace of several musicians (such as Don Byas and Barney Kessel) who would have a tangential relationship with Charlie, and of pianist Jay McShann who was absolutely crucial in his development to maturity. One of her grandparents was born a member of the Choctaw nation and, in the absence of any surviving documentation as to his father's ancestry, this makes Charlie at least one-eighth Native American. According to some of his biographers, Addie had her only child when she was not

more than about seventeen, and yet in one of Charlie's few lengthy interviews, which took place in spring 1950, he stated repeatedly that she was
then sixty-two. However, her listing in the national census conducted in
April 1930 gives her age as thirty-two, not forty-two. A further apparent
complication is her subsequent comment, concerning the over-estimate
of Charlie's own age printed at the time of his death, that it would make
him "older than his mother" – which argues in favour of her being quite
young when he was born. Charlie seems to have been nearest the mark,
however, if one believes her gravestone which bears a birthdate of 1891
(she died in 1967, aged seventy-five by that reckoning). Another discrep-
ancy concerns her son's given name; although there were many references to him as "Charles Christopher Parker," neither his birth certificate
nor his gravestone shows any such middle name. What is certain is that
at some point Addie also found herself bringing up John Parker, nicknamed "Ikey," born of a liaison between her husband and a white woman
and (if it's accurate that he was only two years older than Charlie) born
after Addie's marriage to his father.

Charles Parker Sr.'s own father was an evangelist preacher, and he
himself was said to have been born somewhere in Mississippi but raised
in Memphis. Yet reference to the 1930 census shows him as born in the
state of Kansas to parents who were both from Kansas, and as being
forty-one years old at that point. It is believed that he resettled in the Kansas City area after travelling the country as a singer and dancer who could
also play the piano, before marrying Addie in 1916 when he was twenty-
seven and she was eighteen. He'd worked throughout the Southern states
with touring shows of the kind that provided Bessie Smith and others
with their livelihood including, according to Charlie, the famous Ringling
Brothers circus troupe. While he remained married to Addie, he was still
sometimes working as an entertainer but becoming even more successful
at drinking away his earnings. It seems that, even in the 1920s, Addie was
the one who was bringing in the regular money, from work as a domestic
cleaner and nanny. But, if so, this was concealed in the census entry which
shows Charles Sr. as the one who was in employment – as janitor of an
apartment building – and makes no mention of her working, or indeed
of the existence of Ikey. Given his declining career, it seems unlikely that
her husband ever played the piano at home, as is suggested in some references, any more than he drank alcohol at home. In his 1950 interview,
Charlie explicitly dismissed the idea that his father played an instrument.
Had he done so in Charlie's presence – and given what we know about
his son's incredible ear and all-absorbing mind – we would certainly have
heard of young Charles's musical talent at an earlier age.

Conflicting evidence, and conflicting interpretations of the evidence, surround the next episode of the story. It may be only when Parker Sr. moved his family to rented accommodation near the centre of town – ostensibly to be nearer to potential employers but probably in order to spend more time carousing – that the household began to break up. But this chronology seems more dependable if Charlie's 1949 interview is correct in stating that the move took place when he was seven years old. Charlie's first wife, finally interviewed in the 1980s, maintained that he was still at the Kansas City, Kansas school until 1931, the year that she herself finished elementary school in Kansas City, Missouri but, whichever school he was in, he and his mother were already living in the city and renting rooms at 109 West 3rd Street in early 1930. It is not inconceivable that, despite being listed there by the census enumerator, Charles Sr.'s presence as head of the household was already intermittent, and that he was spending as much time or more with another woman. (In that case, it may be assumed that Ikey had joined this new household, after a period of being raised alongside Charlie.) Certainly, as the Depression hit employment prospects, Charles Sr. began to travel the country again, this time as a chef on the railways or, in Charlie's description, merely a dining-car waiter. The financial implications of his continual travelling, and his disinclination to contribute towards Charlie's upbringing, meant that Addie was now not only a single parent but the sole breadwinner. Since her meagre savings had been wiped out in the bank crash of 1929, she decided to stop paying rent and made a down-payment on her own house at 1516 Olive Street, taking in lodgers on the top floor and taking a second job as night cleaner at the Western Union office in order to pay the instalments.

This meant that Charlie was often left to his own devices at nights, which led within a few short years to him becoming deeply involved in the busy musical life of the city. But the emotional implications were perhaps even more serious. Whatever the relationship with Charles Sr. may have brought to either his wife or his son, they both felt betrayed by his defection. Mrs. Parker's love became centred exclusively on her son, who now channelled his desire for parental affection in the only direction available to him. A parallel might be drawn with the relationship between Billie Holiday and her mother, with the exception that Billie's father had been a top-rank professional musician (playing guitar with the Fletcher Henderson band). The further and perhaps crucial difference is that, at least when she met her father again later in life, his ambivalence towards Billie didn't prevent her from witnessing his pride in her own achievements. Charlie Parker's father seemingly had no further contact with him, except for a fleeting appearance engineered by his mother for Charlie's wedding reception, and it may be that by this time his railway job had already come to an end. Charlie's subsequent wife Doris said, "As far as I can gather, he was a small gambler and pimp," information less likely to have come from Addie than from Charlie. The last time he saw his father was after he was stabbed to death in 1939 by a woman friend, perhaps a prostitute.

The family move had brought Charlie into the Kansas City, Kansas school system but, although at elementary school he was a diligent pupil, learning what he was asked to learn without stretching himself, there was still no music-making. He was interested in music, of course, like many of the kids in the ghetto area, and told saxophonist Budd Johnson many years later, "We were the little cats that played stickball out in front of the house. And when you cats would start to rehearse, we would come up to the window and look in and listen to you guys." This latent interest makes it all the more regrettable that the contacts his father must have had with the already lively Kansas City music scene of the late 1920s were of no benefit to Charlie. At the very least, Parker Sr. might have been expected to possess some kind of collection of early jazz and blues records but, if they were still around the house, there has been no mention of Charlie playing them. Perhaps it is reasonable to assume that Addie had thrown them out, along with her husband and his alcoholic refreshments. Allegedly, the first music that really spoke to Charlie was played on either an alto or the popular 1920s variant, a C-melody saxophone. Another ambiguity in the Parker story surfaces here since his 1949 interviewers, journalists Michael Levin and John S. Wilson, summarized his own account with the words, "Charlie discovered jazz, heavily disguised as Rudy Vallee." This is not wholly implausible, since the then-famous heart-throb (a sort of blond Rudolph Valentino of popular music) was a high-voiced crooner who led the Connecticut Yankees band but also toted a saxophone, an accessory that was virtually mandatory in the late twenties. Yet it is possible to wonder if there was a slip on Charlie's part (or his interviewers'), since one of the most popular saxophonists of the same decade was someone whose music Charlie was actually able to reproduce as late as 1950, namely Rudy Wiedoeft. Neither of these players would be described today as having much connection with jazz, although Wiedoeft's credentials and certainly his technique were more impressive.

Anyway, the result of this initial burst of curiosity was that Charlie began pestering his mother to buy him an instrument of his own. Soon she had saved enough to get a rather decrepit, second-hand alto saxophone for $45.00 from Mitchell's music shop on Main Street, but at the time his enthusiasm was short-lived. As he said in 1950, "I wasn't ready for it then. I didn't get interested in a horn until I got interested in the baritone horn when I was at high school. But I'd had that saxophone for a few years." Thus it was only when Charlie entered Lincoln High at the age of twelve that the flame was lit which kept him burning for the rest of his life. Instruction in the cumbersome baritone horn which he was assigned might have stood him in good stead if he had gone on to specialize in the trumpet or trombone. There is no ambiguity this time, but a simple error on the part of some writers has created references to Charlie starting on the baritone saxophone – although no saxophonist *starts* on baritone, especially at this age, because it's too large. The baritone horn is a valved instrument, not a reed instrument and, like its cousins the alto horn and tenor horn, this member of the euphonium family is largely restricted to backing parts in most band arrangements, which Bird later imitated as "Coop, coop! Coop, coop!" Nevertheless, participating in the school's marching band and "symphonic band" did at least fill his head with the pleasing logic of European harmonies, and gave him a taste for the melodies composed for other instruments than the baritone horn. The graduation ceremony in June 1935, the last occasion on which Charlie performed with the school band, featured them in music by the Afro-British composer Samuel Coleridge-Taylor and even the *Pomp And Circumstance March* of Edward Elgar.

At some point, the band director Alonzo Lewis also assigned Charlie a clarinet, presumably after rather than simultaneously with the baritone, so that he now had to learn the fingering for a reed instrument that is widely thought to be excellent training for the saxophone. Playing written music, however, was nothing compared to the benefits of associating with other youngsters in the band such as trombonist Robert Simpson. Simpson, who was some three years older than Charlie, became, according to Charlie's mother, "his inseparable friend." He not only played the written music accurately and with feeling but, out of school hours, he was playing excellent jazz by ear. Pretty soon, Charlie was dusting off his alto and, by the time he was fourteen, he was taking his first paid engagements with Simpson in a small band called The Deans Of Swing, led by another school friend, pianist Lawrence "88" Keyes, who was also about three years his senior. The influence of such grown-up boys was both good and bad. Charlie was sufficiently fired up to suggest that his mother should undertake the purchase of a new Conn alto, probably in 1935, which she described as "just beautiful, white gold with green keys." Paying off the instalments from the Hurst Loan Shop at 18th Street and

Vine took several years, "but I finished paying for it, [it] was some 200-odd dollars, and that was in Depression times." Equally importantly, he was now able to question Keyes about harmony and see the answers demonstrated on the piano, and to discover that playing jazz was not just a matter of a good ear and a lot of enthusiasm. Even a young amateur band had to meet exacting standards, and Charlie's attendance at school became irregular as he devoted himself to gigging and rehearsing and merely socializing with his companions or occasional girlfriends, who were also older. He was forced to repeat the first year in high school (and possibly his last year of elementary school too) and, when he had to join the musicians' union at fourteen, he pretended to be eighteen and backed it up by dropping out of school without graduating.

There is a suggestion that, at this period, Charlie may have been subject to some minimal supervision by his half-brother (who later went on to become a mail inspector for the Kansas City post office) but, if so, it did little to deter him from spending the night-times with his elders. Some of the more innocent by-products of this street-life involved hanging around outside places such as the Reno club, near the intersection of 12th and Cherry Streets. This was where local hero Count Basie had taken up residence shortly after his employer, bandleader Bennie Moten, had died on the operating table in April 1935. The former Moten bandsmen chosen by Basie for his own outfit included trumpeter Oran (Hot Lips) Page and saxophonists Buster Smith and Lester Young. Young was soon to gain international fame for his revolutionary but seemingly effortless solos and meanwhile, along with drummer Jesse Price, he was one of the musicians who used to smuggle Charlie into the club during the band's breaks. Although far from the remote personality he later became, Lester was eleven years older than Charlie and verbally uncommunicative about his music. In Charlie's eyes, he was like a god – a god who sometimes reached over and passed him the marijuana cigarettes which circulated (perfectly legally until 1937) in the alley behind the club. According to Charlie's observation of him at work, "Pres would sit on the bandstand with a joint between each finger, and when he smoked one, he'd move each one up a finger."

Even if Charlie was growing up too fast for his own good, the great advantage of doing so in Kansas City at this period was the vast number of outlets for music. The city was already well established as the commercial hub of the entire South-west long before it acquired its reputation as a "wide-open town" in the 1920s. This was the decade marked by the passing of the Volsted Act, which became federal law the year Parker was born and attempted to regulate the public sale of alcohol by outright prohibition, the word which gave its name to the whole period. As with subsequent legislative efforts to ban the sale of hard drugs, the net result of Prohibition was to drive potential customers into the arms of illegal suppliers, and to allow the relatively innocent local bootleggers to be swamped by the gangster fraternity, who had a field day that actually lasted fourteen years. So a national network of night-time activities grew up, among which the establishments providing musical entertainment were among the more wholesome, but all of which had direct links with the criminal underworld. Not only were gambling and prostitution rife, but in Kansas City the rule of gangland bosses such as Pretty Boy Floyd was actively encouraged by the connivance of Tom Pendergast, the political fixer who was (both literally and metaphorically) the municipality's monopoly supplier of cement for public works.

Already during the economic boom of the 1920s, Kansas City's active dance-hall and nightclub scene, not to mention its bordellos, catered to visiting farmers and businessmen who either "brought their own" or purchased rather strong "Irish coffee." The venues facilitating these activities supported a growing pool of individual musicians and organized bands. Skilled ensembles such as those of Bennie Moten, or Walter Page and the Blue Devils, or Terrence Holder and the Dark Clouds Of Joy (which eventually became Andy Kirk's band), set high standards and attracted many "territory musicians" from throughout the Southwest and from further afield. At various points in the early 1930s, Kansas City was the operational base for such subsequently significant names as the aforementioned Lester Young; Ben Webster (who soon moved on to work with Fletcher Henderson, Cab Calloway and Duke Ellington); Budd Johnson (later with Earl Hines, Billy Eckstine and Dizzy Gillespie); Basie's Herschel Evans and Buddy Tate – and those are just some of the tenor saxophonists.

The bust that followed the Wall Street crash at the end of the 1920s soon restricted the clientele of the more luxurious establishments, and eventually led to the ending of Prohibition in late 1933, as a spin-off from President Roosevelt's attempts to revive the economy. But demand for entertainment, during what became known as the Great Depression, was high, especially through the "free" medium of radio broadcasts which, along with the sound movies, became the mass medium of the decade. Even records, which had to be purchased separately from their source of reproduction, suffered hugely from the absence of spare money in people's pockets. In keeping with the mood of the moment, the biggest demand was for the allegedly "classy" sweet music of bandleaders such as Guy Lombardo and his Royal Canadians, for whose slumbering saxophones Charlie later expressed an admiration, as did Louis Armstrong. Elsewhere in the country the repeal of Prohibition, meaning that alcohol could now be sold legally once again, had initially accelerated the slump in nightclub business. But the gangster-run clubs of Kansas City thrived under the town's corrupt administration to such an extent that demand for musicians almost outstripped supply, and club managements were prepared to give anyone a try.

The Orchid Room, one of the less famous small clubs in the heart of nightlife district at 12th Street and Vine, was the venue targeted by Charlie and his first musical hero in their attempt to obtain an engagement together. "I tried playing a job at the Orchid Room with my friend Robert Simpson, and they threw us out," recalled Parker. However, the forum for being heard by fellow musicians was the jam session, an important institution in the 1930s and nowhere more so than in Kansas City. This fact was directly responsible for the town's distinctive input to the popularity of the Swing Era. Around the time of Charlie's ill-fated Orchid Room tryout, Benny Goodman's famous August 1935 breakthrough created the start of the so-called Swing Era, a whole decade where white bandleaders became celebrated for playing the most jazz-influenced popular music so far. In the main, Goodman and his brethren such as Tommy and Jimmy Dorsey, Artie Shaw and eventually Glenn Miller were basing their work closely on the achievements of black bands such as Fletcher Henderson, Jimmie Lunceford, Chick Webb and, to a lesser extent, Duke Ellington. But later in the 1930s, both white and black bands became enamoured of the more blues-oriented big-bands such as Count Basie's and Andy Kirk's, which emerged from Kansas City to national fame. The looser playing of these groups, both rhythmically and in terms of ensemble arrangements, was the result of years and years of open-ended jam sessions (such as the ones simulated in the Robert Altman movie *Kansas City*), in which extended improvisations were backed by spontaneously created riffs from the massed horn-players waiting for their own turn to improvise.

Charlie became first a keen observer and then an overambitious participant, while he was still a barely competent Dean Of Swing. His first attempt to sit in on a jam session was at the Hi-Hat club, at the corner of 22nd Street and Vine, joining a group led by tenor man Jimmy Keith who, with fellow group-member James Ross on trumpet (another Dean Of Swing, by the way), would later work with the Harlan Leonard band. Charlie's fullest description of the event was as follows:

> I'd learned to play the first eight bars of *Lazy River* and I knew the complete tune of *Honeysuckle Rose*. I didn't ever stop to think about any different kind of keys or nothing like that. So I took my horn out to this joint

where a bunch of fellows I had seen around were. And the first thing they started playing was *Body and Soul* – Long beat, you know? Shit! So I got to playing my *Honeysuckle Rose* – I mean, an awful conglomeration. They laughed me off the bandstand, they laughed at me so hard.

The issue of different keys is significant because, as Charlie confirmed, he had learned *Lazy River* and *Honeysuckle Rose* in their standard concert pitch of F (the equivalent of D on the alto), whereas *Body And Soul* would almost certainly have been played in its standard key of D-flat concert (as in Benny Goodman's 1935 recording) or possibly E-flat (from Louis Armstrong's 1930 version). The reference to "long beat" is probably explained in an earlier version of the same anecdote by a mention of "double tempo," in the manner of the version that was to appear on a famous 1938 recording of the same song by Chu Berry and Roy Eldridge: "I was doing alright until I tried doing double tempo on *Body And Soul*. Everybody fell out laughing. I went home and cried and didn't play again for three months."

The ability to play improvised phrases at double the original tempo of the piece, though already heard briefly in some 1920s performances including those of Louis Armstrong, was to become one of the distinguishing characteristics of Charlie's mature style. Equally, whether or not Charlie was literally trying to work *Honeysuckle Rose* into *Body And Soul* on this occasion, he was in later years famous for the integration of melodic quotations during an improvisation on another tune, a practice also popularized first by Armstrong (for example, his tongue-in-check reference to *Rhapsody In Blue* on the 1929 *Ain't Misbehavin'*). Even examples as complex as Armstrong's own *West End Blues* introduction, or the theme of Charlie Shavers's *Dawn On The Desert* (one of Parker's favourite cross-references), were to become just one aspect of his fertile imagination and musical self-confidence, but for the moment he had bitten off more than he could chew. Although not playing in public again for the next three months, he practised every day and later acknowledged: "I put quite a bit of study into the horn, that's true. In fact, the neighbours threatened to ask my mother to move once... She said I was driving them crazy with the horn. I used to put in at least 11 to 15 hours a day."

The latter claim may be a slight exaggeration, but similar feats are not unknown among those who acquire a flawless technique (such as John Coltrane or certain virtuosi from the European classical world) and, by the end of this period, Charlie landed a job with saxophonist-bandleader Tommy Douglas at the Paseo Hall ballroom. His improved control of the instrument was put to good use and his knowledge of harmony and repertoire was considerably widened by playing regularly for dancers. Furthermore, Douglas (who later recorded with singer Julia Lee and others) had been conservatory-trained, which was highly unusual for a black musician in those days, and could discuss music with Charlie and provide him with new challenges. No doubt due to Douglas's influence, Charlie came to admire the technical expertise of sax players such as Jimmy Dorsey and, later, even the French "straight music" virtuoso Marcel Mule. When Douglas lent him a clarinet, which he had not touched since dropping out of high school, he was amazed that Charlie mastered the basic differences virtually overnight. There are also mentions of him playing around this same time with trumpeter Oliver Todd at a club named Frankie and Johnny's, where his playing was not to the liking of the management. On the other hand Mary Lou Williams, the great pianist-arranger of the then Kansas City-based Andy Kirk band, heard Charlie in a group led by the wife of her employer, pianist Mary Kirk, and claimed that he was playing "just the way he did when we was in New York."

It was now 1936 and, since beginning to concentrate on his saxophone, Charlie had made up for lost time musically. Intellectually and emotionally, he was still running before he had learned to walk. A considerable appetite for reading, which he felt to be a more adult occupation than school studies had ever been, did not prepare him for a rude shock to his Oedipus complex when he found his mother in bed with a man. It seems revealing that Charlie's outraged and finally understanding reaction was more like that of a deceived husband than a son. And it is surely significant that in the same year he himself became the husband of Rebecca Ruffin, who was just six months older than Charlie with a birthday of February 23, 1920. A light-complexioned, attractive girl whose looks were compared to Lena Horne, she had been a year ahead of him in high school, where she had known him since 1932 and had always had a soft spot for him. But the possibility of a relationship had been unwittingly facilitated by Addie renting her top floor to Rebecca's mother who, in the process of getting divorced, moved in along with her seven children, a son and six daughters. This was in April 1934 and it seems that the closeness between Rebecca and Charlie developed slowly at first, no doubt because he was already spending a lot of time outside the family home. But, when in the spring of 1936 it became clear to Mrs. Ruffin that there was a romantic attachment, she moved her brood out of the Parker house, failing to notice that Rebecca regularly sneaked out to meet Charlie anyway. Unlike her, he was already sexually experienced but, feeling an urge towards some kind of domesticity, he proposed to her on July 24 and married her the following day, Charlie just fifteen years of age.

If this was a gesture of independence from his mother, it did not prevent him from accepting her offer of housing him and Rebecca. Meanwhile, what Charlie required from Rebecca was lovemaking and admiration, in other words some confirmation of his self-esteem. That apart, he was content to let mother and substitute mother get on with it, while he got on with his practising and gigging and sitting-in. Though his ability was increasing rapidly, he was still overreaching himself in jam-session situations and, what is more, gaining a bad reputation for constantly trying ideas he had not really mastered. One night, probably in the summer of 1936, he went so far as to sit in with the major-league men of the Basie band, doubtless with some nodded encouragement from Lester Young. But Basie's recently returned drummer, the brilliant Jo Jones, knew of Parker at least by reputation and, waiting till Charlie had just taken off on his solo flight, gunned him down in no uncertain manner, with a make-believe weapon reminiscent of the famous amateur-night verdicts at Harlem's Apollo Theatre. Lost in concentration on the music, Charlie was abruptly halted by the resounding crash of the drummer's cymbal thrown at his feet. "It fell with a deafening sound," said Charlie's future colleague Gene Ramey, a fellow participant at this session, "and Bird, in humiliation, packed up his instrument and left."

Whether or not he took out his frustration on Rebecca, things went badly from the start. He expected, but at the same resented, her organizing his clothing and his meal-times, as his mother had done, and, once when he needed a taxi and Rebecca had no ready money, he pawned his mother's electric iron. (This was merely the first recorded example of a lifetime habit of either borrowing money or pawning his horn, or borrowing a horn from a friend and then pawning the friend's horn – just sometimes, his mother or his friend would be repaid later.) The frequently violent arguments between the young couple can hardly have been helped by having his mother on the premises, and it didn't seem to bode well when Charlie received another setback. This time it was not a jam-session rejection, but an automobile accident that laid him low on Thanksgiving Day 1936. Somewhere between Kansas City and Jefferson City, Missouri, a car carrying the casually assembled group to a gig, for which Charlie had been promised $7.00, was involved in a smash that left one member dead and the altoist and drummer severely injured. "I broke three ribs and had a spinal fracture... I mean, everybody was so afraid that I wouldn't walk right no more. But everything was alright." The accident brought about Charlie's first mention in the press, albeit incorrectly named as "Jas. Parker, 1516 Olive St.," with a local news report noting that the injuries to bassist George Wilkerson (seventy-two years old, according to Charlie) were fatal.

The promoter who had hired the musicians paid for his medical expenses, while an insurance payout obtained him a new Selmer alto, since the old one was damaged beyond repair in the crash. During his recuperation period, Charlie must have enjoyed being doted on by his mother and his wife and, thanks to visits from friends and colleagues, he had a supply of marijuana which he kept hidden in his pillow. However, when he was back on his feet and back to his old routines, Rebecca was faced with shocking evidence that he was dabbling with heroin:

> He called me upstairs, and he says "Go sit around that side of the bed."
> I thought he had something for me. I looked in the mirror, and I saw
> him stick this needle in his arm. And I screamed, and I got up and I said,
> "Why?" And he just smiled, and he took the – his tie was the tourni-
> quet... [H]e didn't say anything, he just wiped his arm and put his tie
> under his collar, put his jacket on, and come over and kissed me on the
> forehead and he says, "See you in the morning."

Later, she was told by the doctor who had attended him: "I don't know if you can understand it or not, but Charlie has to take heroin to kill the pain from his ribs and his spine." This may have some element of truth, or it may equally be that Charlie was already able to con a member of the medical profession. For his by now long-standing presence on the nightclub scene of Kansas City would have certainly brought him into contact with addicts, and a retrospective explanation offered by Charlie in the 1940s was that "It all came from being introduced too early to night life." He was into alcohol and various pills as early as 1932, he told Leonard Feather, who added that in 1935 "an actor friend" introduced Charlie to heroin. "I didn't know what hit me – it was so sudden. I was a victim of circumstances." The dates given may be a little early compared to the reality, and oral history is notoriously unreliable in this respect, but Charlie was consistent thereafter in stating that he was fifteen when he first tried heroin. Although his mother suggested that it was a bi-racial woman who'd been responsible for getting Charlie involved with marijuana, the jazz-influenced tap-dancer (and addict) Baby Laurence was one of several people who claimed the dubious honour of initiating him into the use of heroin. A drummer named Edward "Little Phil" Phillips, another excellent musician as observed by Kansas City native Bob Brookmeyer ("[He]'d come to sessions with just a snare drum, a sock cymbal, and brushes and play all the drums you'd want to hear"), was later described as Charlie's supplier.

Either way, this development did little to improve his relationship with Rebecca, and it must have been with relief that Charlie accepted a three-month engagement at the resort of Eldon, Missouri, in the Ozarks for the summer of 1937 with the band of singer George E. Lee (the then more famous brother of Julia Lee). Here, with no distractions apart from the occasional female admirer, Charlie spent whole days studying harmony with the band's pianist and guitarist, and experimenting with it on his single-note instrument. As he ran up and down the chords and scales, and for the first time began to *hear* the relationship between the two, he became utterly dedicated to gaining command of his chosen idiom and in the process laid the basis of his subsequent stunning fluency. He told Levin and Wilson that at this point he was practising from books of saxophone, piano and guitar exercises, and it was attested by several later witnesses that, like many horn-players, Charlie actually learned to find his way around the piano as well. When questioned in 1954 about the tell-tale quotation during one of his solos of a phrase from the famous saxophone exercise book by Klosé, he said of his early practice routine: "Naturally it wasn't done with mirrors this time, it was done with books." During the rest of his stay in the Ozarks, he played and replayed the first records to be issued of Count Basie and Lester Young, namely *Shoe Shine Swing*, *Lady Be Good* and *Honeysuckle Rose*. Fingering his instrument in time with Young, he began learning the solos by heart until he could repeat them himself note for note. He could still do so, privately, in the 1950s.

If this single-minded dedication should seem unlikely, given Charlie's academic record at high school, it should perhaps be remembered that he was born under the sign of Virgo (like Lester Young, in fact). Traditionally such people are held to be capable, once their interest has been aroused, of infinite attention to detail and of an almost ruthless pursuit of perfection. Sadly, this was also true, in Charlie's case, of his search for the ultimate in stimulants since, however much the pursuit of musical perfection fed his soul, he was equally devoted to seeking bodily gratification. Kansas City nightclub owner Tutty Clarkin had been aware of him since Charlie first began hanging out, and he commented that

> When I first knew Charlie, he was getting high on nutmeg... From nutmeg Bird went to benzedrine inhalers. He'd break them open and soak them in wine. Then he smoked tea [marijuana] and finally got hooked on heroin. He was the only man I knew who could drink with heroin.

He might have gone on to say that Parker's physical make-up was so out of the ordinary that he was one of the rare individuals not to become instantly addicted to something as potent as heroin. For years, he was able to take it or leave it, although on the whole he preferred to take it. Clarkin did add, however, "When Bird was sixteen he looked thirty-eight. He had the oldest-looking face I ever saw."

2 the jumpin' blues

Musically, Charlie Parker had finally got himself together the summer that he turned seventeen, and the only way to go was up. The fact that Kansas City's own Count Basie band had appeared on records, and was beginning to make it in New York, did not go unnoticed. But, for the moment, no longer being the most unpopular jazzmen in Kansas City became Charlie's incentive for further musical exploration. He found a powerful ally and inspiration in his next bandleader, the altoist and arranger Henry (Buster) Smith. Known as "Prof" to his friends, Smith had been a colleague of Basie's off and on since 1928 and had initially been co-leader of the famous 1935–36 band at the Reno club, until going off to do his own thing just as Basie was being discovered by New York-based talent scouts.

The fact that Charlie would later gain such legendary renown should not obscure his ongoing apprenticeship, but it does explain the vivid recollections of his improvement, following his summer season in Eldon, Missouri. The pianist Jay McShann, for instance, has given three different versions of his sudden awareness of Parker. A typical "territory musician" brought up in Muskogee before moving to Tulsa, McShann worked successively in Arkansas City, Oklahoma City and Albuquerque (briefly giving lessons there to pianist John Lewis) and then returned to Arkansas, finally stopping off in Kansas City in 1937. Heading straight to the Reno club, he was encouraged by bassist Billy Hadnott to stay on in town, and soon found work amid this inspiring environment. "After I got through where I was playing, the joints were still going till five or six in the morning, and I'd go around and hear everybody. It was so exciting I'd not want to go to sleep, because I was afraid I'd miss something!"

As to how McShann became aware of Charlie Parker, we can take our pick. In the last few decades, he has stuck to versions of the following account:

> We were, you know, on 12th Street, and they always piped out music into the street... So I passed by a club called the Barley Duke [correctly, the Bar-le-Duc], and I heard this sound, and I said, "Wait a minute!... Wonder who is that?"... We went in, and Bird was up, was blowing,

you know. So after he finished blowing, I said, "Hey man, where you from?" He said, "Man,... I'm from Kansas City." I said, "Well, what's your name?... I've never heard you around here before." He said, "Well, the reason you haven't heard me is because I've been down in the Ozarks with George Lee's band."

An earlier account for Ross Russell, however, had McShann on the bandstand at a jam session:

> I was in a rhythm-section one night when this cocky kid pushed his way on stage... He had a tone that cut. Knew his changes. He'd get off on a line of his own and I would think he was headed for trouble, but he was like a cat landing on all four feet. A lot of people couldn't understand what he was trying to do, but it made sense harmonically and it always swung.

Another possibility, which first surfaced in an even earlier interview, is that McShann heard Parker on the radio and thought he was hearing Buster Smith:

> I heard a broadcast one night, during the time Bird was working with Prof, and so I told Prof... "You sure did sound good last night." He says, "What do you mean 'sound good last night'," he says. "I didn't play last night... That was Charlie Parker you heard last night."

It seems clear that McShann was impressed. But, if the suggestion is that Charlie's personal "sound" was immediately apparent as soon as he returned from the Ozarks, it seems more likely that what began to show through was the highly individual architecture of his solos. Buster Smith recalled, "He'd improved a good bit since I'd seen him before and of course I wanted him. The only trouble he had was with his mouthpiece. He had trouble getting the tone he wanted to get." What Buster advised Charlie to do was to cultivate power and projection rather than a conventional rounded tone, by using the toughest reeds he could. (He also described himself as having used a tenor saxophone reed on his alto, at a time when Lester Young had a baritone reed on his tenor!) The tiny number of records on which Smith played at this period, particularly *Baby Look At You* and *Jump For Joy* with Kansas City stalwarts Pete Johnson and Joe Turner, show some melodic ideas which went into Parker's vocabulary and especially the flexible but slightly edgy tone with which Parker became identified. In fact, Smith's playing is the only thing on record remotely like Parker, before Charlie himself.

Smith's group that worked (and sometimes broadcast) in Lucille's Band Box at 18th and Woodland grew in late 1937 to a twelve-piece band, with personnel changes that brought in McShann on piano, Hadnott on bass, co-leader Jesse Price on drums and Charlie on second alto. Unselfishly, Buster carried Charlie along with him when the band was fronted occasionally by former Moten trumpeter Dee (Prince) Stewart and, even more surprisingly, Buster kept him on when he obtained a residency at the white-owned Antlers club that only required a seven-piece group. Smith's policy was that:

> In my band, we'd split solos. If I took two [choruses], he'd take two; if I took three, he'd take three; and so forth. He always wanted me to take the first solo... But after a while, anything I could make on my horn, he could make too – and make something better out of it. We used to do that double-time stuff all the time... I used to do a lot of that on clarinet. Then I started doing it on alto, and Charlie heard me doing it, and he started playing it.

This comfortable and stimulating partnership only ended when, in September 1938, Smith accepted an offer to do some arranging work in New York for Count Basie, now resident at The Famous Door on 52nd Street, the hub of midtown Manhattan's jazz nightclub scene. Soon after arriving, he also found himself writing and playing for the band of ex-Basie trumpeter Hot Lips Page. In making this move, Buster was aware that employment for musicians in Kansas City had passed its peak and, hoping to make enough contacts in New York to be able to import his own band, he promised Charlie that he would send for him in due course.

In the meantime, McShann had departed the Smith group sometime before Buster left town, to undertake a long engagement at a whites-only establishment across the river in Kansas City, Kansas, called Martin's-on-the-Plaza. Initially, this was with just a trio including bassist Gene Ramey and drummer Gus Johnson, but he was soon invited to expand the group to a seven-piece with the addition of Parker and other horn-players. As a result of mentions in *Down Beat* magazine by their Kansas City correspondent Dave Dexter, there was interest from Chicago (where the magazine was published) and the band was soon left in the temporary charge of its saxophonist-arranger William J. Scott, while McShann took his trio to the Windy City for six weeks early in 1939. Even before McShann's detour, Charlie had confided to him that he wanted to take a look at New York. However, it is worth noting also McShann's own comment that, during Charlie's early stint in his band, "That is when I realized that he was on this wild kick, because he was always late showing up for the job. So we had to let him go." Whether or not Charlie was already out of the band, McShann's trip to Chicago coincided with the downfall of Kansas City's political bosses, as the corrupt regime that had guaranteed the inner-city nightclubs' prosperity rapidly came to an end and the city's new administration began to close the less law-abiding establishments. Shortly afterwards, many of the musicians still in Kansas City, including Charlie, Little Phil and others, were conducting their nightly jam sessions under the stars in the city's parks.

In addition to the lack of employment, several other reasons have been given for Parker's eventual departure from Kansas City. Around this time, his friend and inspiration Robert Simpson, who had a heart condition, died tragically on the operating table at the age of twenty-one. Fifteen years later, Charlie was still scarred by this loss, saying, "Once in Kansas City I had a friend who I liked very much, and a sorrowful thing happened... He died." Charlie felt too that it was time to get away from Rebecca, who in January 1938 (or possibly a year earlier) had given birth to his son, Francis Leon Parker – the "Francis" chosen by Rebecca and "Leon" chosen by Charlie in honour of Leon (Chu) Berry, perhaps the leading New York-based jazz saxophonist apart from an up-and-coming Lester Young. Far from bringing joy to Charlie's life, this new responsibility seemed more like a burden, and drove him and his wife further apart. After Charlie's desertion, she agreed to his request for a divorce in 1940, leaving Leon in the hands of Charlie's mother until he was ten before eventually taking him to live with her in Baltimore and then Detroit when she remarried. Apparently, Charlie's decision to leave town was hastened by an argument with a Kansas City taxi-driver whose cab he retained for six or seven hours, running up a bill of $10.00, no small sum in those days. During the altercation, he prevented the driver from grabbing his saxophone by attacking him with a knife. He was not only arrested but spent twenty-two days in prison because, untypically perhaps, "His mother, who didn't approve of his conduct then, wouldn't help him out." According to his own later account to Chan Richardson, he may also have been forced to undergo psychiatric tests while in Kansas City, presumably in conjunction with his sentence.

Impatient to shake the hometown dust off his feet, he pawned his saxophone and took a free ride on a freight-train bound for Chicago, where he immediately impressed local musicians by the contrast between his hobo-like appearance and his sophisticated playing. He turned up at the 6.30 a.m. "breakfast dance" at the 65 Club, where the band included trumpeter King Kolax and altoist Andrew (Goon) Gardner. In the recollection of eye-witness Billy Eckstine,

> A guy comes up that looks like he just got off a freight car, the raggediest guy you'd want to see at this moment. And he asks Goon, "Say, man, can I come up and blow your horn?"... And this cat gets up there,

and I'm telling you he blew the bell off that thing!... I guess Bird was
no more than eighteen then, but playing like you never heard – wailing
alto then.

Eckstine added that Gardner (soon to work in the Earl Hines band
and, much later, to record in Chicago with T-Bone Walker), befriended
Charlie and lent him some clothes and a clarinet. As a result Parker stayed
around and made a few gigs, and connections of another kind. "According to what Goon told me, one day he looked for Bird, and Bird, the clarinet and all, was gone."

Shortly afterwards, Parker showed up in New York and decided that
he was staying with Buster Smith and his wife. Smith was tolerant and
conspiratorial, and allowed Charlie to sleep in his bed during the day
while he was out, despite his wife's objections: "I was off at the Woodside
[Hotel] writing music [for Basie], and she'd be down there at Andy Kirk's
restaurant, waiting tables. And she'd come home sometimes, and she'd
see him laying up there with his shoes on. Clothes on, too. So she got to
squawkin'." Charlie spent the evenings and nights looking for paying gigs
and sitting in at jam sessions, for instance with the non-unionized house-
band at Monroe's Uptown House at West 134th Street. He had, however,
not realized the quantity of promising musicians who gravitated to New
York City from all over the country, nor indeed the sheer professionalism
in the upper echelons of the jazz business. He observed the late-night
sessions taking place regularly in the other top Harlem after-hours spots
such as Puss Johnson's. This was where Coleman Hawkins would choose
to make his dramatic reappearance in summer 1939 after a five-year stay
in Europe, a couple of months before making his classic record of *Body
And Soul*. But the standard of the soloists who jammed with each other,
such as Chu Berry, Ben Webster, Lester Young and Don Byas, overawed
Charlie so much that he thought better of trying to play there. And, as
far as actual work was concerned, opportunities were severely restricted
since the musicians' union in New York was the branch most keen on
observing the rule that a new arrival must wait six months before trans-
ferring membership from his hometown.

So, when Mrs. Smith put her foot down, Charlie took various non-
musical jobs for the first and only time in his life, eventually spending
perhaps as much as three months washing dishes, for $9.00 a week plus
meals, at Jimmy's Chicken Shack. This Harlem eatery, owned by bandleader Andy Kirk, employed Mrs. Smith in the daytimes when it was
managed by Kirk's wife Mary, while at night it was run by saxophonist
John Williams who'd recently left the Kirk band in order to do so (and
to separate from his own wife Mary Lou). There were jam sessions here

too, but the real attraction was that it was a favourite hang-out of the great Art Tatum, the blind solo pianist whose harmonic ingenuity perhaps exceeded Ellington's at this stage and whose speed of execution was so dazzling that the ingenuity was lost on all but the more inquiring of his fellow musicians. The influence of this regular exposure to Tatum can hardly be overestimated, and it was just at this period that Charlie made a significant discovery while jamming at Dan Wall's Chili House on 7th Avenue between 139rd and 140th Street. Another devotee of harmony, guitarist Bill (Biddy) Fleet, whom Charlie had met at Monroe's but who also played sometimes at Jimmy's, often led a four-piece group at this inauspicious venue and attracted such high-quality sitters-in as Vic Dickenson, Jabbo Smith and Hot Lips Page.

Fleet, who is not known to have recorded, was apparently expert at playing the sort of mobile rhythm-guitar parts associated with his friend Freddie Green of the Basie band. Some forty years later, Fleet recalled: "Lot of guitar players was playing more guitar than I. But...I'd voice my chords in such a way that I'd play the original chords of the tune, and I'd invert them every one, two, three or four beats so that the top notes of my inversions would be another tune... And Bird had a big ear, and he listened. He say, 'Biddy! Do that again!'" Charlie himself recalled, a mere ten years after the event, "I kept thinking there is bound to be something else. I could hear it sometimes but I couldn't play it." As famously noted by Levin and Wilson:

> At the time, Charlie says, he was bored with the stereotyped changes [i.e. chords] being used then...Working over *Cherokee* with Fleet, Charlie suddenly found that by using higher intervals of a chord as a melody line and backing them with appropriately related changes [alterations], he could play this thing he had been "hearing." Fleet picked it up behind him and bop was born.

Clearly, the last sentence is a case of journalistic hyperbole. But – apart from the fact that Levin and Wilson were using a reporter's notebook rather than a recording device – the rest is obviously from the lips of Parker himself. Representing one of the only occasions on which he spoke about the detail of his music, this statement will be discussed further in Chapter 7. It may or may not be a coincidence that the tune Charlie was working over was later to become the subject of a record justly considered one of his masterpieces (*Ko Ko*, 1945). The song *Cherokee*, a current pop hit in 1939 despite the key-changes of its B-section, became closely identified with him from this time until the last tour on which he played to really substantial audiences, in early 1954.

Still officially restricted to non-unionized venues or out-of-town work, as far as paid engagements were concerned, Charlie accepted a hotel gig of several weeks in Maryland with the not very enthralling Banjo Burney, who also used Biddy Fleet on this trip. It was at this point, in late 1939, that Charlie was summoned home for his father's funeral, following his fatal stabbing. Given the unsalubrious life that Charles Sr. had led in the years since leaving his wife and son, it's not hard to imagine Charlie drawing parallels with his own "dissipation" (the word used by journalist Leonard Feather in the 1947 interview that first discussed publicly this side of his life) and his abandonment of his own wife and son. As well as feeling under some obligation to stay with his mother and young Leon for a while, he apparently effected a brief reunion with Rebecca. It was also the case that Charlie had nothing specific to go back to in New York and had made no close friends apart from trumpeter Bobby Moore who, early the following year, was to be committed to a mental hospital for the rest of his life. Such locations were the last known addresses of a number of jazz musicians, from those who merely indulged overmuch in marijuana (such as Leon Roppolo) to those who acted more violently (including the legendary Buddy Bolden). Charlie would have his own brush with these institutions, as did several African-American players of his generation, including Bud Powell, Thelonious Monk and Charles Mingus.

Probably another reason for remaining in Kansas City was that he wanted to spend some time on his home ground following up his Chili House revelation. It is likely to be around this period that his playing was first preserved, thanks to the portable disc-cutter of a former Tommy Douglas colleague, trumpeter Clarence Davis. The use of such portable recording equipment by private individuals was very new at this point, with most of even the folk-blues or other ethnic music so far recorded being captured in New York, Chicago and Los Angeles, and the rest being documented on brief field-trips to smaller towns and often in hotel-rooms or local radio studios. This informal recording of Parker playing *Honeysuckle Rose* and *Body And Soul*, entirely unaccompanied, was labelled by its subsequent owner as having been made in Kansas City in 1937, but in fact sounds too confident and too typical to date from earlier than 1940 or even 1941. Professionally speaking, he spent a couple of unsatisfactory weeks at the start of 1940 working for the local band of Harlan Leonard, which contained Jesse Price on drums and some friends from the Tommy Douglas period. Soon this band would hook up in New York with a future Parker associate, arranger Tadd Dameron, but at this stage it was a less enticing prospect. However, at just this moment, one of the Swing Era's popular "battles of the bands" pitted Leonard against the augmented group of a returned Jay McShann. As a result, Charlie asked the latter whether he could rejoin him, assuring him incidentally that he was now "clean."

This band was to provide Charlie with a musical home for the next two-and-a-half years, as well as giving him his first opportunity to make commercial records. In fact, he had nearly missed out on a development that would have seen McShann become "the first Kansas City outfit to go on wax since Count Basie and Andy Kirk left town." A first date was indeed reported to have taken place but, according to McShann, "We went into Chicago to do the session, and we ran into some complications there with the union because there was no contract sent in, in front... They told us, 'Come back later when you get this business all straightened out.'" The consequence was that they made no official recordings for a further year and a half. As in Charlie's previous working situations, he was still the youngest band member but the McShann organization's average age was younger than that of the established Kansas City groups. Its members were inspired by his outstanding ability, not only as a soloist but as an organizer since, unusually, he took charge of rehearsing the saxophone section. McShann noted that

> He was an *interested* cat in those days, and I could depend on him to take care of the reed section. He'd be mad at the guys if they were late for rehearsal. Then one night we had played a couple of numbers before he showed, and I knew he was "messing around."

Soon the band was to be heard playing at college dances, for instance at Missouri University (where McShann and Harlan Leonard were the first black bands to appear), and travelling throughout the Southern states as far as New Orleans and Houston. In Des Moines, they drew a larger audience than Ella Fitzgerald's band and, in various band battles, they triumphed over the nationally famous Earl Hines and the territory groups of Milton Larkins and Nat Towles (from whom some of McShann's new sidemen had been lifted). While also promising enough to challenge even the Ellington band and later Cab Calloway, here they lost out to superior musicianship and showmanship.

During 1940, they were based for a while at the Trocadero ballroom in Wichita, Kansas, where another portable recorder was used one evening by two local fans, that preserves – just about – the sound of the band and a few solo bars of Parker. While the band was in Wichita, however, the studio of the local radio station KFBI was used by the same fans (plus local trombonist Bud Gould who was a regular performer on the station) to record seven tracks which were not made public until the mid-1970s.

In an unconscious echo of Basie's first studio session in his own right, these private recordings were made with a small group drawn from the McShann band, with the addition of Gould. McShann himself comes across as an excellent soloist, with hints of Earl Hines in addition to obvious quotes from Basie, and as a superior rhythm-section player inspired by both Basie and Pete Johnson. But the first sizeable solos of Parker in a group context are fascinating for his early mastery of a combined Lester Young/Buster Smith style with reminiscences (and sometimes direct quotations) of Coleman Hawkins and Chu Berry. Comparing them with the contemporary work of Dizzy Gillespie (then with Cab Calloway's band), musicologist Gunther Schuller wrote: "These transcriptions also offer considerable evidence that Parker was well in advance of Gillespie as regards musical consistency, technical poise, and cohesiveness of conception... Nothing quite like it had ever been heard before on the saxophone, and, for that matter, in jazz."

The first commercial recording by McShann was undertaken five months later in Dallas (possibly also at a radio studio) but, though it featured the whole band, it also created a hit single that ignored some of the band's qualities. Shortly before the session McShann heard, allegedly for the first time, a singer at the Kentucky Club in Kansas City named Walter Brown, whose nasal version of Jimmy Rushing and Joe Turner's style had been an asset to the Deans Of Swing six years earlier. McShann had been hoping to record some relatively adventurous instrumentals such as the Parker composition *Yardbird Suite*, then known as *What Price Love?*, but producer Dave Kapp requested blues material. It was only after McShann suggested the instrumental *Dexter Blues* (named for his *Down Beat* cheerleader), *Hootie Blues* (spotlighting Parker and Walter Brown) and a piano boogie feature that Kapp would accept the more jazz-oriented *Swingmatism*, written by ex-sideman William Scott. Once the boogie number was safely recorded with just Gene Ramey and Gus Johnson, Brown was added to the trio for *Confessin' The Blues*, which was the first track issued and became an instant success.

With its mildly suggestive lyrics, this hit dictated that the next McShann studio session, just over six months later in Chicago, was devoted almost entirely to vocal follow-ups with just the rhythm-section and only one piano feature. (The single track with three horns includes an alto saxophone obbligato behind Brown, but it seems likely this is Charlie's colleague, John Jackson.) But it was the B-side of *Confessin'* that amazed musicians around the country, for the 12-bar alto solo on *Hootie* sounded to listeners in the know like a high-pitched yet more earthy version of Lester Young. Also of note was the laid-back playing of the ensemble, as

Gene Ramey pointed out: "If you listen to *Hootie Blues*, you'll notice how far behind the real tempo the horns come in. That gave it a lazy image and a bluesy sound... Most of the sax riffs were set by the two alto players, Bird and John Jackson. Buddy Anderson or Piggy Minor set the riffs for the brass... We looked upon Kansas City jazz as like a camp meeting, where the preacher is singing and the people are replying." Ramey and Gus Johnson, both of whom would work with Basie in the early 1950s, were the hard-driving bass and drums team propelling all these tracks. The trumpeter Buddy Anderson, who had previously been in the Buster Smith band and whose ideas about altered chords naturally interested Charlie, is heard to advantage behind Brown on *Hootie*.

Between Charlie and John Jackson, there was mutual admiration and a piquant contrast. Jackson was a forthright blues player, as his recorded work on *Dexter Blues* and the opening chorus of *Lonely Boy Blues* shows, whereas Charlie's solos on *Hootie Blues* and *Lonely Boy*'s second chorus were more quizzical and laid-back, like those of Buster Smith. Parker's authoritative way of beginning a solo with a striking – often strikingly simple – phrase is reminiscent of Lester Young, for instance on the Wichita small-group versions of *Lady Be Good* and *Moten Swing*. The combining of these factors in the six-beat pick-up *before* the expected start of his solo space on *Swingmatism* is the sort of thing that bewildered and thrilled even his own group several years later. His more overt humour shows through on the saxophone-section quotation from *The Donkey Serenade* behind the brass theme of *Hootie*. The latter is one of two recorded big-band compositions to carry a composer credit for Parker, reflecting his ability at setting riffs, either in rehearsal or during live performances. The other, 1942's *The Jumpin' Blues*, was apparently put together in less than forty-five minutes' rehearsal time. Parker's *Yardbird Suite*, never recorded by the McShann band, is a reminder that the camaraderie in the band spawned Charlie's nickname "Yardbird." Accounts of the actual origin differ, but all except Charlie himself seem agreed that the reference was to a chicken intended for the pot. This later became shortened for general usage to "Bird," although Dizzy Gillespie, when reminiscing about Charlie even late in his life, still tended to refer to him as "Yard."

The five brief Parker solos recorded on the McShann band's 78 rpm singles during 1941–42 were immediately noticed by a handful of fellow musicians as denoting the arrival of something new. But, compared to these commercial recordings, Charlie's live work with McShann was really something to marvel at, as Gene Ramey has described it:

> Everything had a musical significance for him. He'd hear dogs barking,
> for instance, and he would say it was a conversation – and if he was

blowing his horn he would have something to play that would portray that thought to us. When we were riding the car between jobs we might pass down a country lane and see the trees and some leaves, and he'd have some sound for that. And maybe some girl would walk past on the dance floor while he was playing, and something she might have would give him an idea for something to play on his solo. As soon as he would do that, we were all so close we'd all understand just what he meant.

But it was the instant fusion of this instinctual side of Parker's playing with the utterly logical and technically justifiable advances beyond the benchmark developments of Lester Young and Coleman Hawkins that grabbed his colleagues.

His longest surviving solo in the context of the full McShann band is from a New York broadcast, only brought to light almost fifty years later, where he is featured on a swing arrangement of *I'm Forever Blowing Bubbles*. "He used to tell me how he'd stand on the corner, look up at the sign at the Savoy Ballroom and all that stuff," McShann said about Charlie's first New York visit. Now Charlie had made it to the Savoy Ballroom on his own terms, and the McShann debut season there in February 1942 was memorable. The band remembered it because they arrived late for opening night, to find Lucky Millinder already playing his alternating set, yet McShann's men conquered the audience through their driving ensemble work. And New York musicians who hadn't heard *Hootie Blues* remembered it for their first encounter with Parker, particularly through his feature number *Cherokee*, arranged by Skip Hall so that his entrance was preceded by an ensemble quotation from the song *Clap Hands, Here Comes Charlie*. Ramey described the first Sunday matinee:

> Bird started blowing on *Cherokee* at that extremely fast tempo... The programme was going out on the radio and somebody in the studio called the man with the ear-set and said, "Let them go ahead. Don't stop them!"... That night you couldn't get near the bandstand for musicians who had heard the broadcast. "Who was that saxophone player?" they all wanted to know.

Even journalists started to take notice, or at least Barry Ulanov of *Metronome* magazine did, writing that "The jazz set forth by the Parker alto is superb. Parker's tone tends to rubberiness and he has a tendency to play too many notes, but his continual search for wild ideas and the consistency with which he finds them, compensate for weaknesses that should be easily overcome."

The jazz-minded musicians who gravitated to the Savoy to study the saxophonist at close quarters included a select few, such as drummer Sid Catlett and Dizzy Gillespie (by now working with Benny Carter), who were allowed to sit in. But Gillespie was already aware of Charlie, and not just from records. First introduced to Parker by Buddy Anderson in 1940 while he was visiting Kansas City with Cab Calloway, Gillespie had jammed with him at the "coloured" musicians' union hall (the then segregated black branch of the American Federation of Musicians was housed in the same building featured in the documentary film *Last of the Blue Devils*). In the private session with just Buddy, Charlie and Dizzy on piano, the admiration between Gillespie and Anderson was doubtless mutual. McShann later said of Anderson, "He played in the same style as Bird only on the trumpet... He didn't have it with the lip, but he had it here, in his head. He went as far as his lip would take him. He and Diz got real tight." Initially though, Gillespie was not filled with enthusiasm for meeting Anderson's friend: "He wanted me to hear this saxophone player, but I wasn't too interested because I'd been hearing Don Byas, Lester Young, Chu Berry [a fellow member of the Calloway band], Coleman Hawkins and Ben Webster. And I said, 'Not another saxophone player!' Until I heard him. Jesus! Knocked me off my feet. We played all day that day."

Perhaps because Charlie didn't hear Gillespie play the trumpet, either at the union hall or on the job with Calloway, he had apparently forgotten this meeting when asked in 1954 about their early acquaintance:

> Well, the first time – our official meeting, I might say – was on the bandstand of the Savoy Ballroom in New York City... Dizzy came by one night...and sat in on the band and I was quite fascinated by the fellow. And we became very good friends and until this day we are, you know.

When asked if Gillespie's playing at that stage was the same as after working with Charlie, he said, "I don't remember precisely. I just know he was playing what you might call, in the vernacular of the streets, a beaucoup of horn." Answering the same question on another occasion, he replied, "I don't know. He could have been. Quote me as saying 'Yeah'." Now in 1942, having moved on from the Calloway band, Dizzy was a leading light of New York's underground avant-garde, and appearing regularly in the Sunday afternoon jam sessions at Jimmy Ryan's and Kelly's Stable. He had also played famously (and unpaid) with the house band at Minton's in Harlem, which since late 1940 included the innovative Thelonious Monk and pioneering progressive drummer Kenny Clarke. Charlie naturally played on occasion at this "laboratory of bebop" and Monk was quoted to the effect that "Bird's ability and authority were immediately accepted as exciting and important additions." The fact that Charlie was apparently recorded there more than once by amateur sound engineer Jerry Newman is less enlightening, since Newman seemingly didn't appreciate Parker's work and the surviving fragments have yet to be issued publicly. There is available, however, a version of his favourite *Cherokee* from this period, backed by the non-union house band at Monroe's Uptown House. In the competitive give-and-take of such jam-session venues, Charlie now found the locals were no longer so daunting but merely something more that he could learn from and absorb: "I began to listen to that real advanced New York style. At Monroe's I heard sessions with a pianist named Allen Tinney; I'd listen to trumpet men like Lips Page, Roy [Eldridge], Dizzy and Charlie Shavers, outblowing each other all night long. And Don Byas was there, playing everything there was to be played... That was the kind of music that caused me to quit McShann and stay in New York."

Parker's last record session with the band was in the summer of '42, although the previous year he had left of his own accord and rejoined after a harassing tour of the Southern states, during which he and Walter Brown had been briefly arrested together in Jackson, Mississippi for breaking a curfew that was only enforced on black citizens. The jewel of this date is *The Jumpin' Blues*, not only for the excellent contributions by Parker and Brown but the single-minded cohesion of both ensemble and rhythm-section. The famous opening phrase of Bird's solo, echoing an idea that is heard in recordings of Lester Young, was later turned into the theme *Ornithology* by Earl Hines' trumpeter Benny Harris, but it is less often noted that the (Parker-created) saxophone riffs backing the vocal choruses were copied in Dizzy Gillespie's arrangement for the Coleman Hawkins' 1944 recording, *Disorder At The Border*. In a very real sense, this track encapsulates the sources of both bebop and rhythm-and-blues, and of the ultimate conflict between them. Tenor saxist Jimmy Forrest (who much later had a hit record with *Night Train*, the R&B version of Ellington's *Happy-Go-Lucky Local*) joined McShann on Charlie's recommendation around this time, and one writer believes he is already present on the *Jumpin' Blues* record date. Jay himself commented that "Bird would blow that *Body And Soul* till there wasn't anything else to blow, but the people wouldn't even clap their hands. Then Jimmy Forrest would take over, and the house would break up when he got through. It used to make me so mad!"

With Charlie doubling in both the more formalized surroundings of the McShann band and the cut-and-thrust of Harlem jam sessions, with no time for regular sleep or regular meals but a lot of time devoted to scoring drugs, he was becoming less reliable than he had been for quite some time. Although *Cherokee* remained his special feature number with McShann, on one occasion he was absent from the Savoy until, halfway through the number, he appeared playing his solo on the dance-floor. During another *Cherokee*, although seated on the bandstand, he fell asleep instead of starting to play. Early on in the New York stay, he had been sacked and reinstated after a brawl with Walter Brown, and once he nearly set his hotel room alight by falling asleep with a lighted cigarette. Finally, when the band visited Detroit, he had to be left behind suffering from either inferior heroin or an overdose, or both. After recuperating, he joined the Andy Kirk band in order to play his way back to New York, though unfortunately the inspirational Mary Lou Williams had left the group for good a few months earlier. Without any work in prospect, he became a full-time but ill-paid member of the band at Monroe's, now including the young Max Roach – who all played for the kitty that some-times yielded as much as $6.00, although some nights it was more like forty or fifty cents. Then, subsidised by the musicians officially employed at Minton's sharing their pay with him, he also became a supernumary of their band. But, so far, these were virtually the only colleagues who were interested in his welfare or his music.

If Charlie's abundant technique and imagination could have been eas-ily assimilated into the average swing small-groups, he might have found steady employment downtown in the small clubs of 52nd Street, with bandleaders who could have scouted him in Harlem. By contrast, the new elements in his music seemed to be posing a stylistic threat to them, and especially to their saxophone players. Instead, at the end of 1942 he was insinuated into the relatively forward-looking touring band of Earl Hines, who had recently been persuaded to hire Dizzy Gillespie also and who had already expressed interest in Charlie (Charlie likewise, accord-ing to Hines) while he was still with McShann. The largely Chicago-based musicians that populated the band already included two altoists, Goon Gardner and section leader Scoops Carry. So it was agreed that Charlie would play tenor saxophone only and replace the departing Budd John-son, who vouched for his ability to meet Hines's demanding standards. It was probably via Johnson's recollection that we know "The audition took place in the dressing room with Huey Long sitting on the face bowl strumming his guitar while Bird blew one of his favourite tunes, *Cherokee*. Everyone was very pleased... Johnson and Huey Long went to Manny's with Bird to get a horn."

However, except in the eyes of one or two of the band members such as the modernist-leaning Benny Harris and trombonist Bennie Green, he was no longer the leading light he had been with McShann. The fea-tured soloist in the Earl Hines band was Earl Hines, with Charlie just one of several others deserving some solo space each night. His main spot was on *You Are My First Love*, a pop ballad arranged by Dizzy to feature Sarah Vaughan who joined shortly after Charlie, and not all the rest of the band's repertoire was as stimulating as Gillespie's contributions such as *Down Under*, *Salt Peanuts* and *Night in Tunisia*. Unfortunately, no records were made of this transitional band because of the musicians' union ban on recording from August 1942 and, oddly enough, not a single aircheck has yet come to light. But what the eight months with Hines did triumphantly was to cement the relationship between Parker and Gillespie. During occasional weeks when the band was in New York at the Apollo and the two leading modernists were jamming at Minton's every night as well, Charlie put the finishing touches to the synthesis of his Kansas City background and the advanced New York style, a synthesis that within the next couple of years was to become known as "bebop." In 1980, Gillespie told me that Parker was the "catalyst" in establishing this new development:

> My contribution and Charlie Parker's, and all the guys that were involved, are so closely entwined that it's difficult to find out who did what – because we were all conscious of the other ones' contribution. But I would say that my major contribution was in the field of harmonics and rhythm. Charlie Parker's was phrasing, which I think was the most important part of the music, anyway. When you phrase something like someone, you are copying them, whether you're playing the same notes or not... We'd been playing a lot of things, we [the New York experimentalists] had all our rhythm and our harmonies all ready, and then Charlie Parker came on the scene demonstrating *how* it could be done. And then all of us fell in behind that.

A comment made by Hines after Charlie's death pointed to the continuing influence of instrumental exercise books, of the kind he studied in the Ozarks, on both Parker and Gillespie. There was a positive side to Hines' statement that "I think that was where actually Charlie got his particular style from, was from the different inversions and phrases in these exercises he had... Charlie knew what he was playing, and when he made those flatted fifths and what have you, it was written in those exercises." But the statement also helped to create a myth, seized on by detractors of bebop, that the new style consisted merely of technical brilliance. Gillespie, however, when observed in a much later practice-book session with saxophonist James Moody, remarked that the content of an exercise "makes no sense musically, but it sure is hard as hell to play."

While the band was on the road, the collaboration between the two continued non-stop. "We were together all the time, playing in hotel rooms and jamming... The guys who pushed dope would be around, but when he wasn't with them, he was with me... He might smoke a joint or something, but he would never take off in front of me." Although Gillespie was referring to Charlie's extra-musical activities, he can be heard taking off musically in a remarkable group of private recordings that were actually done in hotel rooms. Preserved by the road manager Bob Redcross, who was subsequently Billy Eckstine's assistant, they include a legendary trio performance of *Sweet Georgia Brown*, featuring Dizzy, Charlie (on tenor, of course) and the twenty-year-old bassist Oscar Pettiford, who was then touring with Charlie Barnet's band. Oscar had previously met Parker with McShann, while working with the Pettiford family band, and he recalled in the 1950s: "I saw him again in Earl Hines' band in 1943; they were in Chicago, and Diz was in the band, too. I got word that time that I could be in a jam session with Bird and Diz, and I walked two miles carrying my bass without gloves in ten below zero weather to the Ritz Hotel." The performances, fondly remembered by the participants and even listed in Gillespie's 1979 autobiography, were thought to have been lost or destroyed until they were located and publicly released in the mid-1980s. Fascinatingly, they also contain instances of Charlie practising along with commercially issued records by Benny Goodman and pianist Hazel Scott which, although never intended for wider consumption, amount to a live overdub.

Nevertheless, however much he was focused during such informal sessions, when it came to the job with the Hines band, Charlie was often missing performances altogether or nodding off on stage. Earl Hines was impressed by his seeming ability to improvise by sheer reflex action within seconds of being woken up. In April 1943, as the band finished ten days in Washington, DC, Charlie married for the second time. Geraldine Scott may have met Charlie for the first time a year earlier while he was with the McShann band, although Rebecca claimed to author Carl Woideck that Charlie already knew and had an affair with Gerri in Kansas City. She was a nightclub dancer, described by singer Betty Carter as "a very beautiful girl," when she met her doing chorus-line work in Detroit, probably in late 1947. Gerri was perhaps more in love with the life of showbusiness people than she thought she was with Charlie, while he for his part must have assumed her to be capable of providing money and stability. "When I met him, all he had was a horn and a habit. He gave me the habit," Gerri said later. It therefore must have seemed almost logical to Charlie to borrow back her wedding ring from time to time in order to drop hints about marriage with other girls, especially ones who could "lend" him the money to score a fix for him and his wife. Within a few months at most, they had separated and at the time of Charlie's death, according to Gillespie, Gerri was apparently languishing in a Washington jail. By the end of the 1950s, she was undergoing treatment at the same West Virginia reformatory in which Billie Holiday had been incarcerated.

3 now's the time

By the end of 1943 Parker was, if not yet out of control, spinning slightly out of orbit. He had left the Hines band early in August while they were again in Washington, briefly entertaining the idea of settling down with Gerri in her home town. He worked there for a few moments with pianists Sir Charles Thompson and John Malachi, whose group included a future Parker regular in bassist Tommy Potter. However, he was soon to be found back in his own home town, where he worked for Tutty Clarkin with a compatible sextet including Buddy Anderson and Little Phil Phillips (Clarkin later noted that Phillips was another musician who wound up in a mental hospital after getting in trouble with the law). And early the next year he was heard of in Chicago, in the bands of first Noble Sissle and then Carroll Dickerson, former employers of Sidney Bechet and Louis Armstrong respectively, but whose current musical policy held little attraction for Charlie. While in Kansas City, he was surprised to meet the first new altoist to become a member of the Charlie Parker "school," when nineteen-year-old Sonny Stitt came through with Tiny Bradshaw's band:

> I heard the records he had done with McShann and I was anxious to meet him. So when we hit Kansas City, I rushed to 18th and Vine, and there, coming out a drug store, was a man carrying an alto, wearing a blue overcoat with six white buttons and dark glasses. I rushed over and said belligerently, "Are you Charlie Parker?" He said he was and invited me right then and there to go and jam with him at a place called Chauncey Owenman's. We played for an hour, till the owner came in, and then Bird signalled me with a little flurry of notes to cease so no words would ensue. He said, "You sure sound like me."

While Charlie absented himself from New York during the winter of 1943–44, the first bebop group to be booked on 52nd Street had appeared without him. Led by Dizzy Gillespie and bassist Oscar Pettiford – who, after jamming with Diz and Bird in the Chicago hotel room, had subsequently rehearsed with them in New York – the group opened at the Onyx, playing opposite Billie Holiday with Al Casey's group. Soon after, they moved to the Downbeat, with at first Don Byas and then Budd Johnson on saxophone, pianist George Wallington and a nineteen-year-old Max Roach at the drums. According to Gillespie, he had sent a telegram to Kansas City requesting Charlie's immediate presence, but its intended recipient later claimed that it had never reached him. In any case, Alyn Shipton's research on Gillespie in the Hines band confirms that Charlie, as a recent member of touring bands and with only unofficial work at Monroe's and Minton's in between, had still not transferred his union membership to the New York branch.

However, the survival of one incomplete live recording of the Gillespie-Pettiford quintet (with Budd Johnson as the tenor man) is undeniably exciting as a historic artefact, and a reminder that Charlie should have been there. Meanwhile, the 1942–43 ban on studio sessions had come to an end, as not only some medium-large companies but a rash of newly-formed small labels interested in jazz agreed to the union's terms. Of course, even the small labels thought in terms of established jazz figures such as Coleman Hawkins and Lester Young, but there were some opportunities for the young beboppers, which Charlie missed. When the members of the Gillespie-Pettiford group and others recorded as part of Coleman Hawkins' big-band in February 1944, Dizzy created a number with an archetypal chord sequence for bebop, entitled *Woody'n You*, while Budd Johnson's written contribution epitomized the new rhythmic phraseology in its title-phrase *Bu-Dee-Daht* (with the down-beat emphasis falling on the second syllable). Ironically, the previously mentioned references during the same session's *Disorder At The Border* to Parker's *Jumpin' Blues* – just like Benny Harris's Parker-influenced tune *Ornithology* – gave the impression that Charlie was being analysed and anthologized because his physical presence could not be relied on.

The person who brought him back into the limelight was Billy Eckstine, a vocalist of increasing popularity who had been in his fourth year with Earl Hines while Parker and Gillespie were members, but who had left at the same time as them in order to embark on a solo career. But he was also a part-time trumpeter and a fan of the new jazzmen so, after a few months of working as a single, he accepted the current notion that anybody who was anybody needed his own big-band backing. As a result, Eckstine hired Dizzy as his musical director and personally located Charlie to lead the saxophone section on alto. By the time Charlie joined the band in the spring, he had already missed their first record session in April 1944, which did include Gillespie and Pettiford. However, he joined the band in St. Louis at the same time as their new drummer Art Blakey and, his by now expected unreliability apart, he was full of enthusiasm for Eckstine's personnel and repertoire, both of which were partial holdovers from the Hines band. In addition, Charlie had helped to involve a couple of his own recent acquaintances, Tommy Potter from Washington and Kansas City altoist Robert (Junior) Williams, as well as Buddy Anderson. But, when the band went on tour, it soon became evident that the uncompromising stance of Gillespie's arrangements, even behind vocals, was creating resistance among provincial audiences. Eckstine recalled that

> Diz made an arrangement of *Max Is Makin' Wax*, which was way up there [fast], featuring him and Bird. You couldn't dance to that, but peo-ple would just stand there and watch. But I think that...people weren't ready at that particular time for a concert style of jazz.

During the war also, there was supposed to be less racial disharmony but, when these young musicians acted as uncompromisingly as their music, the lack of servility angered promoters as well as some patrons. Compared to the apparent interest in and support for creative music in New York, the relative incomprehension and intolerance out in the sticks must have been striking. In addition, although Eckstine's was an all-black band, the individual players were used to the idea that many serious white musicians openly admired their black contemporaries, and there was much mixing of the races in both the Harlem jam sessions and the 52nd Street clubs. The latter venues, somewhat controversially for the period, condoned similar attitudes among their clientele, which had already led to problems in the period since the US had been drawn into World War II. Servicemen with time on their hands found the entertain-ment on 52nd Street very much to their taste but, if they were white servicemen from the Southern states with an inbred distaste for racial mixing, they were not slow to vent their feelings in brawls, sometimes involving musicians. Chan Richardson Parker's book instances the occa-sion when "The uniformed side attacked Dizzy Gillespie and Oscar Pet-tiford in the subway on their way uptown after work. Both Diz and O.P. were stripped naked, and left to make their way home as best they could." It was difficult to see any amusing side to incidents like that, even more so when a serving soldier who was black happened to get shot by a white policeman, which led to a full-scale riot in Harlem in the summer of 1943. It also led to Harlem residents electing a city council representative, for whom Charlie would play a benefit concert nine years later.

No matter that black Americans' support for the war effort had been bought with promises, from President Roosevelt and others, that things were going to improve for them after the conflict. The fact of black musi-cians acting as if these improvements were already in position caused resistance even in the rest of New York, let alone elsewhere in the country. Two stories involving Parker at this period are habitually told, the first relating to a Southern gig with the Earl Hines band. At an army camp in Pine Bluff, Arkansas, Gillespie was fooling around at the piano and refused to acknowledge a white audience member's pointed request for *The Darktown Strutters' Ball*, an ancient standard. For his refusal, he was later hit in the head with a bottle but, while other band members held Dizzy and his attacker at arm's length, Charlie pretended to be above the fray and addressed the assailant with an English accent learned from observing film-actor Charles Laughton: "You cur! You took advantage of my friend!" Then, when Charlie caught up with the Eckstine band, they were busily rehearsing for their opening at St. Louis's Plantation Club (which, as the name tells us, attracted a white audience and was run by white owners). The management's instruction to the band not to use the front entrance, and especially not to mingle with the clientele at breaktime, elicited an angrier response from Charlie, as Art Blakey recalled:

> Tadd Dameron [the band's staff arranger] was drinking a glass of water. Out of one of the beautiful glasses they had to serve the customers. Bird walked over to him saying, "Did you drink out of this, Tadd?" Tadd says "Yeah." Bam! He smashes it. "It's contaminated." He broke about two dozen glasses. A guy was glaring at Bird; he just looked back coolly. "What do you want? Am I bothering you?," Bird asks him. "Are you crazy?," the guy asks. "Well, if you want to call me crazy," Bird replies.

However, apart from the indignities of touring, Charlie's main problem with this band was again the comparative lack of solo space. A review of their Chicago appearances commented that the "[d]riving force behind the reeds is Charlie Parker, destined to take his place behind Hodges as a stylist on alto sax. After hearing this band doing six shows at the Regal [Theatre], your reviewer didn't hear repeats on many of the choruses which Parker did." Again, he was the featured instrumentalist on a Sarah Vaughan ballad (apparently still the Gillespie arrangement of *You Are My First Love*) but, even within the reeds, he had to compete with spots for the tenor men Dexter Gordon and Gene Ammons, while the brass included Gillespie of course, Benny Harris, Buddy Anderson and briefly (when Anderson was diagnosed with tuberculosis) the just-turned eighteen-years-old St. Louis resident, Miles Davis. Davis later described his ecstatic reaction to hearing the band and its soloists in many interviews, and in his autobiography: "The whole band would just like have an orgasm every time Diz or Bird played – especially Bird... Sarah sounding like Bird and Diz and them two playing everything! I mean they would look at Sarah like she was just another horn. You know what I mean?

She'd be singing 'You Are My First Love' and Bird would be soloing. Man, I wish everybody could have heard that shit! Back then Bird would play solos for eight bars. But the things he used to do in them eight bars was something else. He would just leave everybody else in the dust with his playing."

The stay in St. Louis was also notable for Charlie's last attempt at a reconciliation with Rebecca. Despite his request for a divorce in 1940, he had asked his mother to let her and Leon remain in her house and, following his return home in 1943–44, had persuaded her to accompany him on the road. But, given that his idea of reconciliation could only take place on his own terms, it's not surprising that it was short-lived. And perhaps it is not surprising that, by the year's end, he had started a new long-term relationship. Though Charlie seldom saw his son again, and regularly defaulted on his alimony payments to Rebecca, he is known to have bought Leon a saxophone when he was around twelve years old. (A singer of the same generation who later appeared under the name "Junior Parker," including on a couple of records with Art Blakey and Phil Woods, was merely befriended by Charlie but unrelated to him.) So, disillusioned both musically and romantically, Parker left the Eckstine band when it returned to New York where, in September, he joined a quintet at the Onyx Club on 52nd Street, put together by the great ex-Ellington tenor man Ben Webster. Less than two years earlier when Parker was acclimatizing to the tenor himself, Ben had heard him at Minton's and, according to Billy Eckstine, told Charlie: "That horn ain't supposed to sound that fast," while nevertheless saying to anyone else who would listen, "Man, I heard a guy – I swear he's going to make everybody crazy on tenor."

Happily for us, the fact that he also sat in further down The Street at Tondelayo's with ex-Art Tatum guitarist and vocalist Tiny Grimes led to Charlie being summoned at less than twenty-four hours' notice for Grimes's September recording date. *I'll Always Love You* provides an example of the saxophonist's work on vocal ballads, which so far had gone unrecorded although a popular feature with the McShann, Hines and Eckstine bands. On *Tiny's Tempo* and *Red Cross* (the latter theme assembled by Parker, although related to a rhythmic figure associated with Sid Catlett and recorded in late 1943 by Coleman Hawkins as *Mop Mop*), we hear the chord sequences of, respectively, the blues and *I Got Rhythm* which Charlie used for so much of his best work. This session represents his longest exposure on records prior to his own first date fourteen months later, with solos on all four of the tracks that were coupled as back-to-back singles. Like most of his remaining sideman recordings, these were later reissued under Charlie's name despite the company's obligation to Tiny Grimes – Charlie later observed that "Herman Lubinsky [owner of the Savoy label] does a gang of things he's not supposed to." But thanks to this fact, the posthumous release of alternative versions (as with the majority of his subsequent studio work) shows Charlie's apparent freedom to build a new solo on each performance, combined with the self-discipline to keep improving from one take to the next.

With Grimes playing four-to-the-bar behind Charlie, the rhythm-section has a pre-bebop feel, as on the several 1945 sessions led by pianist Clyde Hart, Sarah Vaughan, Sir Charles Thompson and Slim Gaillard – all but the Thompson group also featuring Gillespie. Charlie's involved but relaxed playing suited these four-piece rhythm-sections (mostly including guitar) perfectly well, but perhaps better than they suited him. As a result, the one of these casual recording dates that is most beloved by record collectors of the period is the one without a rhythm guitarist. "Red Norvo and his Selected Sextet" was recorded for twelve-inch singles (usually reserved for European classical music), thus allowing more solo space for an "organized jam session" format. It features an excellent mix of advanced swing players including pianist Teddy Wilson and tenor-man Flip Phillips alongside Parker and Gillespie, who probably contributed the Latin-backed bridge-passage idea that distinguishes *Congo Blues*. Charlie is particularly impressive on the slow *Slam Slam Blues* which, in terms of his recorded output, is like a trial run for *Parker's Mood* three years later. The up-tempo standards *Hallelujah* and *Get Happy* both have B-sections whose fast-moving chord cycles are designed to show everyone's harmonic virtuosity, and Charlie's solos on each take of the former have another deliberately premature opening, reminiscent of his entry on *Swingmatism*. (The originally issued take of *Hallelujah* immediately goes on to outline a striking melodic six-bar phrase that Sonny Stitt later claimed as his own composition, *The Eternal Triangle* a.k.a. *The String*.) Attempting to explain the development of his own rhythmic freedom out of the previously accepted swing style, Charlie in the late 1940s said, "I think that the music of today is a sort of combination of the Midwestern beat and the fast New York tempos."

Early in 1945, Parker had begun his first live small-band gigs with Gillespie, after he too left Eckstine the previous December, working briefly with Boyd Raeburn and then being booked on The Street. In the meantime, Charlie himself had played some Monday nights at the Spotlite (run by Clark Monroe of the Uptown House) and deputised in the Cootie Williams band, narrowly missing the young pianist Bud Powell, who had been invalided out of the band by a vicious beating from the police in Philadelphia. But, when Dizzy hired Charlie to complete the front-line of his new quintet at the Three Deuces in March, the altoist was blessed with his first fully compatible rhythm-section. Bassist Curley Russell was joined by two white musicians, including a former colleague of Dizzy's and fan of Max Roach on drums, Stan Levey. Al Haig on piano was, even more than Dizzy's previous quintet pianist George Wallington, an excellent soloist and accompanist and, with no guitarist in sight, Haig and Levey were encouraged by Gillespie to indulge their spontaneous (and seemingly random) reactions to the work of the front-line. These interactions of piano and drums, with the front-line and with each other, complemented the apparent lack of a steady four-four. In the popular swing bands, the pulse was locked down by piano, guitar, bass and drums all working as one, but in bebop it was only heard (if you knew where to listen) through the walking bass-lines and the drummer's right-hand cymbal rhythms. Charlie's comment was that "The beat in a bop band is with the music, against it, behind it... It has no continuity of beat, no steady chugging." Add to that the often deliberately asymmetric phasing of both ensemble statements and improvised solos, and it is perhaps no wonder that many swing-rooted musicians who saw this group in action were baffled and troubled by its incontrovertible evidence of a new stylistic development.

The significance of this first long residency of Bird and Diz together on 52nd St., working opposite Don Byas's group and Erroll Garner's trio, must be measured in terms of the significance of The Street itself. The basement clubs, some of which had begun life during Prohibition, were the undisputed mecca for all types of small-group jazz. Although they were tiny and their amenities such that people in the music business referred to them casually as "toilets," they were where the innovations and reputations established in Harlem and around the country were unveiled to New York's white cognoscenti. Once the partnership of Parker and Gillespie had coalesced and the name "bebop" adhered to it, its recognition by 52nd St. led to record dates and helped the music to gain its first hard-core followers. Also, the habit of performers on The Street of visiting each other's venues during breaks enabled more conservative players to hear the new style fully-fledged and to react either with interest or, in many cases, with alarm and hostility. Charles Mingus once remarked, without undue exaggeration, that "The critics tried to stop Bird... All the guys [musicians] on top except Duke Ellington put down Charlie Parker, because they knew they'd have to change what they were doing."

The live impact of the Gillespie–Parker stint at the Three Deuces is underlined by the fact that the Deuces' residency lasted four months, but can only be dimly sensed from their recording sessions under Gillespie's name that spring. Probably at the request of the record company, the line-ups incorporated swing-style drummers (albeit such flexible and high-class performers as Cozy Cole and Sid Catlett) and on the first occasion a rhythm guitarist. But the perfectly blended and razor-sharp unison playing of trumpet and alto on up-tempo themes exactly mirrors the impact of the succeeding solos by both parties, and betokens their growing collaboration during the preceding three years. The importance of the original themes in codifying the new solo styles was realized by all concerned. Oscar Pettiford was aware of Parker the composer in 1943, saying that "He was writing a lot of things then." However, as to actually notating the things that Charlie conjured up, Gillespie subsequently noted, "I had been putting down Bird's solos on paper, which is something Bird never had the patience for himself." He recalled Parker coming to his apartment in the middle of the night:

> "Not now," I said, "Later, man, tomorrow." "No," Bird cried, "I won't remember it tomorrow; it's in my head now; let me in please." From the other room, my wife yelled, "Throw him out," and I obediently slammed the door in Bird's face. Parker then took his horn to his mouth and played the tune in the hallway. I grabbed a pencil and paper and took it down from the other side of the door.

Although their closeness at the time makes the collaboration with Gillespie hard to untangle, the joint composer credits on many of these numbers probably point to the kind of activity described by Diz. It may well be that Gillespie, with his great ability and interest in the field of arranging, was more than half responsible for the final form of many pieces, especially those that have written ensemble introductions and bridge-passages, such as were common in swing big-band arrangements.

Examples of such structures are *Groovin' High* (with its onomatopoeic two-note "bebop" phrase built into the main thematic phrase), *Shaw 'Nuff*, *Dizzy Atmosphere* and *Salt Peanuts*. The last two have a notable swing feel to the melodic hooks of their themes and their introductions – indeed the riff of *Salt Peanuts*, which Dizzy had been using on record at least since Lucky Millinder's 1942 *Little John Special* (clearly named for Gillespie himself), was a direct quotation from Louis Armstrong's *I'm A Ding Dong Daddy*, while the same tune's first interlude mirrors a solo improvisation of Charlie Christian on *Benny's Bugle*. Perhaps such swing leanings already point towards Gillespie's successful consolidation of big-band tradition and bebop innovation in the second half of the 1940s. Other notable themes from this prolific period that Parker had a hand in include *Ko Ko, Anthropol-*

ogy (a.k.a. *Thriving From A Riff*) and *Confirmation*. It is worth noting here how, in 1949, Parker claimed that Gillespie was "forced to add his name to several of Charlie's numbers, among them *Anthropology*, *Confirmation* and *Shaw 'Nuff*. Dizzy had nothing to do with any of them, according to Charlie." Supposedly this was as a concession to the commercial interests promoting Dizzy in the mid-1940s, in which case Charlie's finger would point at the publisher Leeds Music. While Gillespie demurred over some of the other Parker comments in the same interview, he apparently did not rebut this particular allegation, though it is worth bearing in mind that, at least at this period, the tunes would certainly not have been published at all without Dizzy's name listed as co-composer.

The recordings of this material, plus Tadd Dameron's excellent *Hot House*, were reviewed in *Down Beat* some months later, but the guarded welcome for *Shaw 'Nuff* (backed by *Lover Man* featuring Sarah Vaughan with the quintet) was typical of the general reaction to bebop: "It's exciting and has plenty of musical worth, yet for lasting worth must rid itself of much that now clutters its true value. Dizzy's and Charlie's solos are both excellent in many ways, yet still too acrobatic and sensationalistic to be expressive in the true sense of good swing." Meanwhile, Gillespie and Parker were seeking to expand their horizons and their audience by appearing at least twice in concert at New York's Town Hall (May 16 and June 22), with Levey replaced on the first occasion by Harold (Doc) West – Erroll Garner's drummer and a veteran of the McShann band and the Tiny Grimes record date – and on the second by Max Roach, recently returned to New York after touring with Benny Carter. Incredibly enough, the Gillespie-Parker quintet set from the second concert was not only recorded but, as this book was being prepared for publication, a copy of this previously unsuspected artefact surfaced which bids fair to be the archaeological find of the decade. All the members are on top musical form, though Charlie repeats the frequent pattern of his work for McShann, Hines and Eckstine by arriving late. Dizzy is already playing his tune *Bebop* with the front-line filled out by Don Byas (who was on Gillespie's studio version of this piece from January 1945), when Parker arrives in mid-tune and proceeds to play a high-velocity solo of five choruses. Things get, if anything, better from there on and, when drummer Sid Catlett (the elder statesman who had recorded with the other four musicians the previous month) sits in for a version of *Hot House*, the audience insists on him staying for the set-closing version of the riff attributed to Thelonious Monk, *52nd Street Theme*.

Both of these concerts were reviewed by writers who were enthusiastic about the music but complained about the master of ceremonies, "Symphony Sid" Torin, "a creditable announcer on record shows, but much too anxious to knock you out with hip vocabulary." Covering the first concert, Barry Ulanov noted several tunes mentioned in the last two paragraphs (some of them recorded but none yet released) along with Gillespie's *Night In Tunisia*, *Blue 'N Boogie* and *Bebop*, plus Thelonious Monk's *Round Midnight*. Ulanov, the co-editor of *Metronome* magazine which was generally more favourable to the new sounds, noted that "Charley's solos almost never failed to get a roar from the audience because of his habit of beginning them with four-bar introductions in which the rhythm was suspended (as in a cadenza), then slamming into tempo, giving his listeners a tremendous release, an excited relief." He also complimented such listeners with the comment, "That audience seemed to me the most hip I've ever seen or heard."

Around this same period, the intrepid front-line players also appeared in front of several differently hip audiences, for instance by sitting in with Machito's popular Afro-Cuban band. Furthermore, as Dizzy was proud to point out in 1976:

> Charlie Parker and I were closely connected with the African Academy of Arts and Research from Nigeria, and we became closely acquainted with some of the Africans that were studying in the United States. And we played benefits all over New York, just with the trumpet and the saxophone and African drums. It was never recorded but, man, we used to get into some *grooves*, with those Africans *dancing* and everything while we're playing.

Charlie was to be featured at various 52nd Street clubs frequently throughout the year, even when Dizzy went off in mid-1945 to form his first short-lived big-band with Roach on drums. Now well enough known to be hired as a leader, Charlie was able to return to the Three Deuces in August with the previous quintet but replacing Gillespie with Don Byas. Then in October, he enjoyed a residency at the Spotlite for which he employed a sextet including ex-Eckstine tenor man Dexter Gordon, Sir Charles Thompson and the young Miles Davis who, shortly after playing with the Eckstine band in St. Louis, had persuaded his father to pay for a course at the Juilliard School of Music so that he could listen to and play with Parker on his home territory.

Charlie, however, although a veteran of the big-time and a leader in his own right, soon shacked up in Miles' apartment at 147th Street and Broadway (and looked after some of his allowance and his belongings too), until Davis was joined by his wife and decided to find Charlie a room in the same building. The saxophonist himself was freelancing sexually, and his increasing renown meant that many women, especially those who were on the nightclub scene, took an interest. Two white women in particular became involved with him at this period, and were to be in competition for his attentions for the remaining years of his life. Chan Richardson, a tall and glamorous dancer who was at this point between engagements, worked in the hat-check room of the Yacht Club and shared an apartment with her widowed mother (who did similar work at the 21 Club). Both of these clubs were on 52nd Street, as was their apartment at 7 West 52nd, and Chan was a music fan who made it her business to attend the Three Deuces and Town Hall engagements, and even to be present at band rehearsals. Doris Sydnor, who by contrast admitted that "I didn't know anything about jazz when I met Bird," was also working as a checkroom attendant at the Spotlite and was equally tall though rather gawky. Nicknamed "Olive Oyl" after the *Popeye* cartoon character, she was living at 411 Manhattan Avenue near 117th Street, in an apartment where the pianist Argonne (Dents) Thornton (later known as Sadik Hakim) also rented a room, and was thus able to report back to Charlie when Chan had a dalliance with Thornton/Hakim. Rejecting the independent-minded Chan, Charlie in late 1945 moved into the apartment of the more obviously adoring Doris, who became his official consort for the next five years.

It may be that Charlie's group with Davis also played briefly at Minton's, as mentioned in Miles' autobiography. But by November, Gillespie was back in New York along with Max Roach, and was using Charlie, Max and Bud Powell in his group, plus a new New York arrival, bassist Ray Brown. It seems likely that this quintet line-up worked on 52nd Street before making its historic trip to the West Coast, and that this was the occasion for an attempt by Charlie's peers to make him see the error of his ways. Max Roach has said that "We were all back there in the dressing room at the Three Deuces, and we were telling him how much he meant to us, how much he meant to black people, how much he meant to black music. And for him to throw away his fucking life like that was ridiculous." But when Parker made his benchmark *Now's The Time* recording date that same month – the first under his own name – Miles Davis reported that "All these people kept coming by and Bird would disappear into the bathroom with a dope dealer and come out an hour or two later... But after Bird got high, he just played his ass off." Roach was on drums with Curley Russell on bass, while Dizzy found himself replacing the scheduled Bud Powell on piano for much of the session. Both Powell and Thelonious Monk were at different times alleged to have performed on the session, but it is Gillespie who is the Monk-like player, replaced during *Thriving From A Riff* by Thornton/Hakim. The latter remained unpaid and unacknowledged by both the producer and the record-label owner, because he wasn't a member of the New York union branch, and both pianists were covered by the pseudonym "Hen Gates." As well as these unusual circumstances, there was a need for saxophone repairs early in the session, which were the cause of two bonus warm-up tracks being recorded including *Meandering* (a solo on *Embraceable You*).

Charlie's two blues pieces, apparently composed on the day of recording, contrast the rhythmically involved *Billie's Bounce* theme with the more traditional, riff-based *Now's The Time*, and the latter's improvisation (progressing from the seemingly simple to the relatively complex) shows how far he has travelled since *Hootie Blues*. Davis, making his major-league debut on these tracks plus *Thriving On A Riff*, adds a strikingly new sound different in approach from either Parker or Gillespie which, as trumpeter Benny Bailey pointed out, incorporates a note-for-note copy of the under-recognized Freddie Webster. The masterpiece of the session, however, is *Ko Ko*, for which Gillespie took over trumpet duties and, whoever is responsible for the arrangement (the copyright credit this time is to Parker alone), it is dramatic in itself. Unlike all the other bebop recordings of the period, the opening thirty-two bars does not provide material for the subsequent improvisation, but forms an extended introduction. Between the introduction and the coda, and spurred on by the blistering up-tempo playing of Max Roach, *Ko Ko* is based, like its rehearsal take *Warming Up A Riff*, on *Cherokee*. As such, it takes some of Charlie's favourite ideas sketched on the 1942 Monroe's version a stage further and, for the first time on a commercial record, sets down his new standards for combined invention and execution at high speed – standards which have yet to be surpassed nearly sixty years later.

The audaciousness of *Ko Ko*, as opposed to its mere technical expertise, is still capable of reducing new listeners to awed silence. But, of course, professional journalists do not often take the option to remain silent, and it is revealing that the records from this session helped to confirm a growing scepticism about the new music. The blues tracks, coupled together on the first single, should have been much easier to assimilate than *Ko Ko* but evoked an infamous review from *Down Beat*, perhaps only useful for confirming the feeling already prevalent in some quarters that Charlie was a more important soloist than Dizzy: "Only Charlie Parker, who is a better musician and who deserves more credit than Dizzy for the style anyway, saves these from a bad fate. At that he's far off form – a bad reed and inexcusable fluffs do not add up to good jazz." The brief reed squeaks are certainly there, but the comment focuses on the detail in order to evade the impact of the whole, while the assessment of the then unknown Miles Davis seems merely incomprehensible: "The trumpet man, whoever the misled kid is, plays Gillespie...with most of the faults, lack of order and meaning, the complete adherence to technical acrobatics." Acrobatics, and indeed Gillespie phrases, are completely absent from the trumpet solos, whereas the admirable solidity and supportiveness of the percussion work goes unnoticed: "Drummer Max Roach, who was with Gillespie's ill-fated big band, fails to help as much as he easily could have." Given the multifaceted negativity of such coverage, record sales except to those who were already converts could be expected to be minimal. However, session producer Teddy Reig noted that these "started slowly but it built. In maybe six months it was like the Bible."

Despite Parker's brilliance on this session, his apparent nihilism and irresponsibility were no secret to Gillespie. So, when the quintet set out for the West Coast in December 1945, it was augmented by Milt Jackson who was to share the solo load during the saxophonist's anticipated absences. Charlie lived up to expectations so well that, after a week, the nightclub owner insisted on hiring another saxist, Lucky Thompson, to make up the numbers to six on a regular basis. Later Charlie would rationalize his frequent defections by referring to the uncomprehending response of the Hollywood crowd who patronized Billy Berg's, but who were attuned to and expecting the witticisms of pianist-singer Harry (The Hipster) Gibson and vocalist-linguist Slim Gaillard. In a typical know-nothing media gambit, Gaillard (who was at least hip enough to use Parker and Gillespie on one of his humour-filled record sessions) was described in the press and on radio as a bebop musician, whose verbal "excesses" were deemed sufficient to get "bebop records" banned by LA radio station KMPC. There was, however, considerable acceptance from the local musicians – especially but not exclusively the black musicians – although it proved insufficient to boost the club's takings. And there was interest from other media, with approaches to make records for the Tempo Music Shop (whose owner, Ross Russell, formed his Dial label for the purpose) and live broadcasts from the club every night for the first two weeks of the scheduled eight.

Some special guest appearances on radio followed, including one by the full septet on the Rudy Vallee show, which very occasionally hosted jazz guests such as Louis Armstrong or Art Tatum. This not only gave Charlie the chance to meet his early idol, if he was indeed his idol (see Chapter 1), but led to Rudy's organizing Harry The Hipster to bring his fellow saxophonist to play in person at Vallee's luxurious home. A studio set was also recorded for the Armed Forces Radio Service "Jubilee" series, whose producer Jimmy Lyons (later co-founder of the long-running Monterey Jazz Festival) claimed to have recommended the band to Billy Berg in the first place and subsequently wrote about their guest spot:

They were late. All the studio musicians were already on risers on the stage. And we had a live audience, composed of injured guys from the hospital. Dizzy turned and kicked off the first tune on the roster with his heel, *Hot House*. The place went up in flames. The studio guys just threw their instruments up in the air. They started laughing and holding onto themselves, watching these strange youngsters playing their funny music.

Released on record decades later (though not including *Hot House*, which Lyons perhaps mistook for another tune), this "Jubilee" session has an electric atmosphere and suggests that the house band's reaction was one of elation, rather than cynicism or scorn. As well as a more compatible rhythm-section, the set allows for longer solos than the original studio recordings of *Groovin' High*, *Shaw 'Nuff* and *Dizzy Atmosphere*. But, in the strained and scripted banter between Gillespie and announcer Ernie (Bubbles) Whitman, it becomes evident that the trumpeter is the only musician allowed a name check. Pianist Al Haig many years later highlighted the band name under which they had been booked in Los Angeles, Dizzy Gillespie's Rebop Six: "That was the way they billed the group and I think it kinda put Charlie off and hurt him inside because he didn't show up most of the time."

Another producer destined for fame, Norman Granz, introduced Parker and Gillespie to another enthusiastic non-nightclub audience at one of his Jazz At The Philharmonic concerts. When issued on records, Charlie's blues-filled solo on the pre-bebop style *Lady Be Good*, although typical rather than outstanding, drew attention to the similarities and differences between him and the now detached and withdrawn Lester Young, whose performance on the same set was his first major appearance since being released from his long detention by the military. But it was during the extended collaboration at Berg's that similarities and differences between Charlie and Dizzy became evident as never before. The two most advanced soloists in the country at the time, Dizzy was training for the marathon while his colleague was the man on the flying trapeze. Observing Charlie to be such a profligate spendthrift, musically as much as financially, Dizzy realized he himself wasn't built that way and became aware of the value of organization, both of his own playing and of his bands. Trumpeter Howard McGhee, an ardent admirer of both men, once told me pensively:

> I think Charlie Parker was the most outspoken [musically] out of the whole group, because sometimes he used to make Dizzy sound like a toy. Because he had an unlimited amount of ideas. He's the only man I know who had a photographic mind in music.

The eventual end of their partnership came about through what Gillespie might have considered a typical lack of organization on Parker's part, or may have been a deliberately oblique withdrawal. Dizzy had bought the necessary airline tickets for his sextet's return to New York in early February and, according to Ross Russell, gave them to the band members ahead of their rendezvous at the airport. One of the earliest accounts, on the other hand, has Stan Levey driving around LA trying to find Charlie and eventually leaving his ticket at the desk. Either way, it seems Charlie found a need to exchange it for cash, rather than fly back and continue his partnership with Dizzy. Before that, they had briefly collaborated in what was intended as the first recording session for the Dial label, which Russell later preferred to describe as a rehearsal. A Gillespie group, initially called the "Tempo Jazzmen," in which Lucky Thompson and Al Haig were to be replaced by Lester Young and George Handy, achieved a rough version of Handy's tune *Diggin' Diz*, but without Lester who failed to appear. When the group reconvened with Thompson, it was Charlie who didn't make it to the session, so that his first substantial body of work for Dial was undertaken seven weeks later under his own name, with a group including Thompson and Miles Davis, who had briefly joined Benny Carter's band in order to travel to the Coast.

This March 1946 session proved conclusively that, though temperamentally geared to living (and playing) for the moment, Parker's mind was not only organized but also *capable* of conscious organization. The famous unaccompanied four-bar break on his record of *Night In Tunisia*, which has been hailed by its session producer Ross Russell as a great spontaneous invention during the first take, is repeated note for note on all the takes recorded that day. What is more, most of the live versions extant find Parker repeating the majority of the same phrase, and varying or even improving the overall outline only slightly. By this time, however, disorganization was the keynote of Charlie's lifestyle, and he might well have been recording *Night In Tunisia* five weeks earlier in New York with Dizzy, had he not cashed in his airline ticket. His own session also included the debut recordings of his McShann-era *Yardbird Suite* and Benny Harris's Bird dedication *Ornithology*, plus a new *I Got Rhythm* tune had been created by Charlie in the studio and titled *Moose The Mooche*. Its dedicatee, nicknamed "Moose," was none other than the local heroin connection but, shortly after the session, he was arrested and imprisoned, thus cutting off the altoist's supplies. Charlie began using port, the wino's consolation, and then whisky and benzedrine as an ineffectual substitute. Although doing fairly regular club dates including with Howard McGhee and others, and further concerts for Norman Granz, he was panicked by the realization that he could no longer do without hard drugs.

Davis wrote about the effect on his confidence of the mixed reception he had earned: "When Bird left New York he was a king, but out in Los

Angeles he was just another broke, weird, drunken nigger playing some strange music. Los Angeles is a city built on celebrating stars and Bird didn't look like no star." A regular quintet with Davis and pianist Joe Albany at the Finale Club in LA's Little Tokyo section kept him going for a while, but received little encouragement from the press. "Some chick who was writing for a Negro newspaper came down one night to review the group," noted Art Farmer. "It was their considered opinion that Bird was saying nothing. What's more, his manner was arrogant and he was not too approachable. He had with him, she wrote, a little black, wispy trumpeter who had better technique than Bird." The Finale, which was being managed at the time by Howard McGhee, was then ordered to be padlocked by the authorities: "Howard was constantly being fucked over by the white police because he was married to a white woman," according to Davis. "The police had closed the Finale because they said dope was being dealt from there – and it was. But they didn't never bust nobody. So they closed it down because of suspicion." Miles, however, was not the only person who journeyed West to join Charlie, for Chan also showed up after Charlie failed to return to New York, hearing his group at the Finale and hanging out with such West Coast-based beboppers as Wardell Gray and Sonny Criss. Just a few months later, she wrote "I know the time he was working at the Finale he was trying to be real straight. He practically carried a brief case. When that fell through I dug how much it hurt him... Then at one of Granz's gigs, Bird was juiced and they asked him to get off stage. That was another blow."

But the blow that Chan herself delivered was to announce that she was pregnant with another man's child and, not agreeing with Charlie's suggestion that she should have an abortion, she intended to return to New York. Charlie for his part stayed on in Los Angeles, joining a new Howard McGhee group at the Swing Club, with four saxophones including Criss, and Parker as the section leader. His eventual breakdown is all too well documented, due to the coincidence of a recording session held on July 29, 1946. No longer in a position to play even by reflex action, Parker can be heard struggling valiantly to execute simple phrases on *Max Is Making Wax*, the tune which had previously defeated dancers now defeating the great saxophonist. With a supreme effort of will, he turns the ballad *Lover Man* into an almost coherent solo but, coming a mere eight months after *Ko Ko*, this sounds like the dying words of someone wounded in battle. After his contribution to the session, he created a scene in the lobby of his hotel, was clubbed and arrested by the local police, and finally committed to the California state mental hospital at Camarillo. Charlie was out of orbit, out of control, and now out of circulation for the next six months.

4 parker's mood

When Charlie emerged from Camarillo at the end of January 1947, he was in good health for the first time in ten years. After the rehabilitation effected by regular meals and an absence of drugs and alcohol (and the cure of a bout of syphilis), he had decided to treat his enforced stay as a welcome rest from the pressures of following his chosen profession. Psychologically, he was well-balanced enough, or at least street-wise enough, to avoid giving the doctors any justification for tampering with his personality. If they had really probed beneath its surface equanimity, they would have discovered not only all the normal well-founded resentments of the minority members of an aggressively white society, but an awareness of the burdens of a revolutionary artist. His feelings about the latter were summarized in a comment to Leonard Feather about the period leading up to his breakdown: "What made it worst of all was that nobody understood our kind of music out on the Coast. They *hated* it, Leonard. I can't begin to tell you how I yearned for New York." In his estimation, this probably translated into a generalization that the supposedly hip audiences in Los Angeles were just as bad as the police and the doctors. In fact, Charlie would have been quite capable of alleging that he was locked up *because* he played music that "nobody" understood.

Among those who were his allies, at least initially, must be counted Ross Russell, record producer and subsequent biographer. Certainly, when speaking to Feather in mid-1947 Charlie still had a favourable opinion of Russell, "whose help he recalls with gratitude." After Charlie's arrest, Russell found him in the psychopathic ward of the county jail and, according to Chan, "Ross got him a lawyer who bargained with the judge, arranging for Bird to be committed to Camarillo State Hospital instead of jail. Bird thought Ross had had him committed, and never forgave him for that." Russell also played a part in organizing a benefit concert at the end of the year, which raised several hundred dollars, and when it transpired that, for Charlie to be released from Camarillo, it would have to be into the care of a responsible California resident, Russell agreed to fill this role. Meanwhile, he had issued the five tunes Parker recorded for him the previous February and March and he now pointed out that, since signing a one-year contract early in 1946, Charlie had only done one satisfactory session. Russell obtained his agreement to extend the contract for another year, intending to start with a specially assembled septet as a follow-up to the *Night In Tunisia* date. But, by the time the second year of the contract was completed, Charlie had taken to saying that Russell "wouldn't let him out until he signed the paper."

The fact that the producer had also issued an early version of *Ornithology* under the title *Bird Lore* may have had something to do with this latent animosity. But that was nothing compared to the fact that the next release, in November 1946, was the infamous *Lover Man* (coupled with the even more disastrous version of Gillespie's *Bebop*) from the pre-breakdown session. Miles Davis, who would also play on Charlie's 1947 sessions for Russell, later described him as "Nothing but a leech, who didn't never do nothing but suck off Bird like he was a vampire." Davis, however, agreed with the general assessment that Charlie was now stronger physically and "clear-eyed, not like the crazed look he had," though describing him as slimmer, whereas other observers were impressed that he had put on weight. "But what horrified everybody was that they gave Bird shock treatment while he was in Camarillo. One time they gave him so much that he almost bit off his tongue... But for an artist like Bird the shock treatments just helped to fuck him up more." His mother was aware of the damage to his tongue, if not perhaps of the reason, while Chan heard later about his ingestion of prussic acid, self-administered while in the hospital: "According to Bird, he had put it in chewing gum during his depression."

By the end of his six months, however, Charlie was eager to get back to playing and, despite the working conditions which it entailed, convinced that he could evade the possibility of re-addiction. While waiting for employment to be arranged in New York so that he and Doris (who had moved to the Coast in order to pay regular visits to Camarillo) could return, he was happy to play a series of Sundays at Billy Berg's with the Erroll Garner trio. Then, during the first two weeks of March, he appeared nightly with Howard McGhee's band at the Hi-De-Ho club, where Russell observed the scale of the alcohol problem Charlie faced on his release: "He began to juice (but juice!) right away and within a month was the soggy wreck I saw so often last year. He goofed badly on the sweetheart of a job Howard had lined up at a local club (two bills a week, unheard-of locally at present) and before many nights had passed was unable to blow his horn and was driving business out of the joint." This engagement, however, provided the opportunity for a legendary fan and keen altoist named Dean Benedetti to begin a long series of private recordings which, though far greater in quantity than the Bob Redcross material from 1943, were equally thought to be completely lost (except for a few excerpts that were copied for his fellow musicians and, in a few cases, were released commercially after Charlie's death). They finally surfaced in their entirety, however, in the late 1980s and provided a huge stash of new Parker solos from early 1947 and mid-1948 – but few by any of the sidemen, since Dean Benedetti seems to have pioneered the contemporary notion of "sampling" what he wanted to preserve and omitting the rest.

Such fanaticism became typical of the small group of listeners who were immediately converted to bebop and to Parker in particular. Trombonist Jimmy Knepper was an early associate of Benedetti (and someone at pains to dispute Ross Russell's novelettish depiction of a parasitic hanger-on), saying of Dean and his friends, "These guys were so enthusiastic, all they could listen to was Charlie Parker." It was the same at various jam sessions, such as the one held at the home of trumpeter Chuck Copely to celebrate Charlie's release, a couple of the private recordings from which appeared on one of Russell's early Dial long-play albums. Even more than before his hospitalization, all manner of musicians wanted to sit in with him and get the "word from the Bird." "Who didn't that was searching for new techniques on their instruments?" said Roy Porter, the superior drummer who had been on the 1946 recordings. For Charlie's influence was now spreading like wildfire, partly through live performance but principally through records – not only the *Now's The Time* session for Savoy and the first Dial date, but the two 1945 occasions under Gillespie's name came to be regarded as the touchstones of bebop. Despite the trumpeter's imagination and technique, his style was already diverging from Charlie's and was less of a blanket influence than the altoist, whereas the latter was creating disciples not only on the alto (beginning with Sonny Stitt, Sonny Criss, Jimmy Heath and Art Pepper) but on every other instrument as well. Only Louis Armstrong in the 1920s had caused such a tidal change in the way the music was played.

Parker's last two West Coast record dates for Dial included a homogeneous septet session with Howard McGhee and Wardell Gray, for which his one new theme – written in a taxi on the way to the rehearsal – was a complex blues called *Relaxin' At Camarillo* (so titled by Russell in an allusion to Muggsy Spanier's *Relaxin' At The Touro*, named after the hospital where Spanier had gone to dry out in 1938). On the day of recording, Charlie's playing appeared to reflect the title, even though he was badly hung-over and had slept the night in a bathtub of a rooming house following a row with Doris. The relaxation was even more obvious on one of his few saxophone-and-rhythm-only recordings, done a week earlier although only released after the septet tracks. The accompaniment of the Erroll Garner trio with Doc West on drums, previously heard on the Tiny Grimes date, imparts a pre-bebop feel which throws into greater relief the soaring lines of the alto on *Cool Blues* and especially *Bird's Nest*; the former gained Charlie's first symbolic acknowledgement from abroad as the single was eventually awarded France's Grand Prix du Disque. At the same time he indulged his desire to feature one of the sitting-in breed, an inferior imitator of Billy Eckstine called Earl Coleman, whom Charlie had first known in Kansas City in 1943. The two Coleman features, *This Is Always* and *Dark Shadows*, were treated by listeners and the occasional hip disc-jockeys as being the A-sides, and Charlie's ballad playing behind the vocals made the first tune his most commercially successful record so far, while the second received another kind of symbolic acknowledgement – the alto improvisation was scored by Shorty Rogers for the entire Woody Herman sax-section to play on the appropriately titled *I've Got News For You*.

Charlie and Doris arrived back in New York after an Easter weekend gig in Chicago's Pershing Ballroom, and soon took up residence at the Dewey Square Hotel, just round the corner from Minton's. But it seems that, despite concentrating heavily on whisky in the two months since Camarillo, Charlie resumed his earlier habit while in Chicago. He appeared as a guest soloist with Dizzy Gillespie's thriving new big-band at the Savoy Ballroom and then at the McKinley Theatre in the Bronx, and was being discussed as a permanent addition. But, irrespective of whether this would have been to his taste in the long term, the latter engagement (in the words of big-band member Miles Davis) alerted Gillespie to Parker's condition: "Bird was up on stage nodding out and playing nothing but his own solos. He wouldn't play behind nobody else. Even the people in the audience were making fun of Bird while he was nodding up there on stage. So Dizzy, who was fed up with Bird anyway, fired him after that first gig." Nevertheless, Gillespie's agent at the Moe Gale organization, a former trumpeter named Billy Shaw (the dedicatee of *Shaw 'Nuff*, while *Billie's Bounce* referred to his secretary), indicated his interest in representing Charlie, following an initial engagement at the Three Deuces that had actually been set up through Chan Richardson acting as intermediary for Ross Russell. In addition the Savoy label, which had financed Charlie's *Now's The Time* session, offered to record him again the month after his return to New York.

When made aware by Russell's lawyer of the "exclusive" Dial agreement contracted in February 1946 and renewed a year later, Savoy owner Herman Lubinsky produced a contract with Parker (perhaps drawn up in 1947 and backdated) signed as of November 1945.

In the interval before his nightclub opening, Charlie set about assembling the quintet which was to be his regular working group for the next few years. To the essential ingredient of Max Roach on drums, he added Miles Davis, bassist Tommy Potter and, on the May 1947 Savoy record session, Bud Powell. The playing is of a uniformly high standard in this session, which begat three interesting originals by Charlie, including the straight-ahead call-and-answer riff-blues *Buzzy*, *Cheryl* (a contrastingly asymmetrical blues tune and more chromatic than most of Parker's) and the very unusual *Chasin' The Bird*, the theme of which contains two simultaneous and interlocking melodies played contrapuntally by alto and trumpet. The remaining new item, the *Indiana*-based *Donna Lee*, was an original line put together by Miles, whose authorship was contradicted by the record-label credit "Parker" but confirmed by Gil Evans and many other observers. The fact that its opening idea has been described as deriving from a Fats Navarro solo (on *Ice Freezes Red*, a version of the same chord sequence) at least underlines that this is much more of a trumpeter's phrase than a saxophonist's, especially played at this pitch. Some listeners to these recordings have detected a certain unresolved tension between Charlie and Bud, and Davis subsequently commented: "He told Max and me that he didn't want Bud in the band because he 'got too high.' Now can you imagine Bird saying that somebody got 'too high'?"

This may have caused the choice of pianist Duke Jordan to join the group at the Three Deuces, but he was omitted from several record sessions. For instance, three months later the twenty-one-year-old Davis was awarded his first recording under his own name, with Parker playing tenor for the first time in a studio, using his habitual vocabulary but a tone perhaps slightly closer to Lester Young. The trumpeter elected to use Gillespie's regular pianist and arranger John Lewis, who often sat in with the Parker group that summer while Dizzy's band was booked at another 52nd St. club, the Downbeat, and who contributed his composition *Milestones* to this session. Duke Jordan, who continued with the working band until September 1948, noted that

> Miles...was tight with John Lewis, and he wanted Bird to substitute John for me in the group. But Bird silenced him quietly and firmly saying that he chose the guys and Miles could form his own outfit if anything displeased him. That was all that was heard from Miles.

Such quiet confidence in his own choice of musical direction was relatively unusual in Charlie, as opposed to his sometimes arbitrary authoritarianism. The man described by Miles, Chan, Max Roach and many others as having a natural air of authority habitually relied on this quality to carry him through any situation, and he was not used to being denied. Charlie often seemed almost unaware of his effortless superiority over other players, yet he also used it as a conscious challenge, not only to those who might consider sitting in with him but to his own band, as Roach has noted: "He'd come on the stage and his first piece, his *warm-up* piece, would be the fastest thing we'd play all night. And it would destroy Miles and myself; just reduce us to nothing. I would be scuffling, Miles would be puffing, and he'd just breeze through it." Although now fronting his own group regularly, it was said that no one would ever accuse Charlie of being a good bandleader – something in which Gillespie, and very soon Miles Davis also, were to become extremely skilled. But, whereas the relationship of Gillespie with Parker was one of equality, their different strengths complementing each other, Davis was very much the junior partner with Charlie. No doubt it didn't help that Parker would always take the first improvised solo on whatever piece they played. Still refining his occasionally clumsy technique and searching for his personal style, Miles later said, "Bird used to make me play. He used to lead me up on the bandstand. I used to quit every night. The tempos were so fast, the challenge so great. I used to ask, 'What do you need me for?'" Again, it says much for Charlie's sense of direction at this stage that he recognized Miles' potential and persevered with him despite criticism of his work from others.

Charlie, of course, continued to make guest appearances away from his own quintet, including at a series of Monday-night Jazz At The Philharmonic dates at Carnegie Hall, and a Town Hall concert with Gillespie (plus Powell, Russell and Roach), organized as a salute to the United Negro and Allied Veterans of America. Another venture with Dizzy illustrates graphically the new minority status of jazz. With the end of the war, the popularity of the swing big-bands had waned rapidly, to be replaced in the affections of the majority by either sentimental ballads or dire novelty songs. The black audience for popular music realized that rhythm-and-blues retained some of the values of swing, and had mostly turned its back on bebop as being too difficult to dance to, leaving only a small in-group to appreciate this more demanding "art music." They were joined by a tiny minority of whites, usually of distinctly anti-establishment leanings, while most white listeners who had previously enjoyed instrumental jazz were increasingly drawn to the revival of earlier traditional styles that had been gaining ground since the early 1940s. By 1947, then, the numerically reduced constituency for jazz was being rent asunder by acrimonious debates in the few interested periodicals about the relative merits of the traditional and the modern. One by-product was a new form of "battle of the bands," now staged between a modern bebop group and a traditional New Orleans-style band, and a couple of such battles were broadcast in September 1947 on the Mutual Network, hosted by rival journalists Barry Ulanov and Rudi Blesh. When the second of these occasions allowed the competing line-ups to nominate each other's repertoire, the resulting performances included a convincing Parker–Gillespie adaptation of *Tiger Rag*, incorporating the secondary theme of *Dizzy Atmosphere*!

There was another set with Gillespie the following week during the first all-bebop concert to be held at Carnegie Hall, shared by Ella Fitzgerald and Gillespie's own band, the recording of which preserves a stunning example of Charlie's ability to perform under less than favourable circumstances. The concert's co-producers were Leonard Feather and Teddy Reig and the latter recalled that, as before the *Relaxin'* date, Charlie was asleep in the bath:

> We went to his room [at the Dewey Square] and broke down the bathroom door. We got him out of the tub, dried him, dressed him, got him in a cab, stuck the horn in his hands, and pushed him from the wings on to the stage. The result, which was recorded, can be heard on a record today. It is unbelievable in its speed, ideas, and artistry.

The recording, probably taken from the Carnegie Hall public address system, originally appeared around the start of 1951 under the piratically named "Black Deuce" imprint – with the words "Dizzy Gillespie–Charlie Parker" on the labels and the music identified only as "Part 1" through "Part 6" – and was subsequently reissued by Roost and Roulette, both companies with which Reig was associated. As to the saxophonist's condition beforehand, it seems that Charlie was often drinking heavily, at times excessively, to counteract the desire for other drugs. Duke Jordan reported an instance in Chicago in November 1947 of him becoming incapable of playing due to alcohol whereas, as Gillespie noted (see Introduction), heroin works in an opposite way so that the addict becomes dependent on it to function normally, and it is only the withdrawal of the drug which produces unpleasant physical symptoms. Ross Russell, at this stage still his record producer, observed him using heroin to get "up" for a studio session in October that year. It may be that his untypical physiology again enabled him to take the drug from time to time without actually becoming completely re-addicted. Jordan corroborated Charlie's continued involvement:

> Wherever we would be, the pushers were with us. The grapevine, as far as drugs is concerned, is very quick, very swift; and as soon as Bird hit town, someone would contact him. "I know where something real good is," they would say, sometimes calling the hotel at five or six in the morning, and Bird would go with them. As years went by, Bird started cooling. He went to a doctor in 1948 and was told he had about six months to live unless he took a complete rest for a few years, which he never did.

It has to be mentioned too that, despite this diagnosis, Charlie's notoriety had by now become almost as influential as his music, especially in the eyes of players who persuaded themselves that his apparently superhuman musical ability was somehow the result of using heroin. A full list of those concerned would be too depressingly long for the scope of this book but, for instance, the four altoists mentioned a moment ago (Stitt, Criss, Heath and Pepper, all just a few years younger than Charlie) were to have a serious addiction problem which interrupted their careers, and each of them died in their fifties with the exception of Jimmy Heath, whose involvement was the shortest of the four and who is happily still with us. Of course, the people who made the heroin available are ultimately more culpable, even if they were exploiting a genuine disenchantment with post-war life, as not only African-American aspirations were being choked off but free-thinking whites rebelled against mainstream society's strenuous efforts to bring back pre-war subservience. If you found that the denizens of the night had something to offer that straight citizens didn't, then drugs appeared to offer escape from a world where live entertainment was about to be dominated by the monochrome landscape of television. And, if you were involved in playing some energetic yet intellectual new music that courted rejection by the majority, you were all the more likely to adopt the narcotic most guaranteed to put a wall between you and the rest of society. Unfortunately, as well as heroin use expressing an understandable attitude, its association in musicians' minds with Parker also gave it an air of desirability, no matter what the consequences.

Nevertheless, it was at this period that Charlie made what are not only his finest studio recordings but some of the greatest in the history of jazz. Between October 1947 and September 1948, the quintet took part in six sessions (once augmented by trombonist J. J. Johnson), three each for the two small companies that had been recording him since 1945: Savoy and Dial. The resultant series of performances has the kind of stylistic perfection for which there are very few possible comparisons. Louis Armstrong's Hot Fives, the 1937–38 Count Basies, the 1940–41 Ellingtons, the Miles Davis 1955–56 quintet, the Ornette Coleman 1959–60 quartet and John Coltrane's 1960 quartet virtually complete the list. Already by the time of the last three groups, recording on tape for release on long-play albums had minimized some of the rigid distinctions between studio and live performance which still applied in Parker's day. There are, of course, no live recordings of Armstrong in the 1920s, due to the absence of the necessary technology, but while broadcasts of Basie and Ellington exist from the relevant period they scarcely outweigh their studio sessions in quantity – let alone quality – although their qualities are subtly different. The discography of Parker is extraordinary in that, thanks to Benedetti at this period and to other archivists later, the amount of live material that has been preserved and released to the public now far outweighs the official recordings. Were it not for the frequent deficiencies of the recorded sound, it would be possible to argue that the live output is much more representative and evocative of what it was like to actually hear Charlie in the flesh – and it will be noted that video material is virtually non-existent, so that seeing him in action is next to impossible.

Yet it was the studio work which was thought of by the musicians concerned as their only surviving documentation, and indeed was all that was known at the time. In the studio, according to his Savoy producer Teddy Reig, "Bird was very businesslike with his music. He never prodded his musicians to get what he wanted but he was firm in that he kept going until he got it right. When I felt we had it, we'd listen to a playback and come to a mutual decision." A comment from Dial owner Ross Russell also notes Charlie's leadership role and concern for obtaining the best representation of his music: "On sessions involving Charlie Parker, Bird was always musical director... It was his custom to continue recording until the overall performance was satisfactory and this usually happened on the final take of each number. However, the reason for rejecting earlier takes more often than not lay in defects of performances by sidemen." While the latter statement can be seen as a retrospective justification for the release of alternate takes – a tactic subsequently resorted to by Dial and later by Savoy – the net result of comparing different performances is not only to demonstrate Charlie's own virtuosity and inventiveness but to underline the impressive consistency of the entire personnel involved.

The thirty titles from these sessions, each intended originally for issue in a single version, have the homogeneity and unity of purpose typical of a regular working group at its peak, but also display a rewarding variety both of texture and of material. Some of the latter is discussed in more detail in Chapter 7 but it is worth noting here that, not counting "themeless" improvisations based on standards, there are no fewer than twenty new Parker "originals." (A further "new" item, *Crazeology* a.k.a. *Little Benny* or *Bud's Bubble* was a mid-1940s creation by Benny Harris while, of the twenty, it is now thought that *Steeplechase* is the work of Wardell Gray, and so probably is the introduction to *Klactoveedsedstene* – as to the A-section melody of the latter, it sounds more like the work of Tadd Dameron than anyone else.) Along with some of the Gillespie tunes, and a few Monk and Dameron items, they constitute the most impressive written work of the bebop era. And yet, according to Tommy Potter, their creation was almost as spontaneous as the improvisation of Charlie's solos: "On recording dates he could compose right on the spot. The A & R man [producer] would be griping, wanting us to begin. Charlie would say, 'It'll just take a minute,' and he'd write out eight bars, usually just for the trumpet. He could transpose it for his alto without a score." Max Roach confirmed the need for only one written part, adding "He would tell the harmonic progression to the pianist and the bassist. Then he would look at me and say, 'Max, you know what to do'."

The contribution of the other players should not be underestimated, especially Miles Davis who proceeded undeterred to define his role as an emotional counterweight, but the most impressive aspect of these records is Charlie's authoritative yet mellow solo work. This shows particularly on the numbers beginning without a theme-statement where, after the briefest of introductions or none at all, he establishes the mood with classic composure. It is just as true of the ultra-fast *Merry-Go-Round* (based on the chords of *I Got Rhythm* with a B-section from *Honeysuckle Rose*), *Klaunstance* (based on *The Way You Look Tonight*) and *Bird Gets the Worm* (*Lover Come Back to Me*) as it is of the ballads such as *Bird of Paradise* (*All the Things You Are*) and *Embraceable You*. The latter examples afford an excellent opportunity to observe that, for all Charlie's hard-won harmonic knowledge, his inspiration is above all derived from melodic imperatives and, even at a dead-slow tempo, considerable rhythmic variation. Most notable in this category is the slow blues masterpiece, *Parker's Mood*, where – with no trumpet to act as a foil and even an inappropriately twee piano solo failing to distract – the alto digs down to the roots of black music while majestically updating its language. Despite an Armstrong-like opening and closing fanfare that may be derived from Gershwin's *Summertime*, this is "themeless" in the sense that there is no pre-composed blues tune. It is pure vocal melody transmuted by instrumental virtuosity – involved yet basic, finely sculptured but raw, eminently singable even before the addition of King Pleasure's evocative lyrics some five years later.

Interestingly, the live recordings from 1948 (mainly done by Benedetti at the Three Deuces and the Onyx) tend to corroborate Tommy Potter's statement, insofar as very little of the new original repertoire created in the studio is used in public. *Scrapple From The Apple*, and to a lesser extent *Cheryl* from the May 1947 session, soon became popular with other musicians, and so were often requested during Parker's live appearances. But, in contrast to Gillespie who was using masses of new material in his live performances and broadcasts, Charlie's performing repertoire at this period consisted mostly of standard songs or the bebop classics of a few years earlier, such as *Night In Tunisia*, *Dizzy Atmosphere*, *Hot House* and *Shaw 'Nuff*. This also corroborates Miles Davis's comment that Parker never rehearsed with the quintet, which was at least partly related to a disinclination or even an inability to rationalize about his music:

> See, when Bird went off like that on one of his incredible solos, all the rhythm-section had to do was to stay where they were and play some straight shit. Eventually Bird would come back to where the rhythm was, right on time. It was like he had planned it in his mind. The only thing about this is that he couldn't explain it to nobody... When he called the rehearsals, nobody believed him... We waited around for a couple of hours and I ended up rehearsing the band... Bird never talked about music, except one time I heard him arguing with a classical musician friend of mine. He told the cat that you can do anything with chords.

A lingering trace of Miles' embryonic organizational ability may be the trumpet-led introduction to *Don't Blame Me*, heard on the Dial studio recording and preserved in an afternoon rehearsal at the Onyx of the same tune (which was seemingly not retained in that evening's set). Davis also noted the amount of sitting-in with the quintet:

> Musicians were constantly sitting in with the band and so we were always adjusting to different styles... But Bird had come from that tradition in Kansas City and kept it going up at Minton's and the Heatwave in Harlem, so it was something he always liked to do and felt comfortable with. But when somebody who couldn't play the tunes sat in, then that was a drag.

This aspect of the group's work is partly confirmed by Benedetti's club recordings, with one-off appearances by guests such as Thelonious Monk and vocalists Earl Coleman and Carmen McRae, after whose performance Charlie admonishes the audience for their lack of attention (pre-dating Charles Mingus's activities in this regard by several years). It seems likely he was equally influenced by his swing-era background in realizing that singers often communicate with an audience more easily than instrumentalists. Despite what was said earlier about bebop being seen as an art music – by both performers and listeners – the cross-fertilization between pop and jazz continued, but less obviously than in the previous decade. For instance, one of the non-bebop tunes Charlie frequently played in 1948 was not a standard song from the 1920s or 1930s but the current hit *Slow Boat To China*. In the same year the world of cartoon music, which had frequently reflected jazz sounds in the past, incorporated a favourite Parker phrase (heard in the originally issued version of *Now's The Time*, for instance) as the hook of the 1948 novelty hit, *The Woody Woodpecker Song*. Whether conscious or not of the irony, as early as July 1948 Charlie added this phrase to his armoury of quotations.

The incorporation of even hints of bop into more popular music was a very gradual and totally underground development, brought about largely through the "backroom boys" who wrote the songs and the arrangements that populated the charts, and especially the film and television music of the next decade. Otherwise, this radical new style was perceived as wearing its alienation on its sleeve, and was soon typecast by the media as being just right for anti-social addicts, but not for anyone else. Even Charlie, for all the blues base of some of his work and the genuine melodic architecture of all of it, was ambivalent about its popular potential. In his 1949 sessions he would attempt to exploit it, after observing that some of his improvisations on standards (such as *Out Of Nowhere*, the only song soon to be re-done with strings) were so popular that audiences could sing along with his recorded improvisation. But by 1948, he had formed the habit of ending his live ballad performances, not with an out-of-tempo cadenza as Coleman Hawkins did (for instance, on *Body And Soul*) but with a rapid unison statement of the English folk-tune *Country Gardens*, ending in a long-drawn-out antepenultimate note followed by an abrupt cut-off. While Charlie may not be responsible for this song becoming a pop hit a decade or so later, the distinctly "post-modern" irony of its use by him may be intended to distance himself from the profundity of his preceding improvisation. Or it may just be a way of signalling the time for a reaction from inattentive club audiences, to avoid the indifferent response to his ballad work already noted by Jay McShann. Charlie may also have been the first player to make the kind of ironic announcements beloved of Dizzy Gillespie, Ronnie Scott and others, such as "Thank you, ladies and gentlemen, ordinary applause will be sufficient."

Meanwhile, Charlie as a bandleader managed to create other problems for his sidemen, often concerning money. Now he was in a position to withhold their salaries arbitrarily or even, as Max Roach said:

> Because of some of his irresponsible acts, the rest of the men would
> be docked or the owner would try to get out of paying the rest of us
> anything. I would start beefing to Bird, "I was here all night and working
> for you." I would chide him about his responsibilities as leader.

Some of the more drastic actions which Max complained about included Charlie throwing his saxophone out of an upper-floor window which, according to Davis, led to the immediate acquisition of a new horn funded by Billy Shaw. However, this was almost certainly arranged in exchange for the use of Charlie's image in advertisements for King Super-20 saxophones. In Miles' account, the incident took place while the quintet was appearing at the El Sino in Detroit in December 1947, while the previous month at Chicago's Argyle Lounge (or, according to Miles, on a later return visit the following year) Charlie attained a new notoriety by taking the colloquial description of a nightclub as a "toilet" literally, and peeing on the floor. The consequence, recalled by both Davis and Duke Jordan, was that the club's white manager threatened to withhold payment and Charlie, in what was probably his first direct confrontation with the American Federation of Musicians (AFM), sought redress. In order to do so, he presented himself with other members of the group at the local black branch office (the union's slow integration would only begin in the 1950s but the Chicago branch, which for decades provided the union's national president, held out longer than most in favour of retaining segregated branches). However, the black branch official Henry Gray, who had earlier acted to break Earl Hines free of a long-term contract controlled by gangster interests, on this occasion took the club-owner's side. Pulling a gun on the Parker quintet, he dismissed them from his office and, though Charlie was all for defending himself with his fists (again foreshadowing Mingus), Duke Jordan wisely restrained him.

In the face of such suicidal provocation of authority figures, both Max and Miles realized that at times they were just pawns in Charlie's power games. While both prepared to suffer for the privilege of working with Parker, it was a different story when that hit them in their pockets. There were intra-group tensions during a further fortnight at the Three Deuces starting at the end of March 1948, and they both resigned from the band during what should have been a lucrative spring tour with Norman Granz's Jazz At The Philharmonic concert package with Sarah Vaughan. Completing only two weeks of the four weeks contracted, they were announced in *Down Beat* magazine as being replaced by Stan Levey and another young white musician, trumpeter Red Rodney, both of whom probably stayed on for another tour arranged by Billy Shaw for the Moe

Gale agency, billed as "Bop versus Boogie" and featuring the quintet opposite pianist Freddie Slack. Before undertaking these tours, Charlie and Doris had found it wise to move out of the Dewey Square hotel (when the former was raided by the narcotics squad and Charlie was informally notified that he was under observation) into a hotel near Times Square, the Marden, where Lester Young also resided. It was around this time that Davis and Roach both became involved with the group of instrumentalists and arrangers gravitating around the more senior figure of Gil Evans, which led to Miles becoming the leader of a nine-piece band, later associated with the album title *The Birth Of The Cool*. Their separation from the quintet was by no means final, however, for Charlie was another who often hung out at Gil Evans' apartment, and both Miles and Max were back in the group for its week at the Onyx in July 1948 and a week at the Apollo Theatre opposite Buddy Johnson's R&B-leaning big-band. Charlie then appeared as a special guest with Miles and Max, during the opening weekend of the nine-piece group's two-week stint at the newly bebop-oriented Royal Roost club on Broadway, where bands were also able to broadcast once a week between the unscripted chatter of "Symphony Sid" Torin.

After recording the last two sessions with his most famous quintet line-up in the autumn of 1948, Charlie capitalized on his growing reputation by signing a new exclusive record contract. Norman Granz had already secured two Parker contributions to a forthcoming compilation of specially commissioned tracks called *The Jazz Scene*, featuring Duke Ellington, Lester Young, Coleman Hawkins and others. He noted that Charlie's conflicting obligations to both Dial and Savoy had expired, and added him to the growing stable of Jazz At The Philharmonic-related artists whose records he produced and leased to the Mercury label. At the same time, Charlie earned what was then very generous payment, by taking part as a soloist in the latest month-long JATP tour, with Howard McGhee, Coleman Hawkins, Sonny Criss and Flip Phillips. Parker's bassist Tommy Potter was part of the package, as was Al Haig who became Charlie's regular pianist immediately after this tour. While the group was on the West Coast, he first of all missed one show in Vancouver and then nearly missed another in what had been his temporary home, Los Angeles. Seemingly after the concert in Long Beach, California, he took Doris down to Tijuana and got married for the third time, returning to LA (according to Doris) in time for that evening's performance. But the recollection of Tommy Potter was that this was a couple of days later and, when he was in no fit state to play as the concert neared its end, Granz has confirmed that he pushed the saxophonist's head under a cold tap and said "Charlie, if you don't get out on that stage I'm gonna kill you."

Charlie had recently been told by the doctor that, even if he was cooling on the drugs front, relatively speaking, his alcohol consumption had given him a serious ulcer condition. This may have influenced his sudden decision to formalize the three-year relationship with Doris, although she apparently felt they were already drifting apart: "I really had no strong desire for marriage, but Charlie was going through a jealousy period, a romantically insecure stage with me; so I said yes." There was further change in the air as the New Year approached, for Billy Shaw was preparing to leave his job at the Gale agency and, whether as cause or effect, the bookings of Dizzy Gillespie's big-band were taken over by Willard Alexander. Shaw rationalized his special relationship with the remaining leading modernists – such as Charlie, the newly independent Miles Davis and one or two others – by setting up his own Shaw Artists Corporation. As a sort of wedding present and in recognition of the fact that Bird was beginning to "make it," Shaw decided that Charlie should have his own Cadillac ("The one he was gonna get rid of, anyway, you know," in the words of Budd Johnson). But, according to Doris Parker, the money to pay for the vehicle (licensed in January 1949) came from Charlie's earnings with the agency, and this is certainly possible since his period of less frequent drug use coincided with a considerable increase in income. Aware that some of the comparative squares who came to see him in concert did so because of his junkie status, he frequently admonished both musicians and fans against the fascination of stimulants:

> Any musician who says he is playing better either on tea, the needle, or when he is juiced, is a plain, straight liar. When I get too much to drink, I can't even finger well, let alone play decent ideas. And, in the days when I was on the stuff, I may have *thought* I was playing better, but listening to some of the records now, I know I wasn't.

When Charlie re-formed the quintet to return to the Roost in December for a long stay of fourteen weeks, Al Haig was on piano and both Davis and Roach rejoined – Miles for a couple of weeks, Max for most of the next year. But Davis too was aware that Charlie's behaviour was gaining attention for the wrong reasons:

> Bird always said he hated the idea of being thought of as just an entertainer, but like I said, he was becoming a spectacle... When he started cutting off the band just for the hell of it...that was too much for me to take... I loved him as a creative, innovative musician and artist. But here he was turning into a motherfucking comedian right before my eyes.

There were problems about the money too, so by Christmas Miles was out for the last time, to be replaced by trumpeter Kenny Dorham. Max also took a leave of absence, but only for a couple of weeks, during which he too got married. Perhaps because Charlie wanted the drummer back, he turned up at the church and turned on his charm, according to Max: "There was Bird with this beautiful smile on his face, and a great big black Cadillac with a chauffeur to take us to the wedding party."

While Charlie never forgave Ross Russell for issuing the *Lover Man* solo, it is just as well he was unaware that technology, through wire and then tape machines, now enabled the unauthorized recording of certain of his apparently ephemeral live appearances and broadcasts. The post-humous release of such material has given us dazzling moments such as the 1947 Carnegie Hall concert, as well as some merely indifferent per-formances such as a recently discovered JATP guest appearance in Febru-ary 1949. The fifteen Royal Roost broadcasts of 1948–49, of which several tracks trickled out over a period of twenty-five years before the arrival of a comprehensive issue, provide new insights into Parker's playing barely hinted at in his studio work, such as the casual, open-ended invention of the February 12 *Barbados*. But the set-up for these live shows was pretty relaxed, as shown by the March 12 *Slow Boat To China*, introduced verbally by Charlie himself because announcer Symphony Sid is elsewhere and can be heard laughing and talking as the number is played. On the other hand, the January 29 version of *Groovin' High* includes a single incoher-ent phrase from Charlie before he lapses into silence (and, according to Sid's recollection, sleep) for the rest of the broadcast. Four weeks later, *Night In Tunisia* finds him audibly losing his nerve during the famous alto break, and sounding every bit as uncoordinated as on the *Lover Man* session.

5 celebrity

By the start of 1949 the outlook for Charlie did not seem bright. He knew that he was ignoring the doctor's advice, and he knew that he was sometimes not performing to the best of his ability. But this was at least partly related to the conditions under which he was obliged to perform. After his return from the Coast in 1947, he expressed satisfaction that at least in New York bebop had achieved some popularity with younger listeners, and this satisfaction was undoubtedly reinforced by touring the nation's concert halls with Jazz At The Philharmonic. Before this positive development, however, Duke Jordan had observed that:

> Bird knew the limitations of his success and felt annoyed that he was confined to just playing nightclubs. He was also bugged by the fact that, being a Negro, he could go just so far and no farther. Once he finished a set to great acclaim, ducked out, and went quietly to a bar around the corner on Sixth Avenue between 51st and 52nd Street, called McGuire's. The paradox of his life was brought into focus when the bartender asked what he wanted and addressed him as a "nigger." Parker vaulted over the bar to teach the fellow manners.

Clearly, many whites in post-war America longed for a return to the old values, in part because, during the "war on fascism," blacks had been encouraged to think the US Constitution's promise to treat everyone as equal might eventually be honoured. An influential early-1940s book by black writer Roi Ottley, taking its title from the old spiritual *New World A-Comin'* (and inspiring Duke Ellington to write a piece of the same name), made a plea for the abandonment of racial discrimination. But this underestimated the strength of opposition to such ideas, and not just in the Southern states. In 1949 a former jazz disc-jockey in Detroit could be fired from a "white radio-station" for broadcasting a "black record" by vocalist Nat King Cole. The fact that, by now, America was locking into the Cold War mindset also made it easy for those in favour of a hierarchical society, with blacks at or near the bottom of the heap, to dismiss any moves towards greater integration as being just as dangerous as – and indeed very similar to – the "evil of communism."

One sharp ray of sunlight during the stay at the Royal Roost club was the invitation for the quintet (now including Kenny Dorham and Al Haig with Potter and Roach) to the second Paris Jazz Fair in May 1949. Howard McGhee's group had been to the festival the previous year when Dizzy's big band also appeared in France, while Don Byas and Kenny Clarke had gone so far as to settle there. A number of other African-Americans had decided to live in Paris during the 1920s and 30s, writers as well as musicians, although their number had decreased to vanishing point by the time of the Nazi occupation. But now, in the hopeful climate of post-war Europe, France was widely believed to be a country without any racial prejudice, and certainly the longevity of jazz appreciation there had created an awareness that all the historically significant contributions had been made by black musicians. The joint organizer of this second Paris Jazz Fair, namely the pioneer jazz discographer Charles Delaunay (son of a noted Impressionist painter), was also editor of *Jazz Hot*, the one French jazz magazine that had opted for bebop in the increasingly bitter feud between fans of modern and traditional jazz. So it was hardly surprising that the festival's bebop representatives – the Parker group and the Tadd Dameron–Miles Davis quintet – were lionized just as much as the other guest soloists, Sidney Bechet (who also ended up staying on in France) and Hot Lips Page.

Coverage in the foreign press was equally positive, with reviews in Britain's *Melody Maker* and in *Down Beat*, the latter written by pianist Marian McPartland: "The band had a tremendous beat, and Parker, displaying his prodigious technique and originality of ideas, wove in and out of the rhythmic patterns laid down by Roach to the accompaniment of ecstatic cries of 'Formidable!' from the fanatics." The overwhelming effect of their acceptance was recalled by Tommy Potter: "The reception in France was lavish. Autograph-signing parties in record shops and lots of press coverage topped by a press party in Bird's hotel room. Charlie ordered a bottle of champagne, and he tipped the waiter generously; and well he might, because he had that waiter make five trips for five buckets of champagne." New York musicians noted that Charlie not only returned with a beret but temporarily exchanged his British accent for certain Gallic mannerisms, and a *Down Beat* correspondent, speaking to Charlie after his return, observed that "Bird described the [French] language as being beautiful, with interesting rhythms and musical sounds. 'You know, some of the French cats sounded better than the guys in New York,' he remarked." One "French cat" was actually British saxist-arranger John Dankworth who, having already journeyed with fellow fanatics including Ronnie Scott to New York to hear the Parker quintet at the

Three Deuces, now made "an educational trip" to Paris. Charlie's brief appearance at a jam session in the Club Saint-Germain found him borrowing Dankworth's alto to play *Anthropology*: "When my turn came around to solo he listened carefully. As I finished I handed the Conn back to the master. Then there began a series of badminton-like exchanges, with my alto as the shuttlecock, as we each contributed in turn to the 16-bar (and later 8-bar) mini-solos... Bird surrendered my now-sanctified Conn back to me, gave me a handshake accompanied by a reassuring wink, and disappeared into the throng of besieging admirers."

While in Paris, Charlie was delighted to attend a concert by the classical guitarist Andres Segovia which, in Gary Giddins' words, "exemplified his belief that the artist should be able to hold an audience without theatrics." He was introduced, also at the Club St-Germain, to the French philosopher Jean-Paul Sartre, who was being educated as to jazz by his partner Simone de Beauvoir and by writer and occasional musician Boris Vian. Charlie's rather inscrutable reaction to Sartre was to greet him with the words (translated back to English from Vian's translation): "I'm very glad to have met you, Mr. Sartre. I like your playing very much." Chan Richardson noted that "Bird had also met the great [classical] saxophonist Marcel Mule... He had been idolized and he had a new dignity." (Indeed, it may be during the period following his European trip that he actually took saxophone *lessons* with the noted teacher Henry Lindeman – presumably with a view to improving his tone production rather than his already awesome facility!) The interview done in the summer of 1949 by Levin and Wilson found Charlie saying that:

> For the future, he'd like to go to the Academy of Music in Paris for a couple of years, then relax for a while and then write... Ideally, he'd like to spend six months a year in France and six months here. "You've got to do it that way," he explains. "You've got to be here for the commercial things and in France for relaxing facilities."

It has been suggested that, at some point, Charlie had gone so far as to write a letter to Charles Delaunay, asking about accommodation in Paris so that he could study with the composition teacher Nadia Boulanger. Whether or not Charlie would ever have had the discipline to "write" in a premeditated way, he had, since settling in New York, become deeply interested in European music. His photographic mind enabled him to incorporate specific quotations from Chopin or Debussy into an improvised solo (probably only when there was someone in the audience who would understand the reference), and in interviews he mentioned his liking for Bach, Beethoven, Bartok and Shostakovitch, often naming particular works such as Milhaud's *Protée* or Schoenberg's *Pierrot Lunaire*. Teddy

Reig mentioned Charlie borrowing his classical records: "I had three copies of the *Concertino Da Camera For Saxophone And Orchestra* [by Ibert] and Bird got every one." Younger, more formally educated musicians were also impressed, such as the teenaged Wayne Shorter, who heard Charlie in concert (possibly in May 1948) and said: "I remember that while Bird was doing his solo, he'd go into Stravinsky. Real quickly, he did the little phrase from *L'Histoire Du Soldat* and the other one from *Petrouchka*, put it in his solo and keep going around." And Charles Mingus, who described Parker improvising along with the record of a Stravinsky piece, attempted a similar combination on his recording of *The Chill Of Death*, a work Charlie admired as evidence that Mingus was "a good writer."

Now that Charlie's association with Norman Granz had led to signing with Mercury Records, such large-scale efforts seemed more possible. But, unfortunately, the results were musically disappointing, as in Charlie's first studio recording for Granz for a project entitled *The Jazz Scene* which, though only released in late 1949, had been assembled over a period of three years. One of his two tracks featured him improvising over the second half of a tedious, Stan Kenton-style big-band-with-strings piece by Neal Hefti (who later went on to write such gems as *Girl Talk* and *Batman* but, as a teenager, wrote charts for the black Nat Towles band and, according to Buster Smith, also used to hang around the Kansas City jam sessions with Charlie). The lack of inherent connection between the solo and the arrangement led many listeners to suppose that the solo was overdubbed (a technology that was then in its infancy) but, in fact, Parker had dropped by during the big-band recording session and had created his alto part by ear, while glancing at the conductor's score. For the same project, with just a rhythm-section, Charlie cut his longest solo ever on a commercial record, an improvisation on the Basie number *Topsy* called *The Bird* and containing a fund of ideas, marred only by an apparent uncertainty as to just how long the recording would run. Hank Jones, about to become the regular pianist for Jazz At The Philharmonic and for Ella Fitzgerald, was accompanying Charlie for the first time, an experience he described as follows: "You just try to align yourself or even to anticipate. I don't think I managed to do that, but it was enough to be on the same planet as him. When you're playing behind Charlie Parker, he pulls you along so that you play at his level – I think the expression is 'over your head'."

But the idea of doing a whole album (in those days, this meant a group of 78 rpm singles sold together and often available separately as well) featuring Parker with strings was met with immediate enthusiasm by both Granz as his recording manager and Billy Shaw. Part of the subtext was resistance from within the record industry to the idea of black artists being allowed such a "white" background – Nat King Cole and Billy Eckstine had just recently begun to achieve the necessary cross-over status and, prior to them, only Lena Horne and Billie Holiday had received this apparent accolade. As to instrumentalists, Shaw and doubtless Charlie were aware that Dizzy had already recorded with strings on the West Coast in 1946, only to have the releases blocked by the publisher of the Jerome Kern songs concerned – so much for the idea of jazz musicians being allowed to pay tribute to the composer of *All The Things You Are*, who had recently died – and, as a result, Gillespie didn't do a successfully issued string-based session until 1950. Charlie was clear that the idea was his and, possibly exaggerating the time-scale, he once said: "I asked for strings as far back as 1941, and then, years later, when I went with Norman, he okayed it." Not only did the musical texture appeal to Charlie but, like Louis Armstrong in his late twenties, he may have felt a need to pull back from advanced exploration and reconnect with the wider audience for jazz.

In addition, it would be a way to capitalize on the popularity of his ballad improvisations, only recently heard for the first time on record without the accompaniment of vocalists, in tracks such as *Embraceable You*. The single version (that is, the "B" take) of the latter had been released early in 1949, to a sympathetic response from *Down Beat*: "*You* is a prime example of the heights of originality that the Bird can soar to when he's in the mood. He plays impeccably with a richness of ideas and change of pace that at once astounds you and then enables you to coast a bit while assimilating what went before." The way the album turned out, however, it was definitely one of "the commercial things" and not necessarily in the way that Charlie intended. Despite his lyrical solo on *Just Friends* with its beautifully integrated quotation from *My Man* in the last half-chorus, this is the only improvisation longer than sixteen bars and elsewhere his decorative ideas are deliberately reined in, often cut off in mid-phrase. However, the really dispiriting thing is the way the piano solos and the rhythm-section slot into a businessman's bounce at every opportunity. The unashamedly schmaltzy arrangements by former Alec Wilder sideman Jimmy Carroll are fairly inoffensive, although Charlie apparently liked Joe Lippman's writing for a subsequent session better. Mitch Miller, another Alec Wilder alumnus who has gone down in jazz discography as the oboe player on the first session, was actually Mercury's successful A&R producer for pop music, and Carroll and Lippman were the arrangers he regularly used for backing such stars as ex-jazz singer Frankie Laine.

A virtual co-producer of these recordings, Miller would also have played a significant role in ensuring they were well promoted, and promoted as being the acceptable face of Charlie Parker. There must have been a knowing irony in Charlie's telephone call to his mother, "Mama, I'm going to the top, my name's going to be in lights, and you're going to be there to see it" (which just may have been a conscious allusion to Jimmy Cagney in the 1949 movie *White Heat*, exclaiming "Look, Ma, top of the world"). Yet, on the strength of his statement of the melodies, *Just Friends* and the later string-backed version of *Autumn In New York* did respectively become his biggest- and his third biggest-selling records ever, the first album even earning a listing on the popularity charts. The preparation period for the first recording with strings was seemingly quite long, and there are stories of sessions being called, where Charlie didn't contribute to any extent before leaving the studio again and disappearing. Miller told Ira Gitler: "It turned out that he had been so overwhelmed by the sound that he felt he couldn't work with it" and there may be some corroboration in the viola-player Frank Brieff's statement: "He felt that we were greater musicians than he was and that wasn't true at all... He was, himself, an extraordinary man in the sense that he did things and he didn't know how and why he did them." There could well have been other reasons for his departure, yet an odd parallel exists with the Miles Davis/Gil Evans *Sketches Of Spain* (begun ten years later to the very month) where Davis also did not perform on the first studio date.

It is intriguing too that this high-profile and ultimately popular venture came to fruition shortly after the publication of Charlie's lengthy *Down Beat* interview, in which he severely criticized Dizzy Gillespie. Doubtless the timing of this publicity was partly inspired by Granz, whose first single of "Charlie Parker with Machito" had recently appeared at the time that Mike Levin and John S. Wilson got together with the altoist for a series of conversations, probably during his August residency at the club Bop City. But the background to some of Charlie's remarks undoubtedly lies in the publicity surrounding Dizzy Gillespie in the past couple of years, including pieces in *Life* magazine and the *New Yorker*. Already in 1947 Chan Richardson had observed, "I'm sure if Bird were given the opportunity that Diz was, he could straighten himself out. He knows how much he blows and he's hurt [']cause Diz is making all that gold." In addition at the start of 1949, coinciding with his change of agency, Dizzy had joined the Capitol record label which, as well as recording the Miles Davis and Tadd Dameron groups, had decided that slightly "modernized" big-bands were the next big thing. So Benny Goodman "had yielded to Capitol's blandishments about 'We'll make hit records with you'" (in the words of George Avakian), as well as Gillespie, Woody Herman and Charlie Barnet

– none of whom actually achieved any hits before Capitol changed their policy again at the end of the year.

Charlie may have felt this sort of activity could fatally dilute the impact of bebop, as he believed some of the more entertainment-oriented aspects of the Gillespie approach already had. At pains to distinguish the creativity of "bop" from the big-band style that still for many people represented "jazz," he tied himself in several knots while trying to establish that they were entirely separate styles. And, seemingly more in sorrow than anger, he speculated about the publicity process and its effect on his former companion, in not very veiled terms:

> "Some guys said, 'Here's bop'", he explains. "Wham! They said, 'Here's something we can make money on.' Wham! 'Here's a comedian.' Wham! 'Here's a guy who talks funny talk.'" Charlie shakes his head sadly... "A big band slows anybody down because you don't get a chance to play enough. Diz has an awful lot of ideas when he wants to, but if he stays with the big band he'll forget everything he ever played."

It is interesting to compare the reactions, after Charlie's death, of two non-playing observers who were nevertheless close to the scene. Symphony Sid said that "Dizzy was with the big band and making a lot of money, and Bird was scuffling, because he was negligent in his work... He was the character that made modern jazz possible. He was the first on. He started Dizzy off" – but Sid also added, "The successful musician is not a junkie." Teddy Reig commented, "It is possible that Charlie was a bit jealous of Diz's commercial success, but Parker could have had it, too, if he had had the self-discipline for it." The usefulness of Dizzy's sense of humour in ingratiating him with audiences may also have alienated some musicians but, for instance, John Dankworth has spoken of its positive side: "I think Dizzy's clowning was rather reassuring. When bebop came in, it was not only startling music – and, to me, very joyous music – but everybody seemed so poker-faced about it. You don't imagine Charlie Parker with a smile, or Miles Davis for that matter – even less, Miles."

The other reason for the timing of this interview was undoubtedly the intended opening of a new high-class jazz nightclub scheduled for September 8, 1949, the same week as publication of the article. Birdland was probably the first club to be named not after its owner but in honour of a musician, with specific reference to Charlie as a symbol of quality. It was located on Broadway, not only further north than other recently opened Broadway clubs such as Bop City or the Royal Roost but, symbolically, very near to the corner of 52nd Street. Promoter Monte Kay (who set up the 1945 Town Hall concerts, along with Symphony Sid) claimed to have spent $8,000 of his backers' money in converting the former Clique club, and to have taken a six-year lease on the premises. The opening acts were to be the Parker quintet, the Lennie Tristano sextet, Stan Getz, Harry Belafonte (at that time working as a jazz singer) and Bud Powell. However, the state liquor authority (or Alcohol Beverage Control Board) refused to award a licence and, while the other would-be performers were soon redeployed at various 52nd Street venues, *Down Beat* noted that the "only element of the Birdland show not working at month's end was the Charlie Parker group." Charlie himself was able to join the autumn tour of Jazz At The Philharmonic in September as a soloist, and the gradual proliferation of almost portable recording-machines helped to underline that it was not only in Paris that Charlie was seen as a kind of Pied Piper. Following the JATP concert in Detroit, he showed up to sit in at the Blue Bird Inn and a local fan reacted immediately:

> I said "Wow!" and jumped in my car... Went home and got my machine and came back. When I got back, I couldn't get in the place! I wasn't gone for more than fifteen minutes! I was outside, so I took my microphone and passed it inside to somebody.

It was not until December 15 that Birdland finally opened, with what was described as a change in management although the principals seem to have remained the same. By then, it had undergone further refurbishment, including the introduction of bird-cages suspended from the ceiling with real live inhabitants, who nevertheless didn't survive for very long in the smoke-filled atmosphere. It also introduced a non-alcohol section of the premises where under-age or impecunious listeners could enjoy the music without being hustled to buy drinks, which was seen by some as conferring a little dignity on the proceedings. Naturally, the quintet was re-hired as one of the opening attractions together with Lester Young, Hot Lips Page and Lennie Tristano, the first two choices underlining not so much a Kansas City theme as the intention of featuring small-group swing and even traditional jazz alongside bop. That was another policy that didn't long survive, as the focus soon shifted towards "modern jazz," but the idea of live broadcasts during Symphony Sid's record shows was carried over from the Roost with great success. It was not before time that Charlie should look for a more prestigious outlet than the so-called "toilets," especially since the lively and fraternal scene which had once been 52nd St. was dwindling by the end of 1949. With the exception of the remaining modern stronghold, the Three Deuces, where the quintet played from early October to mid-November (and of the traditional-jazz venue Jimmy Ryan's, which weathered the next decade), many of the clubs on the Street were turning themselves over to striptease. The introduction of jazz to more big-time Broadway clubs begun by the Royal Roost and the short-lived Bop City, which also featured the quintet for a week in late 1949, was significantly boosted by the establishment of Birdland, which was to fly the flag for a decade and a half.

Charlie's group for this engagement had trumpeter Red Rodney replacing Dorham (as at the Deuces and Bop City) with Roy Haynes now taking over from Roach. The quintet was also on hand to take part in Symphony Sid's Xmas Eve concert at Carnegie Hall, which was recorded and later broadcast on the cold-war propaganda station, the Voice Of America, soon to influence a generation of music fans in Europe. After the opening three weeks at Birdland and a fortnight there in February 1950 with J. J. Johnson added on trombone, the quintet performed at dance gigs in both New York and North Chicago, one of which was partially preserved on tape. Saxophonists Don Lanphere and Joe Maini recorded excerpts from the engagement at St. Nicholas Arena, switching off *à la* Benedetti when Charlie was not playing, and the copy of these tapes passed to Maini's friend Jimmy Knepper later appeared on LP and CD as *Bird At St. Nick's*, historically the first of the amateur live recordings to be released after Parker's death. Further concert presentations on Jazz At The Philharmonic's next nationwide tour in March took the quintet from Buffalo to Minneapolis. During the tour, a day off enabled Charlie to invite members of the group to visit at his mother's house in Kansas City, and Rodney and himself to take part in a late-night jam session at the Playhouse Club. But, while the rhythm-section took the next day's train to St. Louis for the concert, the two horn-players missed it and were flown there by one of Charlie's friends who owned a small plane. As Tommy Potter heard the story, "Red told me that Bird asked if he could take the controls; his friend said yes. Now, Charlie never flew a plane before, but there he was, blithely flying the ship, a broad smile on his face. Suddenly, Bird leans left, and the plane banks to the right... Bird said he just wanted to hear the motor when he banked the plane."

On their return to New York, Charlie rehearsed his role as star soloist with an ambitious twenty-seven-piece band put together by ex-Stan Kenton arranger Gene Roland, including Red Rodney, Zoot Sims and Al Cohn as well as Lanphere, Maini and Knepper. Unfortunately, this organization never obtained any bookings, although its rehearsals were the subject of several photos and an amateur tape-recording that Charlie himself initiated. (Also recorded privately was the famous and much-quoted interview carried out by Marshall Stearns and John Maher, around this period, and which is largely concerned to verify the stories of Charlie's upbringing and previous musical history, that had surfaced the previous year in the *Down Beat* article and in Leonard Feather's book *Inside Jazz*.) But a specially assembled quintet – often stated as appearing at Birdland in May 1950 (though possibly somewhere in the Bronx) – was a different matter altogether. The group Charlie fronted was so evenly matched that the participants seemed determined to outdo each other in excellence. The personnel included Bud Powell, Art Blakey, bassist Curley Russell and trumpeter Fats Navarro, opposite whom Charlie had played at the Royal Roost, then on a Metronome All Stars recording and on the Carnegie Hall JATP concert in February 1949. Navarro, sadly, was to die in a few weeks' time aged only twenty-six, of tuberculosis aggravated by the effects of heroin addiction – although you would never know it from his fiery playing on the surviving recordings. Of Charlie's own work, the mobile yet serene extended solo and the series of alto and trumpet exchanges on *The Street Beat*, as well as his new ideas on *Ornithology* and *Embraceable You* (which also features vocalist Little Jimmy Scott), are outstanding.

The following month, the regular quintet then went into another plush nightclub, which had not previously taken any interest in bebop, the downtown Café Society. The plan was originally for this to be Charlie's first live engagement with strings (which had already been postponed at Birdland) and, sartorial elegance never having been his strong point, the occasion was marked by the acquisition of an all-white suit. Unfortunately, the status symbol of the string section was again postponed, so the quintet was used, with the exception that Rodney had been hospitalized for appendicitis and Kenny Dorham was asked to return briefly. The repertoire of the strings ensemble was retained, however, in order for patrons to dance, as Charlie mentioned in his on-stage announcements – all delivered in a smooth-talking 1950-disc-jockey style: "And now for your listening entertainment pleasure, we bring you...". The star attraction was the Art Tatum trio but, after being rebuffed in his desire to play along with Tatum, Charlie decided to step outside the format, as drummer Al Levitt observed:

> After the [Tatum] show, the quintet was supposed to play for dancing.
> Bird pulled up a chair and sat right in the middle of the dance floor
> and played all the bebop you wanted to hear. The audience loved it,
> especially all the musicians who had come to check out the scene. The
> quintet played a storm, it was great, but needless to say the manage-
> ment didn't feel the same way.

Also in June, another significant all-star session took place. The new Norman Granz recording reunited Charlie with Dizzy Gillespie, for the last time in a studio, and Thelonious Monk, whose only studio session with Charlie this was. As it happens, although it is a joy to hear his accompaniments Monk was allowed little space by the producer, and the choice of Buddy Rich (in order to minimize the rhythmic intricacies for listeners accustomed to Charlie's strings recordings) detracts from the group sound, if not the work of Parker and Gillespie individually. During the same month, Charlie was guest of honour at a series of private jam sessions organized by Knepper, Maini and friends, who were busily creating another stash of live Parker recordings. In public, Charlie was also a magnet for sitters-in, some of whom later admitted that he was in a different league. British-born pianist George Shearing, recently relocated in the US, committed the social gaffe of trying to be too hip: "I said to him, 'What'll we blow, Bird?' So he replied, '*All The Things You Are* in five sharps'! Well, I survived, and even emerged with some honour. But what I should have said was, 'What would you like to play, Mister Parker?'"

During this period of relative success Doris Parker, despite priding herself on keeping Charlie straight, at least financially, had begun to take a back seat emotionally and eventually went home to her mother, recalling subsequently that

> I was in no physical condition to cope with the erratic life of a jazz musician. I was nervous and bothered by low blood pressure and anaemia. I just couldn't take the anxiety of wondering where he was the nights he came home very late or not at all. Visions of him hospitalized or in jail would come into my mind...When we broke up, I was very sick, and Charlie never sent me a penny. I had to depend on my family for help.

Addie's view of this situation was that "Once when Doris was sick, Charles told her to go home, stay awhile, and then come back. He wanted more children." Perhaps this is why on May 29 Charlie consolidated a relationship which had restarted several months earlier, and moved Chan Richardson into the apartment he'd shared with Doris at 422 East 11th Street. As mentioned, Chan had known Charlie in the mid-1940s and, after his ill-fated California trip, had been instrumental in arranging his New York comeback gig at the Deuces. The three-year-old Kim, Chan's reason for leaving California, was readily accepted by Charlie as his stepdaughter (and indeed, by the 1980s, she was singing professionally under the name "Kim Parker"). Now, in this new period of relative domesticity for Bird, Chan preserved a much greater quantity of memorabilia from his career – as well as operating the tape-recorder Charlie had bought her, for instance during the Stearns/Maher interview.

In early July, the second album with strings was recorded and, two days before the funeral of Fats Navarro, Birdland booked the enlarged group into the club for five weeks (though only the lead violinist Sam Caplan was held over from the record date, the other players being perhaps too busy with session work to be available for an extended engagement). A *Down Beat* review observed: "To date the string backing has done a lot for the Bird so far as general public acceptance is concerned. The album has made several appearances on the best-selling albums list, an unusual experience for a musician as determinedly esoteric as Parker." The anonymous staff writer went on to say, however, that "His tone becomes a flat, monotonous, squawking thing, and his work in general appears to have little relationship to what is going on around him." Already at Café Society, Charlie had been plugging the first strings album verbally, and the popularity of the concept enabled the new group to appear at Carnegie Hall and Harlem's Apollo Theatre, with the Haig–Potter–Haynes rhythm-section being shared by Stan Getz. At the end of August, the Birdland management threw a party for Bird's thirtieth birthday, to publicize a return booking for the strings unit. There were subsequent extended stays in Philadelphia, Brooklyn and Chicago, where Charlie's reputation for foreseeable unreliability led to a penalty clause being inserted in his contract. And then Al Haig, the only other jazz soloist apart from Charlie within the confines of the string arrangements, left the group.

The Carnegie Hall appearance was again just the opening night of a Jazz At The Philharmonic tour, but in the same month of September 1950 he recorded two numbers for a studio-based Norman Granz film of JATP stars, one featuring Charlie with Coleman Hawkins (titled *Ballade*, it was a themeless improvisation on one of Hawk's favourite chord sequences, *As Long As I Live*). A few years later, after Charlie's death, these were issued on vinyl – for some reason, a completed film was not released at the time, and the material was deemed lost. Nevertheless the silent footage of Charlie miming to the playbacks (and shot by Gjon Mili, who was the cinematographer on Granz's famous *Jammin' The Blues* short) was rediscovered in the late 1970s and used in various compilations and documentaries, without anyone confirming that it corresponded to the issued records. Only in the 1990s did Granz manage to marry the footage with the sound and incorporate it in a video programme called *Norman Granz Presents Improvisation*, shown once on French television and then commercially issued in Japan. It shows not only Parker's charismatic performance but an insight into his physical presence, expressed in a ready smile as Hawkins takes over the solo duties, although this apparent reaction shot may be the result of clever editing. Very much at the other end of the spectrum, during a Birdland engagement now seemingly without the strings, Charlie was seen guesting on a local New York television show with comedian Jerry Lester, who presumably played the part of a caricatured bebopper since the script describes him appearing "in wig and trombone." Perhaps it's fortunate that this is one of a couple of TV shots for which poor-quality audio has survived but no video documentation.

Pending further strings engagements, Charlie was made available as a single artist to work with local rhythm-sections, as he had done occasionally in the past – for instance, on a one-nighter in Chicago with the Freeman brothers, guitarist George, drummer Bruz and tenorist Von. For Charlie, perhaps the most rewarding result of this policy was the second brief trip to Europe in November 1950, promoted by the editor of the jazz magazine *Estrad*, Nils Hällström. The reception during the week in Scandinavia was enthusiastic and knowledgeable, and Charlie was particularly impressed to find that Sweden's budding beboppers were on the whole more competent than the Europeans he had heard the previous year. Doubtless he was also looking forward to his last-minute booking at the third Paris Jazz Fair in early December but, according to Chan, "He kicked his habit shortly before he left...and he satisfied his cravings for drugs with alcohol." Instead of staying at the hotel arranged by Charles Delaunay, he opted for the flat of Kenny Clarke and singer Annie Ross, who was expecting Clarke's child in a matter of weeks and chose Charlie to be a godparent. Thus, Delaunay could not contact Charlie, who subsequently claimed he had not been able to collect his advance. It seems he sampled the nightlife at historic venues such as Le Boeuf Sur Le Toit and became so overwhelmed by gifts of free drugs and a wide variety of alcohol that he ended up taking an urgent flight back to New York. Ironically, a little over eight years later, Lester Young was to take a similar uncomfortable journey, as he flew home from Paris to die. In Charlie's case, his bleeding peptic ulcer merely put him in hospital for a while and made him think seriously about mending his ways: "The doctor told me if I don't quit drinking, I'll die. I've had my last drink."

In the Christmas issue of *Down Beat*, Charlie was announced as winning for the first time the magazine's readers' poll for best alto saxophonist but, inevitably, his abstinence had already been broken long before he went back to work on a series of one-week engagements with the strings. This tour ended at Birdland in late March with the strings unit playing opposite Dizzy Gillespie who, according to Dan Morgenstern, "made fun of Bird's conducting behind his back; Bird heard the laughs, turned, and reflected hurt feelings on his face." But the belief that his physical constitution was after all superhuman receives considerable support from broadcasts during the three weeks at Birdland, especially the quintet (without strings) in which he was joined by Dizzy and Bud Powell. The opening *Blue 'N Boogie*, with its ensemble riffs presumably deriving from a Gillespie arrangement for Earl Hines or Eckstine, sets the tone for a sparkling twenty-five minutes which put in the shade all the other quintet performances of the period, except for the previous year's Parker–Powell–Navarro occasion. Three other early 1940s classics, in the shape of *Anthropology*, *Round Midnight* and *Night In Tunisia*, constitute the rest of the repertoire on this occasion, but the first of these three is taken extremely fast and notable for the controlled exhilaration from all participants. Its opening Parker solo contains an anthology of his favourite phrases as well as some new invention, and quotations from other songs such as *Tenderly*, the New Orleans march *High Society* (a frequent reference on up-tempo performances in B-flat, ever since its use in *Ko Ko*), and the song *Temptation*. The last-named conveys some irony – in retrospect, though not necessarily in Charlie's intention – because of its strong association with rhythm-and-blues alto king Earl Bostic.

Still some years away from its rock-and-roll crossover, black rhythm-and-blues retained an ambiguous relationship to the new jazz, with many of its saxophonists striving to emulate aspects of bebop, such as the excellent Eddie Vinson (whom Charlie had temporarily replaced in Cootie Williams's 1945 band). But, apart from introducing the occasional bluesy buzz to his tone, Charlie rarely leant in the opposite direction, preferring to try and expand his established style. A jam session with Wardell Gray at Christy's outside Boston, a fortnight after the broadcast with Gillespie, is more uneven but distinguished by Charlie's extended improvisations, including nine consecutive choruses (lasting nearly five minutes) on *Scrapple From The Apple*. The day after this April session, he began a week at the Apollo Theatre fronting a big-band that included such players as Benny Harris (his new regular quintet trumpeter), Bennie Green (another former Earl Hines colleague) and saxophonists Sahib Shihab, Charlie Rouse and Gerry Mulligan, whose hour of fame had not yet arrived. Mulligan had alreadyS arranged two of his pieces for the strings unit (*Rocker* and *Goldrush*), as also had George Russell (with his *Ezz-thetics*), but there is no documentation of what the big-band actually performed. Being even more expensive than the strings, and probably less well rehearsed, this idea was not repeated. The following month in Philadelphia, a temporary association with another trumpeter – who briefly replaced Harris and would also become famous and influential within a couple of years – found the young Clifford Brown being highly praised by Charlie: "Bird helped my morale a great deal. One night he took me into a corner and said, 'I don't believe it. I hear what you're saying, but I don't believe it.'"

Taking into account the more inhibiting nature of recording studios, there are bright moments in the January 1951 reunion date with Miles Davis and Max Roach, which introduced Charlie's new pianist and bassist, Walter Bishop and Teddy Kotick, and included a particularly successful themeless *K. C. Blues*. Similarly, the only studio session with Red Rodney was notable for three blues, two of which (*Si Si* and *Blues For Alice*, the latter named for Norman Granz's secretary) each refer to a descending chord sequence first outlined in Charlie's *Confirmation* but which was fashionably referred to in the 1950s as "the Swedish blues." But, according to Chan, Charlie felt his most significant achievement from this date was a new, more contained version of *Lover Man*: "He took me into a listening booth in a record shop, and proudly played it for me." (The fact that, on the latter, pianist John Lewis reproduces the five-bar introduction from the 1945 Dizzy Gillespie/Sarah Vaughan version helps to explain why Charlie makes a late entry on his 1946 recording, after Jimmy Bunn's four-bar introduction.) There were also many bright moments in Charlie's new home life, including the birth on July 17 of a daughter named Pree and, preceding this event, a move to the ground-floor apartment at 151 Avenue B on the Lower East Side, now popularly known as the East Village. But there were problems too. The lengthy tour with the strings during the first five months of the year had underlined the anti-improvisation nature of the scores and had necessitated using sometimes inferior local players to read the parts, while the "novelty" appeal of the group led to them being booked opposite rhythm-and-blues vocalists such as Ivory Joe Hunter.

Furthermore, Charlie's guest spot at Birdland in June 1951 with Machito's band, on whose new album he also played briefly, marked his last New York club appearance for fifteen months, because the state liquor authority (as well as licensing premises selling alcohol) also then had the power of licensing all performers in such premises. Hence, the all-important "cabaret card" could be withdrawn from anyone convicted (or even suspected) of unlawful behaviour, and this is exactly what happened for a while to numerous artists from Frank Sinatra to stand-up comedian Richard (Lord) Buckley. It may be significant that Charlie's bust happened not long after an article in the February 1951 issue of the aspirational black magazine *Ebony*, in which Cab Calloway complained about the effects of drug use within the jazz milieu. As Carl Woideck has pointed out, Calloway's text named no specific individuals, but the effect is undercut by the editor appending captioned photographs including those of Art Blakey, Miles Davis, Dexter Gordon, Billie Holiday, Howard McGhee (all of whom had already come to the attention of the police) and the late Fats Navarro.

Of course Calloway was not wrong, but it is possible to wonder if he was in some way being used by the authorities. Within the next few months, musicians not featured in the magazine were affected, as not only Charlie was arrested but, in a separate incident in August 1951, so were Bud Powell and Thelonious Monk. Monk was found in possession and, though probably he took the rap for Powell, he spent sixty days in confinement.

When Charlie (according to Chan's account) appeared in court at an unspecified date, it is not clear what the charges were but they must have been comparatively minor – or else the judge was particularly lenient – for he was given a three-month suspended sentence. The immediate consequence of this was that his cabaret card was rescinded. As a result, Billy Shaw sent him out to play guest spots on a tour with Woody Herman's big-band in Kansas City and St. Louis. But he began missing dates and, by the time he was due in early September in Chicago, home of the musicians' union national boss James C. Petrillo, the latter sent a telegram dated August 29 (Charlie's birthday) saying, "Your agency tells me they cannot locate you. You are directed to contact your agency immediately and play the engagement mentioned above. Your failure to do this will place your membership in jeopardy." (This same year Slim Gaillard, the boppers' nemesis from Billy Berg's, recorded for Norman Granz a tongue-in-cheek homage to the union's power called *Federation Blues*: "You may play an instrument/And think that you're a killer/But you still ain't got nowhere/Till you see J.C. Petrillo" – Slim's track remained unreleased until the 1990s because it was too political.) The Federation's subsequent investigation of Charlie's "activities" seemingly only managed to turn up a fine owing to the Los Angeles branch from some years before, but this harassment from the union and the events leading up to it may be what forced Billy Shaw to carry out one of his frequent threats not to seek further bookings. Already in early 1951, Charlie told Leonard Feather, "I guess you heard I'm breaking with my manager," but the initiative came from Shaw, especially since he pointed out in writing that Charlie always found ways to extract more money from the agency than he had actually earned.

At a loose end professionally, Charlie accompanied his regular pianist of the last few months, Walter Bishop, to a Miles Davis record session in October, only too well aware that his former protégé was now struggling with a serious heroin habit. To add a further touch of irony, Charlie once again won the *Down Beat* readers' poll in December, which resulted in the otherwise underemployed altoist making his only television appearance to have been preserved in sound and video, and only the second video documentation currently known. Around the end of the year, possibly

The Kansas connection – (left to right) Parker and Gene Ramey, seven years older than Charlie and an early friend and supporter, pictured in Wichita, 1940

The Kansas connection – The Jay McShann band on stage at the Savoy Ballroom, Harlem, early 1942. McShann, far left; Ramey, 3rd from left; Walter Brown, 4th from left; Gus Johnson, 6th from left; Parker, 7th from left; John Jackson, 9th from left

A rare photo by Charles "Teenie" Harris of the *Pittsburgh Courier*, sometimes cropped to show the two central figures. (l–r) Lucky Thompson, Dizzy Gillespie, Parker and bandleader-vocalist Billy Eckstine, probably at Pittsburgh's Savoy Ballroom, summer 1944

One of two historic concerts at Town Hall, New York, May 16, 1945. (l–r) Doc West, Curley Russell, the left hand of Al Haig, Parker and the group's leader, Gillespie

The 52nd Street connection – Charlie's first steady gig in New York was with a similar Ben Webster group, Onyx Club, late 1944. (l–r) possibly Eddie Nicholson, Bill DeArango, poss. Rail Wilson, Webster and Parker (the unseen pianist would be Argonne Thornton aka Sadik Hakim)

The 52nd Street connection – Charlie's first official booking as a leader, Spotlite Club, October 1945. (l–r) Stan Levey, Leonard Gaskin, Parker (obscuring pianist Sir Charles Thompson), Miles Davis and Dexter Gordon

A posed picture taken when recording *Dark Shadows*, C.P. McGregor Studios, Los Angeles, February 19, 1947. (l–r) Parker, Ross Russell, Doc West, Earl Coleman and songwriter Shifty Henry

A version of the classic quintet plus Latin drummers (of unknown family name), at the Three Deuces, New York, 1947–1948. (l–r) Parker, percussionist Guillermo, Nelson Boyd, Diego, Duke Jordan, Max Roach and Miles Davis

The Norman Granz connection – Bird prepares to take flight with members of the Jazz At The Philharmonic touring group, LaGuardia Airport, New York, November 1948. (l–r) Howard McGhee, Flip Phillips and Parker

The Norman Granz connection – Another posed shot from the first session with strings, Mercury Studios, New York, November 1949. (l–r) Buddy Rich, Ray Brown, Parker, violinists Max Hollander and Milton Lomask, and co-producer/English-hornist Mitch Miller

The setting for an important series of live broadcasts, the Royal Roost, c. March 1949. (l–r) Parker, Kenny Dorham and Tommy Potter

Revisiting Kansas City with Red Rodney who, at 22 years old, was already ignoring his leader's advice and becoming addicted to heroin. (l–r) Rodney, unknown friend and Parker, outside the Playhouse, March 1950

The European connection – Jamming for the edification of British fans (saxist Harry Klein is seen behind Charlie's right shoulder), Paris, May 1949

The European connection – Charlie's first gig in Scandinavia, Konserthuset, Stockholm, November 20, 1950

Looking the worse for wear at a Boston-area roadhouse where he was informally recorded in extended jam-session performances, Christy's, 1951 or 1952

With the plastic saxophone at one of his last great all-star appearances, Massey Hall, Toronto, May 15, 1953

coinciding with the news that Chan was pregnant again, Charlie went back briefly to Kansas City to visit his mother and to "rest," and as usual he immediately ran through whatever money his mother had put by ("I always had $150 to $200 around the house for his emergencies"). Fifteen months earlier in Detroit, he had been picked up by the FBI for non-payment of alimony, but this particular trip almost had consequences that were potentially more serious. During his visit, he was playing on a semi-regular basis at Tutty Clarkin's, with Addie usually in the audience – which was a first for both her and Charlie, since she had clearly been far too busy to attend any of his teenage gigs. Charlie's mother recalled a red-headed girl who "pushed dope, and he had met her through one of those numbers on a match cover people were always slipping him... She worked for the Italian [mafia]." But the owner noted: "We got word somehow that she was trying to frame him on a narcotics charge for the government. He only had time to play eight bars of *How High The Moon* when we motioned him off the bandstand and helped him to skip town." Presumably his escape was not made by plane this time, but the attempt by the authorities to set up an arrest confirms that the heat was on nationally for addicts such as Charlie.

6 i remember you

Back in New York, no agent had come forward to fill Billy Shaw's shoes. After fulfilling previously contracted engagements, Charlie's only live appearances in the first few months of 1952 were arranged informally or by friends, with local bands at out-of-town venues such as the Silver Saddle in Newark and the Times Square Hotel in Rochester. On his opening night at the latter, Charlie had to put up with "A piano player playing the melody of *Honeysuckle Rose* in a style that could not be classified as jazz of any type by any stretch of the imagination...and, after the piano had finished his chorus, Bird went into the riff *Scrapple From The Apple*. The drummer was about equal to the pianist. They were probably two high officials of the Rochester local [union branch]." Clarinettist Buddy DeFranco recently observed that "Through the years Charlie Parker has played with some of the worst rhythm players. But when you hear him, you're convinced that he's got a great rhythm-section. He blanks it out. He's so dominant, so positive." Fortunately in this instance, Charlie persuaded the manager to hire Walter Bishop and drummer Art Taylor to finish the week, and even played a return date there the following year.

Norman Granz helped out with a batch of record dates which provided some income, and it was probably at this period that Granz, who unlike some of his competitors did pay royalties, put Charlie on a weekly salary of $50.00 as a retainer and an advance against future earnings. There was, however, little musical stimulus in these occasions, although the big-band and the big-band-plus-strings sessions were doubtless thought to be image-boosting. Potentially more interesting was Charlie's second small-group session with Latin-American percussion. It has been noted already, but not sufficiently emphasized, how wide were his musical sympathies. Not only was he increasingly interested, and in some ways inspired, by European classical music but at this period he also expressed a desire to study composition, mentioning this intention to the émigré composer Edgard Varèse and a couple of fellow jazzmen who were students of Stefan Wolpe. Equally, he had an encyclopedic memory for all eras of jazz and the American songbook. Kenny Dorham recalled him unexpectedly playing a spontaneous version of *I'm Painting The Town Red (To Hide A Heart That's Blue)*, one of the least remembered songs covered by Billie Holiday and Teddy Wilson, while two of his originals from this period (*She Rote* and *Cardboard*) are based respectively on such uncommon vehicles as *Beyond The Blue Horizon* and *Don't Take Your Love From Me*. But he was just as likely to hear what was good about a polka band or a klezmer outfit, and Red Rodney told the story of Charlie being more than happy to improvise with the band at a Jewish wedding. It made sense, then, for him to take an interest in Latin dance music and, given the African roots it shared with jazz, to see no difficulty in playing with such a backing.

He had already proved his compatibility as a guest soloist on sessions by the Cuban bandleader Machito, recorded at the end of 1948 and late 1950. While the segmented nature of his assigned role on the latter date's *Afro-Cuban Jazz Suite* (written by Chico O'Farrill) is slightly unsatisfactory, his blowing on the more straightahead *Okey Dokie* (by the band's pianist René Hernandez) and *Mango Mangue* from the earlier set sounds completely at home. The first such session under his own name in 1951 had an extremely varied programme, including two Latin classics (of which *Tico Tico* had been tried out at the Onyx rehearsal three years earlier), a Jerome Kern standard and an original (*Fiesta*) by the subsequent Coltrane collaborator, trumpeter Cal Massey. Its remaining item was the most successful, credited to Parker as composer because it was thought to be in the public domain, but actually a song from the French Caribbean that Charlie picked up in Paris, entitled *My Little Suede Shoes*, or *Mes Souliers De Daim* – reportedly, it became his second biggest seller after *Just Friends*. Now, in early 1952, apart from Cole Porter's *Begin The Beguine*, he concentrated on the Latin songbook (*La Paloma* etc.) and, on a live dance date later this year, he reprised *Suede Shoes* and included the calypso standard, *Sly Mongoose*. Unlike the extremely restrictive arrangements commissioned for the larger ensembles (swing or Latin), this combination could have formed the basis of a rewarding regular group. The interest in Latin music shown by the bop pioneers in the mid-1940s, and the references in several of the classic Parker quintet records, point to a compatibility never fully explored until the 1970s. Charlie was one of the few soloists, along with Gillespie, who could adopt yet still dominate a Latin-American accompaniment and, though less "up-market" than the strings, such a partnership if pursued in depth might have ensured a more lasting popularity, as well as a more stimulating musical environment.

In late May 1952, Billy Shaw came back into the picture and sent Charlie to the West Coast for his first residencies in five years, working as a single with local groups for fortnights at the Tiffany in Los Angeles and the Say When in San Francisco. The local trumpeter he chose for these two engagements was a young unknown named Chet Baker, who observed that "Bird was a flawless player, and although he was snorting up spoons of stuff and drinking fifths of Hennessey, it all seemed to have little or no effect on him." But, after an exciting session with popular tenorman Flip Phillips at the San Francisco club, he managed to get himself fired several days before the end of the booking, for speaking his mind about the club-owner. Baker told it like this:

> It just so happened that during our engagement there was a big tel-ethon benefit... Bird got on the microphone and announced that he was passing the hat among the customers, with the proceeds to go to the Muscular Dystrophy Association [actually, the Cerebral Palsy Fund], and that the club had agreed to equal whatever was collected. He did this, of course, completely on his own, without having spoken to the manager of the club, who was a tough guy named Dutch... Naturally, Dutch refused to kick in his $125. People began yelling, banging on tables, etc.; there was almost a riot, and as I said, that was the end of our engagement.

Baker also noted that the same night Parker fell asleep and once again set a hotel mattress on fire. "Oh Bird, never a dull moment," commented Baker. Unfortunately, this became the first of a series of disputes lodged with the AFM by club-owners for breach of contract, and counter-charges from Charlie for non-payment – which, in this case, dragged on until the following February, when the union fined him $100.

Idle for a week, he sat in at a competing club, the Blackhawk, with saxophonist Vido Musso, who was then threatened by the union for paying Charlie while he was still under contract elsewhere. But, before this blew up, Charlie had a letter from Billy Shaw waiting for him at the Say When, referring to the Tiffany engagement: "When you were in my office, you signed deduction orders, and asked me to have your money sent here; now, I understand you threatened to walk out if there were any deductions, etc." At the San Francisco after-hours club Bop City, which he was already frequenting before the dispute with the Say When, he found himself in another jam (in both senses of the word) with Buddy DeFranco's rhythm-section including Art Blakey. According to reedman Jerome Richardson,

> He was very drunk but he was persuaded to go up on the stand and play... "Anything you want to play," Parker muttered. Blakey said "*52nd Street Theme*" and with that he started a rhythm at a murderously fast tempo. Bird was all tied up. False starts, uncoordinated fingering. He stopped. "Give me an hour, I'll be back." No one knows how he did it, but in one hour, he returned cold, deadly sober.

During the stay in Los Angeles, he also took part in the first studio-recorded jam session produced by Norman Granz, who not only had tenor saxophonists Phillips and Ben Webster under contract but all three undisputed giants of the alto, Johnny Hodges, Benny Carter and Charlie. It is worth recalling that the "jazz wars" were still very intense at the period, and probably no one except Granz would have considered or seen the validity of this line-up but, no doubt put on his mettle by the company he was in, Charlie played with a brilliant combination of relaxation and invention. On the famous *Funky Blues* (incidentally, probably the first use of the adjective in connection with a musical performance), he can be seen to incorporate both the blues-based power of Hodges, who plays first, and Carter's graceful lyricism along with the stylistic innovation that was all his own. Crucial to this session was the new-found freedom of long-play recording, but this freedom was never seriously applied to any of Charlie's own dates, as it would have been had he lived just a couple of years longer.

Meanwhile, after staying on the Coast long enough to take another guest engagement in Altadena, Charlie returned to New York, where he was often just showing up at other people's gigs. One of the more satisfying sets must have been with Mary Lou Williams at the Downbeat club, where the former queen of Kansas City was working with an excellent rhythm-section of Oscar Pettiford and Kenny Clarke. According to her,

> Charlie Parker came in one night and he said to me, "Lou, let's get a band or something together. You know all the cats always want me to get a band with you." I said, "No, man, not in the condition you're in." He said, "Mary, anything you tell me I'll do... You know I'm not allowed to play in Birdland or any of the clubs."

In this period of relative inactivity, Charlie made one of his attempts to enjoy the straight life, and Symphony Sid heard him at the Downbeat talk about wanting to learn golf. Singer Sheila Jordan, on the other hand, was taken by Charlie for horse-riding lessons, while he himself studied painting with Harvey Cropper. A development that could have been financially important, if Charlie had able to take it seriously, was his hiring in the winter of 1952–53 as a teacher at the Hartnett Music Studios, where he also appeared on at least one of the New York Jazz Society's Sunday afternoon jam sessions. However, outside of a tape preserved by one musician who had already worked with Charlie Barnet and Stan Kenton (the tenor player Dick Meldonian), there is precious little evidence of Charlie giving music lessons.

However, starting from when Chan gave birth to their second child Baird on August 10, 1952, Charlie made several more discreet forays to New

York clubs, including Birdland. Since he was still officially unemployable in such venues, it must be assumed the management was trying to be helpful, while making sure that he was technically "just sitting in" (even for their live broadcasts in September and November). For other appearances, he was quite willing to provide a reconstituted string group, a quintet hand-picked (or thrown together) for the occasion, or just his alto saxophone and his charisma. All of these were present on the dance engagement at Harlem's Rockland Palace, which was actually a benefit performance for Benjamin Davis, the black secretary of the American Communist Party, elected to the city council in 1943 but now sentenced to five years in prison for "sedition," i.e. advocating his ideals during the McCarthyite hysteria of the early 1950s. Chan commented sardonically that "The communists paid better than the capitalists and this was one of his highest paying gigs." Private recordings were made both from the house mike by Chan, and seemingly from the auditorium by another amateur engineer, whose machine suffered from speed fluctuations but whose tapes were first issued in the 1960s, including a dynamic up-tempo version of Lester Young's *Lester Leaps In* with Max Roach back on drums. Chan's recording came into general circulation only after her collaboration on the *Bird* movie, and in 1996 there was an attempt to combine both tapes of *Lester Leaps In* into the only "stereo" track of Charlie.

However, the accompaniments provided on his solo gigs in Chicago, St. Louis (with former Jay McShann colleague Jimmy Forrest), Washington, Boston, Montreal and elsewhere varied considerably as to format and competence, the appearance at Boston's Hi-Hat Club boasting an excellent rhythm-section of Roy Haynes, Charles Mingus and pianist Dick Twardzik. The trip to Montreal in February 1953 would be the first of two visits in three months north of the border, and seemed to hint at the growth of a more serious interest in bebop similar to what Bird had seen in European countries. The Canadian pianist Paul Bley had moved in 1950 to study at the Juilliard School in New York, where he soon met Charlie at the sessions organized by Joe Maini and Jimmy Knepper, and, while back home in the summer of 1952, he helped set up the Montreal Jazz Workshop. Its concerts initially featured local players and then, after Bley was back in New York, he brought guest musicians including Charlie, who also appeared on local television with fellow Americans Brew Moore and Dick Garcia (both in town for a club gig). By this time, Charlie had begun regularly using a white plastic saxophone, the Grafton Acrylic made in England and apparently "a gift from an Englishman about three years ago," according to its owner. Red Rodney said it was in Detroit that "The manufacturer's representative came up and gave it to him... I think he could play a tomato can and make it sound great... Every once in a while Charlie, like most of us, needed some money and...once the guy gave him the plastic horn, he pawned his." Journalist Dave Gelly underlined its significance for Charlie: "No pawnbroker would offer him anything against the poor old Grafton," so as a result it was always available.

From at least this period onwards, when working away from home Charlie got into the habit of cabling small amounts of money to Chan as soon as he received them, rather than risk the temptation of mis-spending them. When back at home the same month, Charlie wrote a letter to the state liquor board referring to the loss of his cabaret card:

> My right to pursue my chosen profession has been taken away, and my wife and three children who are innocent of any wrongdoing are suffering... My baby girl [Pree] is a city case in the hospital because her health has been neglected since we hadn't the necessary doctor fees... I feel sure when you examine my record and see that I have made a sincere effort to become a family man and a good citizen, you will reconsider. If by any chance you feel I haven't paid my debt to society, by all means let me do so and give me and my family back the right to live.

Pree's health indeed continued to give cause for serious concern, demonstrating symptoms that Chan later related to cystic fibrosis, a diagnosis that didn't "exist" at the time. On the work front, Chan in her book notes that various people with underworld connections, including the Birdland management, had been trying to sort out Charlie's employment situation: "One day two detectives came to our house, and offered Bird a cabaret card in exchange for names. Bird refused." So the process is unclear by which the liquor authority were persuaded to reconsider their decision but, within five weeks of his letter, Charlie was being officially rehabilitated at another Broadway club next door to Birdland, called the Band Box. This had first opened in January 1953 and Charlie was booked in February, playing opposite the Ellington band (with Charles Mingus on bass) and at least once sitting in with them. But, according to *Down Beat*, "Charlie Parker...left the Band Box abruptly last month owing to cabaret card trouble, straightened things out and went back into the club in a show also spotting the Milt Buckner Trio." Despite Charlie's renewed New York employment and his continued authoritative playing, the very next week's broadcast found him very inebriated and, none too subtly, taking a rise out of announcer Leonard Feather.

Having no regular group of his own any more, Charlie was still on the flying trapeze, but now without a safety net – he once said, "I need a good rhythm-section like old people need soft shoes." As to choice of repertoire, a few of his tunes such as *Now's the Time* and *Scrapple* were known to most musicians who had any pretensions to sharing a band-stand with him and, for the rest, it was a mild form of challenge for him to play anything the locals could suggest – even their own original arrangements – and still outshine them. The most striking example so far available of this ability is the Washington concert with "The Orchestra" where, with no rehearsal whatsoever, he fits himself in, over and under the big-band scores of *Willis*, *Roundhouse* and others as if they had been written expressly for him. Additional out-of-town gigs with just a rhythm-section usually contained a majority of local players mixed with the occasional sideman recommended by Charlie, such as Max Roach (for a quick return visit to Washington) or Roy Haynes (at the Storyville Club in Boston). But, concerning things written expressly for him, what Charlie had on his mind at this period was seemingly more ambitious, and partly inspired by a European classical work he'd already mentioned admiringly back in 1949, as he told Nat Hentoff:

> Now, I'd like to do a session with five or six woodwinds, a harp, a choral group, and full rhythm-section. Something on the line of Hindemith's *Kleine Kammermusik*. Not a copy or anything like that. I don't want ever to copy. But that sort of thing... But in 50 or 75 years, the contributions of present-day jazz will be taken as seriously as classical music. You wait and see.

Norman Granz obviously agreed to this latest suggestion from Charlie. However, even with such an intelligent arranger as Gil Evans, who was then trying hard to make it in the commercial music world, the wood-winds-and-choir record date in May 1953 was disappointing. The amount of effort spent in achieving a sound balance and a passable performance resulted in only three tunes being completed rather than the usual four (although a fourth score, of *Yesterdays*, had been prepared by Evans and vocal-group leader Dave Lambert). Granz eventually abandoned the session rather than pay for overtime. But already, ten days before this session, the historic concert at Toronto's Massey Hall had taken place, put together at the initiative of another group of Canadian fans.

As recorded by Charles Mingus and Max Roach and issued on their Debut label, the Massey Hall performance was the only one of the numerous "live" releases of which Charlie was aware (apart from the Jazz At The Philharmonic concerts and the Black Deuce release of the 1947 Carnegie Hall appearance). Since it was offered to and declined by Granz, its issue required the use of the pseudonym "Charlie Chan" to get around his exclusive recording contract. No one made much money from the record, at least before its 1970s' reissue, as the Debut label soon went out of business, but Charlie was the only one to get full payment for the actual concert – seeing the unexpectedly small attendance, he had cashed his cheque through the company that sold the concert tickets, whereas the cheques accepted by the others bounced. (A monograph on Parker's 1953 Canadian visits suggests that Charlie also asked for and received an advance before leaving New York.) The historical significance of the event was simply that of the last-ever quintet performance of Parker, Gillespie, Powell and Roach together and, with the addition of Mingus, they were billed by the organizers as "The Quintet Of The Year," shortened on reissue albums to "The Quintet." Although none of the material was written later than 1944, the musicians' exciting rediscovery of each other makes it sound absolutely fresh. Despite the overdubbed bass added by Mingus to make the balance slightly closer to studio quality, the live feel of a unique occasion comes through strongly. Though much has been made of supposed rivalry between Charlie and Dizzy on this occasion, Charlie's solo work is perfectly relaxed throughout and especially on *Perdido* and *Hot House*.

It is worth noting, however, that while Dizzy had just come through a difficult period artistically, and was about to become a valuable property in Granz's touring stable, Charlie had not been part of Jazz At The Philharmonic since 1950 and his career – unlike his playing – had completely lost its impetus. Charlie's studio tracks from the same period do not even hint at this, though, perhaps because with one exception they all have Max Roach on drums. The Miles Davis session for Prestige is different in featuring the explosive Philly Joe Jones. This too would have broken his record contract, and he received an advance payment to do so, rather than just turning up unexpectedly. However, it was not issued till after his death, due to a shortage of material not unconnected with the fact that Charlie fell asleep during the recording. (Davis noted that "In place of his normal big dosages of heroin, now he was drinking an enormous amount of alcohol... I got so angry with him that I told him off, told him that I had never done that to him on one of his recording sessions.") This second and last time he was to be heard playing tenor saxophone on record is naturally of interest and, if his tone is somewhat unfocused, this is doubtless because he needed a much harder reed than the borrowed instrument provided. As for Charlie's own quartet dates (in December 1952 and July 1953) they are filled with buoyant solos on previously composed themes such as *Confirmation, Now's The Time, Chi Chi* (written as a gift for Roach's own record session three months earlier) and another "Swedish blues" dedicated to his son, *Laird Baird*. Of the two themeless improvisations *Cosmic Rays* and *Kim*, the latter is of course named for his stepdaughter, while the up-tempo standards *The Song Is You* and *I Remember You* may be intended for Chan.

If it was a question of the external realities of his life rather than his confident and commanding performance here, it would be tempting to think of the last tune as referring to the former Charlie Parker. However, at this stage, not only his playing but his attitude to and love of music remained absolutely undimmed. In the Hentoff interview, he was as enthusiastic about Dave Brubeck and Lennie Tristano as about Monk and Powell, and said "What you hear depends on so many things in yourself. Like I heard Bartok's *Second Piano Concerto* over here and later, I heard it again in France. I was more acclimated to life, then, and I heard things in it I never heard before." Talking to John McLellan during his latest Boston visit in June 1953, he was even more expansive: "Most of the things...coming out of a man's horn ad-lib, or else things that are written, original things – they're just experiences, the way he feels – the beauty of the weather, the nice look of a mountain, or maybe a nice fresh cool breath of air... But I can definitely say that the music won't stop, you keep going forward." It was an uphill struggle at times, though, despite playing with the Bud Powell trio (alongside Gillespie's quintet) at Birdland for a fortnight after Massey Hall. Finishing two further weeks at Birdland in late June, he succeeded in alienating the management and was barred from the premises named after him for something like a year. He was again dependent on friends, including Dave Lambert, to arrange appearances such as those at the Sunday night sessions at a Greenwich Village coffee house called the Open Door, produced by Robert Reisner.

Family life was, however, far from buoyant and the financial and emotional strain was beginning to tell on Chan, for at some point (most likely during 1953) she wrote an extremely troubled letter to Charlie, saying among other things:

> I know how unsettled you are as far as every day living is concerned. How unable to forgive the hurts of the world... And, although I want with all my heart to believe in your moral reform, I know that there would be backslides. I found out that you were juiced one night the week before we went to Boston. I know how intolerant I'm being in letting that bother me, for – every step back you take I realize the four steps forward that go along with it. But I'm afraid. Somewhere during our three years I lost my courage.

While this refers to Charlie's behaviour, Chan's letter makes it clear the main worry was about the lack of income, as well as the income that went on backsliding rather than on the family. Probably the previous year, they had been refused welfare payments by the ADC (Aid to Dependent Children) Board, and Chan subsequently wrote: "The woman who took our application at the relief board must have thought we were crazy when we told her we had a Cadillac and a maid. But we had no money." (Though the story rings hollow that Charlie ever dumped his children at the welfare board with the words "Here! You feed them," Chan notes that at Christmas Charlie sold the Cadillac in order to buy Kim a bicycle.) The other side-effect of Charlie's involvements was on Chan's equilibrium, and her book mentions taking herself and the children more than once to seek refuge in her mother's West 52nd Street apartment. In consecutive chapters, she writes "Life with Bird wasn't all fear and violence" and "Although Bird had never harmed me, I was afraid of him when he was drunk" – giving a clear impression of what today would be called an emotionally abusive relationship. In fact, there is a distressing parallel with Doris's description of her break-up, in the comment from Chan that, by 1953, "I was not in good health: I weighed 103 pounds, had chronic bronchitis, and was working on my sixth pneumonia. A doctor I had seen in a sleazy office on 125th Street across from the Apollo Theater had diagnosed possible tuberculosis." And she was pregnant again – until her mother convinced Charlie to agree to an abortion, which took place at the apartment of his drug connection.

Although Shaw Artists was still listed as being Charlie's agency in *Down Beat*'s annual directory published in July 1953, by October the Shaw office was writing to Chan with a reminder that, while Charlie was now working for others, they were still awaiting reimbursement of their outstanding advances. Charlie's bookings had in fact been taken over by the Moe Gale agency (Billy Shaw's former employer), probably at Chan's suggestion. She cannot have been too pleased when, on one of his first dates for them, he managed to get reported to the musicians' union after the first day of a week in Montreal, and then summarily fired on the third day. The reasons boiled down to the fact that Charlie brought an unrehearsed and unkempt pick-up band and was personally uncooperative. As with the Say When incident, news of this dispute leaked out to the music press, further harming his already terrible reputation, and despite Charlie's counterclaim, the union's financial adjudication nearly six months later went in favour of the Montreal club. Yet the music was still superlative when conditions were right. In September he had played a week at the new location of Boston's Storyville, where the young promoter-pianist George Wein, leading a more traditional-jazz band with Doc Cheatham and Vic Dickenson, witnessed Charlie jamming with them and choosing the classic tune *Royal Garden Blues*:

> I'll never forget the energy of Bird's solo chorus that seemed to lift the whole song... Bird was reinventing the blues, but without stripping away the essence. And his rhythmic drive was enormous; from my perch behind the piano, I could feel him surging ahead on the homestretch like a thoroughbred horse.

Further appearances in Chicago, Baltimore, Philadelphia and Boston, at least one in concert with the strings, kept Charlie reasonably busy into the New Year, augmented by an eleven-day tour with an all-star package called "West Coast In Jazz." This involved the increasingly popular Dave Brubeck quartet, whose altoist Paul Desmond took after Lee Konitz rather than Parker but admired Charlie enormously; while Charlie himself fronted an ad-hoc quintet comprising Chet Baker, Shelly Manne, bassist Carson Smith and pianist Jimmy Rowles. These Los Angeles-based musicians were sent together to Northern California by bus for the opening date, where Parker was due to meet up with them. "We were all saying, 'He'll never make it.' We were playing this job in Olympia[, Washington] and Bird showed up about twelve o'clock at night," according to Rowles. The short tour also took in dates in Seattle, Eugene, Portland and at least one in Canada, for Rowles recalled them being cross-examined at the border by a Mountie:

> All of a sudden, right in the middle of the whole thing, Bird looks behind him – cigarette papers and some tobacco. He says, "Give me that." Bird takes one paper out, lays it down, takes the other side and takes the sack [of marijuana] and throws a bunch of it in there and closes up the bag and goes like this – zip – one movement and he had a Camel. And then he went like this – "Match?"

While in Boston again in January to play at the Hi-Hat, he went for the second time to John McLellan's radio studio, on this occasion joined by a rather overawed Paul Desmond (concurrently performing with Brubeck at Storyville). Interestingly, although the records played during the interview included the Gillespie-led *Groovin' High* and tracks from his own sessions for Savoy and for Granz, there was no Dial material. This was very much a live issue at that point, since already during recent years Ross Russell had released, without further payment, several alternate takes of Charlie's Dial dates. Now, at the start of 1954, he issued an LP that contained a 48-second extract from the first take of the 1946 *Night In Tunisia* (under the title *The Famous Alto Break*) as well as three partial performances of amateur recording quality from the following year's Chuck Copely jam session. Granz, who was active in protecting his interests and those of his artists, wrote to Charlie:

> This is one time that I am so incensed that I am going to make it a special point to go after Russell myself for you... Don't worry either about whether or not you have a copy of his contract, because my lawyers will make him produce one in court, and he will regret that he ever started this kind of chicanery with you.

At this point, Charlie also heard that he was to become a member of the "Festival of Modern Jazz" tour with the Stan Kenton orchestra, Erroll Garner, Dizzy Gillespie and others, joining them in Wichita Falls, Texas. The nationwide concert package had just been deprived of Stan Getz, following his arrest for drug offences but, because of Charlie's own reputation, it took a Charlie Parker *and* a Lee Konitz to replace one Getz. Kenton's saxophonist Dave Schildkraut recalled that "In one Southern town, a restaurant would not serve Negroes, so Bird had to wait in the bus while the rest of us were wolfing down steaks. Finally, after persuasion, the eatery relented. Dizzy and Erroll Garner left the bus, but Charlie held out and refused to go in and eat." On the concerts, all the soloists except Garner had to play separately, backed by the Kenton ensemble, and Charlie's slot (like Dizzy's) comprised three short numbers, completed in under ten minutes. Though a live recording exists, there is a certain irony in the fact that the following year (1955) Kenton recorded the arrangement Bill Holman wrote for Parker on *Cherokee*, as a feature for his own altoist Lennie Niehaus. Niehaus became something of a star during the brief 1950s vogue for West Coast jazz but also, by a neat twist of fate, was to be the musical director for the film *Bird* in the late 1980s. Another irony is that, the same month Charlie was touring, Art Blakey made his first live recording at Birdland, including extended versions of *Now's The Time*, *Confirmation* and *Night In Tunisia*, and preparing the return to popularity of hardcore bebop that Charlie would not live to see.

There is a final, distinctly non-musical irony in the fact that, in his last cable to Chan before the end of this tour, Charlie was eloquent and affectionate, ending with the words:

> THANK YOU FOR MAKING A MAN OF ME I WILL ALWAYS LOVE YOU
> GUESS WHO

As the tour ended on the West Coast, Norman Granz arranged a recording session which might have been one of the greatest in jazz history or might have been a disappointment, but though Charlie was present and correct, his co-star Art Tatum was indisposed. In the light of subsequent events, there was no time to reschedule the date. Immediately after the last concert of the tour on February 28, Charlie was booked again for a week at the Tiffany, but he was soon in trouble with the club management for disappearing on the first night. Charlie's explanation was simple: he had been "taken to a Los Angeles Police Station on suspicion of being a user of narcotics. I was held there over night, and after it was found out that the charges could not be substantiated, as a substitute, I was booked on a drunken and disorderly charge which was unfounded." Apparently, he earned the attentions of Los Angeles Police Department's narcotics boss John O'Grady, the notches on whose gun eventually included Stan Getz, Gerry Mulligan, Billie Holiday and Lenny Bruce. O'Grady later claimed that "I could have nailed him... I decided it wasn't worth wasting the time nailing Parker just so the City of L.A. could pay for his keep." The suspicion that he was using again was, however, correct despite the lack of evidence, and he was drinking very heavily. He had indeed been fired yet again by the time he received word that two-year-old Pree had died in hospital of pneumonia. Charlie's telegrams to Chan betray the sobering impact of this tragic news:

> [Time of dispatch] 4.11 AM
> MY DARLING MY DAUGHTER'S DEATH SURPRISED ME MORE THAN IT
> DID YOU DON'T FULFILL FUNERAL PROCEEDINGS UNTIL I GET THERE
> I SHALL BE THE FIRST ONE TO WALK INTO OUR CHAPEL FORGIVE
> ME FOR NOT BEING THERE WITH YOU WHILE YOU WERE AT THE
> HOSPITAL YOURS MOST SINCERELY YOUR HUSBAND
> CHARLIE PARKER
> 4.13 AM
> MY DARLING FOR GOD'S SAKE HOLD ON TO YOURSELF
> CHAS PARKER
> 4.15 AM
> CHAN, HELP
> CHARLIE PARKER

As if this weren't enough, there were still financial worries. Chan has said that he accepted the tour with Stan Kenton because it paid so well, but there was still $500.00 owed to Billy Shaw and a sum not much smaller for funeral expenses (the music he chose to have played at the ceremony was by Bartok). As a result, he was once again in debt to his new agency, and was pursuing claims against various promoters who had failed to pay him in the last year or so, several of which the union resolved in his favour. In the matter of the Tiffany Club's complaint, however, the union's award went against Charlie. There was still recording as a source of immediate income, but he made only two studio sessions in 1954 – intended for an album devoted to Cole Porter songs, the kind of concept album Norman Granz was beginning to pioneer – but little was produced that was not rather ordinary by Charlie's own standards. He was still obliged to take gigs in Philadelphia, Baltimore, Chicago and Detroit to defray his expenses. The early morning of May 18, 1954 seems to be when the following anguished telegram was sent to Chan at her mother's apartment, as opposed to the Avenue B address:

> MY DARLING I JUST WANTED TO LET YOU KNOW REGARDLESS OF THE THINGS WE HAVE TO EXPERIENCE IN LIFE I WANT YOU TO KNOW THAT I AM IN THE GROUND NOW I WOULD SHOOT MYSELF FOR YOU IF I HAD A GUN BUT I DON'T HAVE ONE TELL MY WIFE THE MOST HORRIBLE THING IN THE WORLD IS SILENCE AND AM EXPERIENCING SAME. IM TIRED AND GOING TO SLEEP
> CHARLES PARKER

After the latest reconciliation, a pleasant interlude in July and early August at Brewster on Cape Cod saw Charlie, when he was free between provincial engagements, join Chan (and Kim and Baird) to attempt to repair their relationship. Symphony Sid, by then bounced from the New York airwaves and working in Boston, commented that

> Brewster is one of the most exclusive places – not only is it restricted, but the poor are prohibited. I don't know who Charlie knew there. Someone must have dug him very much to allow him and his wife to have a cottage on their property. Bird did a gig out there at a place called The Red Barn... He looked beautiful and healthy, and he said, "Say, Sid man, we're havin' a ball, the baby's havin' a ball. I don't care if I work."

But the self-destruction began again at the end of August on an engagement with the strings at Birdland, Charlie's first appearance there in over a year. According to Tommy Potter, the fourth night of the engagement was Dinah Washington's thirtieth birthday, coinciding with Bird's thirty-fourth, and he consumed a large quantity of alcohol at Dinah's backstage party. As if to demonstrate the inflexibility of working with non-jazz musicians, he asked for *East Of The Sun* but followed the strings' introduction by playing *Dancing In The Dark*. And then, as if to prove that he didn't desperately need this gig, he publicly fired the band for their incompetence. Not unnaturally, Birdland then fired Bird.

Realizing that the union was now quite likely to order him to pay the musicians' salaries for the rest of the scheduled three weeks, he next tried to commit suicide by swallowing iodine and was committed to Bellevue, the New York mental hospital. (Later he claimed that he had faked the suicide in order to evade his responsibilities, but this seems to amount to the same thing.) Despite evidence of genuine emotional problems, he was discharged ten days later in the care of Chan and the family doctor. And, despite having been cancelled from a European tour due for late September, he was added instead to a concert bill in both New York and Boston with Birdland regulars including Count Basie, Sarah Vaughan and the Modern Jazz Quartet. Two days later, in other words less than three weeks after leaving Bellevue, he was back again at his own request, seeking an escape from both chronic alcoholism and the broken promises to Chan. Two-and-a-half weeks later, he was discharged again against Chan's wishes but this time, according to her, "He had conned the shrink." Chan and the children moved to a small house near where one of her girlfriends lived, in a locality with the implausible name of New Hope, Pennsylvania. Charlie joined them and, two weeks later on October 30, he took part in Robert Reisner's concert at New York Town Hall, "looking fit" according to eyewitness Ira Gitler, who recalled: "Bird played brilliantly that night. All in the audience were extremely regretful when the stagehands rang the curtain down as he was still blowing. The evening had started behind schedule, and union regulations do not sit still for spontaneous art."

The other performers at the Town Hall included Thelonious Monk, Horace Silver, Art Farmer and, in the person of Sonny Rollins, one of the most important younger musicians who would extract new findings from Charlie's methods. Charlie, for his part, claimed to be getting used to spending all his free time in the country and commuting to the city to visit his agency and the psychiatrist at the hospital. But it was not to last. As soon as he started doing out-of-town gigs again, he started missing the train back to the country and began living on the charity of friends and chance acquaintances, while early the following year Chan moved again with the children to a house in Lumberville, Pennsylvania. A week after the Town Hall concert Hot Lips Page, once the trumpet king of Kansas City, died aged only forty-six and Charlie, in the company of his disciple Jackie McLean, paid his respects at the funeral parlour, already wondering out loud whether he would see 1955. Later, he took to visiting the city morgue alone to survey unidentified corpses, claiming that he was looking for a friend of his. Soon after, he was taken in, in a state of semi-collapse, by a young African-American student Ahmed Basheer, who lived in a small apartment on Barrow Street in Greenwich Village. Basheer recalled waiting for Charlie when he visited Chan's mother's apartment to retrieve some of his clothes: "Charles Parker came walking down 52nd Street with a contemplative air, like he was passing through a ghost town. He looked at the Deuces, the Onyx, all the clubs he used to play, and they were all strip joints."

While based in the Village, Charlie took to sitting in for free at a 7th Avenue bar called Arthur's Tavern. Drummer Al Levitt noted that

> Pretty soon, different saxophone players would also come in to play, and when they finished their solos, Bird would borrow their horn and play too... Jackie McLean sometimes came in, and they would both play Jackie's alto, or Brew Moore's tenor, or Larry Rivers' C melody or baritone sax, or Sol Yaged's clarinet. Bird just played on whatever reed instrument someone handed him. Sometimes when there was no one there with a saxophone, Phil Woods, who was working across the street playing for the strip show...would come over with his alto during his intermission, and they would both play on Phil's alto.

Woods recalled these occasions, adding that he was at the time dissatisfied with the state of his instrument. But, after Charlie had blown the bell off the thing, "That's when I knew there was nothing wrong with my saxophone!" according to Woods.

In a foretaste of some of the coverage after his death, the tabloid *Daily News* had managed to photograph Charlie being bundled into an ambulance after his suicide attempt, while a press picture taken later in the year of him dressed as a Mau Mau "cost him a couple of jobs," according to Charlie. Journalism about jazz music in the more heavyweight newspapers was very much in its infancy in the mid-1950s, while coverage on radio and television had diminished considerably. *Down Beat* and *Metronome* continued to review Charlie's records and, in the former, he still won the critics' and readers' polls for 1954, but the next mass acknowledgement of modern jazz was in a November 1954 issue of the hugely popular news magazine *Time*. They featured a cover story on the popularity of West Coast music, with Dave Brubeck pictured on the front (their only previous jazz cover was of Louis Armstrong five years earlier). When asked why it wasn't him in the picture, Charlie replied, "My watch doesn't work that well. I don't show up to all my gigs." Robert Reisner recalled running into Charlie on New Year's Day 1955 and having a conversation in which the saxophonist quoted his favourite lines from the nineteenth-century poem, *The Rubáiyát Of Omar Kháyyám*:

> Come, fill the Cup, and in the fire of Spring
> Your Winter garment of Repentance fling;
> The Bird of Time has but a little way
> To flutter – and the Bird is on the Wing.

More poignantly, perhaps, at this same period he encountered the increasingly stable and successful Dizzy Gillespie, who later said, "Shortly before I left for Europe [with Jazz At The Philharmonic], I ran into him at Basin Street [East]. He sat down and talked to me about our getting together again. The way he said it, it was as if he was saying 'Before it's too late.'" In Chicago in February 1955, he was advised to wear an overcoat but declined with the words, "I don't want to see another winter – pneumonia's next for me." According to the African drummer Guy Warren it was during this same weekend that, after spending most of the evening delaying his performance and simultaneously getting in a state where he was unable to perform, he had to endure an effusive hipster who told him how well he had played and what a great guy he was generally. He finally rounded on his sycophantic tormentor and yelled, "Look, man, I *goofed*. And I know it!"

At this point, he probably knew that he had accidentally been pronounced dead, in what was undoubtedly a side-effect of the critical battles on the French jazz scene. A journalist on the newspaper *Combat* "for a joke...was told that Charlie Parker had just died," and the report was apparently picked up by several other French papers, before it was confirmed as false. As February turned to March, Parker's mood had not exactly improved. When he unexpectedly met Sonny Stitt, who was then enjoying some success but by and large neglecting the alto saxophone in favour of tenor and baritone, Charlie allegedly said, "Man, I'm not long for this life. You carry on. I'm leaving you the keys to the kingdom." Whether he felt flattered or patronised, Stitt soon found himself taking up alto again, once Charlie was no longer on the throne. Meanwhile, there was a final engagement at Birdland for two days at the start of March. Not so much a comeback, more a come-back-all-is-forgiven-one-more-once. A special all-star quintet was assembled with Art Blakey, Charles Mingus, Kenny Dorham and Bud Powell, and on the first night the performance was, at the least, perfectly adequate. Dan Morgenstern recalled Charlie "very much in charge and trying his best to get Bud to focus," when Powell kept repeating the A-section of a tune and had to be cajoled into remembering the B-section. But on March 5 the pianist, who was frequently more disturbed than Charlie was, also got drunk quicker. There were verbal altercations and not much music. Finally, as Powell was being helped from the bandstand, the leader announced his name, repeatedly, ironically, contemptuously. No one applauded for Charlie, ever again.

The following week, before setting out for a gig in Boston, Charlie felt unwell and called at the apartment of the Baroness Nica de Koenigswarter, sister of Lord Rothschild but also a friend to Art Blakey, Thelonious Monk and others in the jazz community. She had Charlie attended by her doctor, who insisted on him remaining where he was since he refused to enter hospital, and for three days Nica and her daughter took care of him. Though he had continued to talk openly of the desirability of suicide to friends in recent weeks, he now said to his benefactor, "I've been dead for four years... I'm just a husk." On the last day of his life,

March 12, 1955, Charlie let Nica play a few of his records for the doctor, giving pride of place to *Just Friends* and *April in Paris*, with strings. And the heart attack which ended his suffering came while watching the Dorsey Brothers on television, in order to admire once again the technical efficiency and emotional vacuity of altoist Jimmy Dorsey.

Apparently Charlie had been granted his wish and had contracted pneumonia, the immediate cause of death on the certificate. But, as well as his long-standing ulcers, he now had advanced cirrhosis. The narcotics had left fewer marks, especially during the year since the loss of Pree, but as Charlie once said, "They can get it out of your blood, but they can't get it out of your mind." From the condition of his thirty-four-year-old body, the doctor estimated Charlie's age at the time of death to be fifty-three.

7 the song is you

The rootless confusion of Charlie Parker's private life and the waste of his undoubted intellect can perhaps be written off by some as the fault of society (though no less of a tragedy for him or his nearest and dearest, of course). But, whether it is seen as imposed on him or totally self-inflicted, his downfall ultimately pales into insignificance before his musical legacy. A mere six years after his death, Dizzy Gillespie was moved to write: "What he did was enormous. You hear his music everywhere now... But people talk too much about the man – people who don't know – when the important thing is his music."

Regarding the ubiquity of Charlie's influence, there was already a considerable consensus at the time of his passing. Duke Ellington, who was reputed to have offered employment to Charlie (and at different times to Fats Navarro and Miles Davis), was quoted as saying "There are countless records and performances by innumerable artists in which you hear a certain phrase, and you immediately see Charlie's picture in your mind's eye." Lennie Tristano's statement, made even before the altoist's death, was more categoric: "If Charlie Parker wanted to invoke plagiarism laws, he could sue almost everybody who's made a record in the last ten years." And Charles Mingus expressed the same thought in more picturesque language, with the lengthy subtitle to his tribute piece *Gunslinging Bird*: "If Charlie Parker were a gunslinger, there'd be a whole lot of dead copycats." More poignantly, on another occasion he said of the copyists: "They don't know that Bird had to escape into his horn or *die*."

The Gillespie article also included a challenging suggestion, which perhaps goes some way to explaining the apparent superiority of Charlie over all the copycats: "I doubt, though, whether he knew *everything* he was playing. I'll bet that 75 per cent of his playing he thought of, and the other 25 per cent just fell in place, fell under his fingers." Granted that he had to have extremely talented and well-trained fingers for things to fall in place the way they did, there is both an element of routine and also an element of luck in the use of improvisation, especially if that improvisation is (as with bebop and post-bop) in some sense collective. The more chances are taken, the more chances there are of something going wrong, but also the greater the possibility of being lucky – which is part of the excitement that communicates to its listeners. A number of observers, from musicians who worked closely with him such as Miles Davis and Red Rodney to those who asked him for advice such as the saxophonist Dick Meldonian, found holes in Charlie's theoretical knowledge. In this context, it is interesting that quite early on (starting from his interrogations of Lawrence Keyes when he was fourteen, and culminating perhaps in the Ozarks in 1937) he picked up a working knowledge of the piano. Gillespie mentioned this in connection with their very first meeting in 1940: "You didn't find many [horn-playing] musicians who could show you on the piano what they were doing. But Charlie Parker could, even then." These days, this would probably imply that he also had an excellent command of harmonic theory and that the piano was just an adjunct to exploring that theory. But, in the period when Charlie came to musical maturity, it was still far more common to acquire the necessary harmonic ability by ear, so that being able to see laid out on a keyboard the sounds that you heard would act as a very efficient way of bypassing a lot of theoretical description. The other comforting implication of Gillespie's comment is that the reader of the present work does not need a knowledge of theory to follow the drift of the ensuing discussion.

Charlie's legacy has two distinct aspects, of which his overwhelming influence is one. The profound effect on other instrumentalists and composers, although in some cases difficult to separate from the influence of the bebop movement as a whole, has been mentioned from time to time in the foregoing chapters. As it happens, the first edition of the present book expressed the sentiment that the time was ripe for a detailed study of Charlie's relationship to the rest of his contemporaries and followers. In the meantime, this has been accomplished with considerable success in Thomas Owens's 1995 work *Bebop: The Music and Its Players*, which devotes a chapter to Parker and then discusses everyone else relevant. None too surprisingly, his brief musical examples show how prevalent certain short motives were in Charlie's work and that of his followers. However, the next year also saw the publication of two musicological volumes that are more specifically devoted to the altoist. Carl Woideck's *Charlie Parker: His Life and Music* has a short but efficient biographical chapter, but otherwise is the only book to cover in detail the evolution and implications of Charlie's music, with the addition of four lengthy solo transcriptions. Somewhat more narrowly focused is the essay by Henry Martin, *Charlie Parker and Thematic Improvisation*, which brings to bear a particular kind of analysis originally developed in connection with European composition, in order to discover how far Parker's solos are directly related to the songs on which they are based. In addition, 1997 saw the second edition of Larry Koch's *Yardbird Suite: A Compendium of the Music and Life of Charlie Parker* which – despite the fact that one has to be a discographer and a hardened record-collector as well as a musician to appreciate it to the full – has obvious relevance to a theoretical discussion. These four books are the ones that define the current state of Parker musicology and, to the extent that the following commentary may whet the appetite, they are the most valuable choices for further reading.

The most we can achieve, within the scope of the present chapter, is to study Parker's own style briefly, virtually ignoring its later influence but not its antecedents. The aim is to evaluate it in terms of such major areas of expression as tone qualities, rhythmic values, harmonic language, melodic sensibility and compositional considerations, and to do so through the tangible evidence of a limited number of examples drawn from the many studio and live recordings that have been made publicly available (so far). They afford not only a joyful voyage of discovery but a considerable challenge to anyone wanting to penetrate beneath the dazzling surface and the direct emotionalism. And even these aspects present their problems, since they have often proved too strong meat for listeners coming from different backgrounds. The following comment from Julie McDonald, a fellow artist though working in a visual medium, addressed the emotional message of Charlie's actual sound on the horn, little spoken of by those who focus mainly on the notes:

> No wonder many who heard Bird play recoiled from his brilliant exposure of human emotions and found his music too painful a mirror of their inner selves. Yet those who listened more carefully found identification; they found release in knowing their anxieties – rage, even – were shared; found comfort in hearing their longing for love played back to them.

Because the listener's reaction to tonal nuance is so much more likely to be instinctual than intellectual, it is hard to rationalize its effect. Yet pianist Hank Jones, who first experienced it by hearing Charlie in the mid-1940s at the Spotlite and the Three Deuces, has insisted on its significance: "What a lot of people nowadays don't realize is that, as well as his fluency and his blinding speed – that incredible technique – he also had an incredible tone. It comes across better in newer records, which have been remastered." Among Parker devotees, his instrumental tone means diverse things to diverse people, and the most profound musical comment in the whole of Ross Russell's biography is relevant here: "The sound has its double edge, the two tones combined in one, the thin transparent tone and the fat thick tone, one on top of the other, blended into a single textured sound. It is at once veiled and clear, cloudy and incandescent." In historical terms, this sound can be described as one of the ways in which Charlie achieved an amalgamation of Coleman Hawkins and Lester Young. Perhaps because of Hawkins' pioneering role and perhaps also for more subtle reasons of personal development, his tone varied considerably over the length of his career, but its spectrum ran from confident and sometimes blustering declamation to more fulsome, even over-ripe, romantic outpourings. Young, on the other hand, sounded laidback and sly and insinuating and, when he edged closer to the declamatory, there was the suggestion of tongue-in-cheek or even of briefly putting on an act. It is fascinating to realize in passing that both of these hugely important musicians developed their approach in part from the example of Louis Armstrong, and that such variation of tone was just one of the aspects Armstrong had brought into play, using an instrument less adaptable in that respect than the saxophone.

Like that of all the major jazz soloists, Parker's personal sound is emotionally ambiguous, and indeed this is the nature of his relationship to the music of the blues. There is, of course, a painful historical scenario explaining the existence of a folk music in which words of pessimism and cynicism can be contradicted by the determination and lightheartedness of their vocal expression (and in which, conversely, verbal optimism can be undercut by musical resignation). The fact that Charlie was able to tap into this fundamental attribute of the vocal blues, just through subtle variation of his tone, meant that on an emotional level he turned everything he played into a blues – an observation made about him by musicians as different as Jay McShann and saxophonist Teddy Edwards. He rarely employed blues phraseology as such and, when he did, it formed a deliberate contrast to his predominantly diatonic melodic style, but it also showed clearly his knowledge of the whole tradition that lay behind his allusions. For instance, the solo on *Hootie Blues*, which first turned the heads of musicians who became aware of Charlie through records, contains in bars 7–8 (heard at 0:50 from the start) a riff that, in some form or other, went back probably for generations before him. It is instructive that such a simple phrase formed part of his huge vocabulary and that, nearly five years later, he would repeat it in a different key on the non-blues sequence *Lady Be Good*, at 1:38 of the JATP version. What's more, the original issue of *Billie's Bounce* has the phrase in bars 5–6 (1:41) of a blues chorus in yet another key while, on his first published version of *Now's The Time* from the same session, he begins the phrase at 0:43 but develops each half of it into a longer, more convoluted contour, covering all of bars 5–8. (A further reason to study this early *Now's The Time* is that the three-chorus alto solo presents a gradual transition from phraseology that is relatively straightforward – the first three phrases fall neatly within the four-bar divisions of the blues chord sequence – to much freer, more asymmetric phrasing typical of the mature Parker.)

Ex. 1a

Ex. 1b

Ex. 1c

Ex. 1d

Ex. 1: Four rhythmic variations on the same blues phrase: (a) starting at bar 7 of the *Hootie Blues* **solo; (b) bars 17–18 of the** *Lady Be Good* **solo; (c) bars 41–42 of** *Billie's Bounce* **(take 5 solo); and (d) bars 5–8 of** *Now's The Time* **(take 4 solo)**

Therein lies an example of the versatility and openness of the blues form, and of Charlie's openness to it. While discussing *Now's The Time*, Woideck mentions the use (on the originally unreleased Take -3 at 0.55) of a favourite and more singable blues phrase, sometimes associated with traditional words such as "You told me that you loved me, but you told me a lie/I told you that I loved you until the day I die." Charlie frequently employed this same phrase in a manner comparable to his song quotations, often (as here) playfully varying its timing, but its relevance to this paragraph lies in his speech-like variations of timbre, especially the slightly strangulated tone and vibrato on the final note of the phrase. Also in connection with *Billie's Bounce*, it is worth noting the variations of tone quality and articulation in the opening phrase of Charlie's solo (at 0:40), which has not been identified as a quotation from something previously known but was later borrowed by many others. Further, in bars 1–4 and also bars 11–12 of the theme-statements (0:06 and 0:20), the falling-off articulation of the harmony notes he plays under Davis is crucial to their effect, and the same is true of the extraordinary bluesy gesture going into his fourth and last solo chorus (1:33) – which, again, has been later used by others as a tribute to Parker. While the expressive use of tone and variation of articulation, sometimes almost from note to note, ought to be part of every saxophonist's armoury, it is surprising how often this is overlooked when considering the effectiveness of Charlie's communication. Because it was an inbuilt factor of his playing, probably acquired more from Young than from anyone else (including Hawkins), it needs to be acknowledged as informing everything he played, no matter how involved its contours.

With a view to meeting the challenge of the contours, a bit of detail on the rhythmic front may be of help. In fact, it is the absolute primacy of rhythmic variety in his playing which is now totally accepted – in theory, at any rate – as being one of his key achievements. As a result, it is so familiar in a superficial way that it becomes hard to appreciate until one attempts an actual imitation. Even Dizzy Gillespie, a performer of great rhythmic intensity but before the mid-1940s a trifle stiff, has said, "Rhythmically, he was quite advanced, with setting up the phrase and how you got from one note to another... After we started playing together, I began to play, rhythmically, more like him. In that sense he influenced me, and all of us, because what makes the style is not what you play but how you play it." Interestingly, this is the aspect which shows the clearest derivation from Lester Young, and the art of creating an improvisation with an apparent rhythmic life of its own was, once again, derived ultimately from Armstrong. However, in Lester's case, this art was deployed in a constant ebb and flow of tensions between on-the-beat playing and behind-the-beat playing. Parker's comparatively "hard" approach produced a consistent level of rhythmic tautness by playing continually just a fraction behind the beat, and maintaining the same relationship to the stated pulse of a rhythm-section unless, very occasionally, he allowed a phrase to fall much further behind for effect. In addition, there was a constant tendency to push just a little harder on between-the-beat eighth-notes (sometimes described as the "and," as in "1-and-2-and-3-and-4-and"), despite all the cross-accents he introduced.

It was undoubtedly these accents that threw the first generation of listeners, who found their sense of rhythm dislocated by his playing, and similarly the first generation of musicians who learned to play with him. Yet, if the jazz world had acquired a sense of its own history, this polyrhythmic phenomenon would not have seemed so hard to grasp. The accentuation of every third beat or every third half-beat during two or more bars (counting in a four-to-the-bar meter) is fundamental to all Afro-American music from ragtime to hip-hop, and goes back at least as far as the opening bars of both Scott Joplin's *Maple Leaf Rag* and *The Entertainer*. In Parker's compositions it appears, for instance, in the same opening bars of *Billie's Bounce* discussed above, coinciding exactly with the previously mentioned harmony notes played by the alto (bars 1–4, 11–12). These repeat the rhythmic motive every third beat (or quarter-note or crotchet, depending on your terminology), as does the onomatopoeic title-phrase in bars 1–4 of *Another Hair-Do* (0:05). But the accentuation in the *Billie's Bounce* phrase comes on every third half-beat (or eighth-note or quaver), like that in the theme of *Moose The Mooche* (bars 1–4, 9–12, 15–16, 25–28 and 31–32, equivalent to 0:09, 0:18, 0:25, 0:36 and 0:43). It is particularly useful to be able to draw examples from Charlie's written melodies because, except for the occasional simple riff tune such as *Buzzy* and *Cool Blues* (the latter another quotation from the common stock), they relate directly to his improvisational style and, as we have seen, some of them were created almost as fast. But the staggered repetition is also true of the riff-like phrase discussed above in connection with *Hootie Blues* (which repeats after the third beat) and of its re-use in the *Billie's Bounce* solo (where, it will be noted, the same overall timing starts one beat later).

Ex. 2a

Ex. 2b

Ex. 2c

Ex. 2: Basic polyrhythms in written Parker themes: (a) *Billie's Bounce;* **(b)** *Another Hair-Do;* **and (c)** *Moose The Mooche*

During Parker's improvisation, in fact, this kind of polyrhythmic phrasing became such a central principle – constant yet constantly varied as to the starting note – that the effect is overlooked in its total integration with the harmonic and melodic shapes. Two relatively simple examples in the famous *Ko Ko* are found, firstly, at bars 5–6 (0:28) of the main saxophone solo (a repetition at the third beat, heard again at bars 7–8) and, secondly, in the phrase resolution at bar 34 (0:51, with accents every third half-beat, echoed in bar 38). Both of these instances are comparatively easy to feel, because they involve exact repetition of the same phrase shape (and, talking of rhythm, the use of silence between the repetitions in each case is very impressive). But the ongoing redistribution of accents, especially at the level of the half-beat/eighth-note/quaver, is so ever-present that it is also almost more perceptible through singing along (or dancing along) than by reading a written transcription. This is, of course, what makes Parker's music so comparable to – and compatible with – the work of a present-day Afro-Latin rhythm-section. Unfortunately the Machito band of Parker's day, though "modern" for its time, largely reflected a Latinization of swing-band formulae, prior to the influence of bebop itself on Latin music, and as a consequence stuck to specific dance beats with a minimum of rhythm-section improvisation. Hearing the classic Parker quintet play the Latin-blues themes of *Barbados*, *Bongo Beep* or the remarkable *Bongo Bop* (with its first, fifth and ninth bars in Afro-Latin "even" timing and the remainder in "swing"), one realizes that Max Roach was actually the most compatible Latin drummer to play with Parker. But it is also obvious that these particular themes could well be played with a swing rhythm-section, whereas all the others such as *Billie's Bounce* or *Moose the Mooche* can be played in Latin (or its soul and funk derivatives), without altering the melody line or the accentuation.

There is less evidence of Charlie playing Afro-Latin or Caribbean music in his early years than Dizzy Gillespie, doubtless because the latter was based in New York from 1937 and not out in Kansas City. But the accuracy of both of them when doing "that double-time stuff," which Parker first picked up from Buster Smith, may well have been enhanced by their openness to Latin rhythms relying on an even eight-to-the-bar feel. With that as a mental basis, it's not hard to see how at medium tempos Charlie could sometimes double the feel again to 16th notes or how, at ballad tempos, he could sometimes make 16ths the norm and incorporate 32nd notes. Certainly, the use of multiple parallel pulses (e.g. 4/4 and 12/8 or 8/8 and 16/16) gradually became fundamental to jazz, and there is a surprising hint as early as *Hootie Blues* from 1941, for which the head arrangement was put together by Charlie. The unison saxophone allusion to *The Donkey Serenade*, responding to the bluesy brass section at 0:14, mirrors the song being quoted by suggesting a Latin rhythm and being played with "even" rather than "swing" timing. There are all manner of "Latin" references in the New York small-group sessions, for example the 1953 *Now's The Time* which has, in the second chorus of the theme at 0:23, a brief interpolation of *Ornithology* that pointedly goes from "swing" eighth notes into "even" eighth notes and effortlessly back. As well as the three original blues mentioned in the last paragraph, Charlie flirted confidently with Latin rhythms on themes such as *Cardboard*, *Visa*, Cal Massey's *Fiesta* and the introductions to *Dexterity* and *Segment/Diverse*. Similarly, the B-section of his *Bird Of Paradise* slips easily into a bolero pattern (perhaps mirroring some "straight" arrangements of the original Jerome Kern background theme *All The Things You Are*), while his live performances of *How High The Moon* and both different introductions to *Star Eyes* each have their Latin tinge.

It is important here to emphasize the collective nature of the creation on virtually all the recorded performances we have of Parker. Even in a big-band setting, whether it be the McShann band or one of the 1950s guest appearances, the stylistic feel of the horn-sections and the energy and pulse of the rhythm-section have a direct input to what Charlie plays. As for the small groups, listening to or looking at a soloist's line in isolation from its interactive "accompanists" is something we're all prone to do, but it is a falsification. The *Ornithology* reference in the 1953 *Now's The Time*, referred to above, could be interpreted as a humorous, or even slightly defensive, reaction to the driving beat that Max Roach is laying down, before Charlie backs off and digs in along with him – or maybe it is not this at all, but it's undoubtedly a reaction to something that's going on in the moment. When commentators refer to the "tension" surrounding his recordings with Bud Powell in May 1947 (usually described as a negative factor) or to the "tension" surrounding his live sets with Powell in May 1950 (usually described as a positive), what they hear are details of tone and timing in Charlie's playing provoked by Powell's playing. In other words, his exciting accompaniments are as pushy as Roach's in the previous example. Whether welcome or unwelcome (to Charlie or to the listener), they are different from the accompaniments provided by Duke Jordan or Al Haig or the safe pair of hands that is Hank Jones. If further proof is required of the prime importance of rhythm in Parker's music, it may be found in Sadik Hakim's comment that, when demonstrating a new tune, "He had a funny way of humming the rhythm of the tune instead of the melody."

Harmonically speaking, there are manifest misconceptions in the received view of Charlie's contribution, misconceptions that derive from texts written in the 1940s and 1950s and that prove surprisingly tenacious, even in the age of the Internet. As Martin Williams already commented in 1970,

> It has been said that the boppers often made their compositions by adopting the chord sequences of standard popular songs and writing new melody lines to them. So they did, and so had at least two generations of jazzmen before them. It has been said that they undertook the similar practice of improvising with only a chord sequence as their guide.

Williams pointed out that this too was the norm by the late 1930s, but in fact saxophonists and clarinettists had been doing it since the late 1910s, and indeed everyone who improvised on the blues was obliged to do so. Similarly, received opinion seems to be that harmonic chromaticism was essential to bebop in general and to Charlie's music in particular, and there is much potential confusion in the statements of other musicians (perhaps because it excited or baffled them, as well as potential listeners). Drummer Gus Johnson has said of the Jay McShann period, "We would play a number in five or six different keys – what we call chromatics. We'd start in B-flat and then take just a half-step [i.e. to B], to C, to C-sharp... Charlie would just run all through 'em." This sort of thing, presumably for a chorus at a time, was put on record later by people such as Sonny Stitt or Stan Getz (in his *Crazy Chords*) and goes to illustrate the kind of practice regime which went into another aspect of the same early-period Parker, described by Gene Ramey: "Bird had a way of starting on a B natural against the B-flat chord, and he would run a cycle against that – and probably it would only be two or three bars before we got to the channel (middle part) that he would come back to the basic changes." The reference this time is to a rapid series of substitutions drawn from the key-cycle, and outlined in one of his rare interviews by Don Byas: "Bird got a lot of things from me... I played all that stuff from Tatum. That F-sharp, B-natural, E, A, D, G, C, F, like in [*I Got*] *Rhythm*, instead of playing [the first four bars of] *Rhythm* chords."

Most revealingly, however, it is hard to find recorded examples of anything so straightforward or elementary in Parker's playing. Tatum seems not to have put this use of the key-cycle on record until his 1944 *I Got Rhythm* although Monk, who doubtless also got it from Tatum, can be heard doing it on *Rhythm Riff*, a 1941 live recording at Minton's, as well as on later items such as *Humph* and *Rhythm-A-Ning*. (For the historically minded, it was also documented by other representatives of the New York piano tradition, Clarence Profit [1939] and Garnet Clark [as early as 1935], and Byas himself did it on record in his 1945 *I Got Rhythm* and in Gillespie's version of the Monk tune *52nd Street Theme* in 1946.) But, out of all Parker's output, it is hardly found at all during his mature period, apart from brief references in *Merry-Go-Round* (0:38), the December 12, 1948 *Salt Peanuts* (2:17), Jazz At The Philharmonic's *The Closer* (8:52) and in the recordings from the 1950 Swedish tour. Intriguingly, though, this approach may be said to survive in the cycle-based chord sequence of Charlie's classic piece *Confirmation*, and the related idea heard in the themes of what were known for a while as "Swedish blues," such as *Blues for Alice* and *Laird Baird*. But it was unusual for him to compose lines that relied on complex harmonic movement, obviously preferring to reserve an optional complexity for his spontaneous improvisations. His use of harmony was extremely sophisticated, but what distinguished his mature style was the ability to take *any* principle of chord complication, whether derived from Tatum, Ellington, Gillespie or Young, and make it work in a totally non-programmed and non-schematic way. Put more succinctly, the polyrhythmic approach was fundamental but the polyharmonies were less so.

Ex. 3a

Ex. 3b

Ex. 3c

Ex. 3: Flexible timing of the same passing-chord arpeggio, marked x, in (a) bar 11 of the *Shaw 'Nuff* solo; (b) bar 35 of *Thriving From A Riff* (take 3 solo); and (c) bars 3–4 of *Anthropology* (Birdland 1951 solo)

Kenny Clarke was quoted as saying of Charlie, "He was twice as fast as Lester Young and into harmony Lester hadn't touched" and, while the first half of the statement is true, the second half reveals a rather misleading impression. Many of the passing-chords that were familiar from the work of Hawkins and Tatum were less often heard on alto (Biddy Fleet compared Charlie to other players by saying, "Where they would go from one chord to another, Bird played that in-between"). But the comparative strangeness of his interpolations was obviously underlined and exaggerated, in people's reactions, by the rhythmic freedom previously discussed. Looking, for instance, at a couple of solos based on the unamended *Rhythm* changes, the arpeggiated chromatic passing-chord in bars 3–4 of Parker's solo in *Shaw 'Nuff* (0:50) begins on the fourth beat, i.e. one beat later than expected, but in bar 11 (0:57) it reappears early at the second beat. By contrast, when the same arpeggio is used in the original issued take of *Thriving From A Riff*, it falls on a "strong" beat (beat 3 of bar 3 of the alto's second chorus, at 1:14) and immediately sounds more "normal" – even though, in theoretical terms, it would be described as based on the famed flatted-5th substitution, implying a D-flat root rather than G. In fact, what appear to be substitute chords are often merely anticipated or delayed chords, as in the first eight bars of the 1951 Birdland solo on *Anthropology* which include both a similar arpeggio heard one beat late (end of bar 3, 0:30) and a further example delayed by two beats (end of bar 7, 0:32). For examples more easily heard at a slow tempo, both takes of *Embraceable You* have, at the start of the B-section in bar 9 (0:42 in take A, 0:36 in take B), a melodic phrase that belongs with the dominant harmony of the previous bar. Similarly in take B of the same song, the start of the C-section in bar 25 (1:30) is observed by the rhythm-section but delayed in the solo line, which still refers to the previous chord.

As to the actual "new" harmony Parker was alleged to have incorporated, a statement by Dexter Gordon was fairly specific. As well as noting that Lester Young had already popularized the use of the 6th and the 9th in his solos, Dexter commented as follows: "I would say that the chords were extended and altered. The flat 5, the flat 9th and the 13th chords, whereas you could play changes on top of changes by perhaps playing the top of the chord of an extended chord first, and into the basic chord and continuing in this vein." To illustrate the impact of what Gordon meant, one could look again at *Ko Ko* and that second example of simple polyrhythm described a while back (i.e. bar 34 or 0:51), noting that the interval of a 13th above the root used by Charlie derives from the background tune of *Cherokee* – whereas, if one were to imagine Young playing a similar phrase on this song, he might instead have aimed for the 9th. Already common in Tatum's and Ellington's harmonizations, these, of course, are the "higher intervals" referred to in Parker's own statement about his discoveries. But the perception that he plucked something out of the air that no one had previously found is highly erroneous. For instance, not only did the published song of *Cherokee* abound in 13ths, but the hit instrumental version by Charlie Barnet – which Parker could not have failed to hear – even has an interlude (arranged by Billy May) with prominent alternating raised 9ths and flatted 9ths. These would not have found their way into even a hip big-band score, had they not already been common in the work of soloists such as Roy Eldridge, whose work Charlie was very familiar with.

Similarly, the use of phrases based on the flatted-5th substitution seems less extraordinary when one realizes that they were so prevalent in the work of Ellington and Tatum in the 1930s, and that there is even an allusion by Benny Goodman and Teddy Wilson as early as 1935 (*After You've Gone*). Precedence would not be much of an issue unless Charlie claimed that he had found an entirely "new" way of playing, but in fact he merely described hearing "something else" that he personally could not previously realize. Even that is nevertheless more than somewhat misleading, since it implies that he then started using it extensively and prominently but, except again perhaps during his apprenticeship, this is not the case. As implied by the Gordon quote above, there is a sense in which temporary reference to an alien key-signature (i.e. bi-tonality, or what became known in the post-Coltrane era as "side-slipping") might be construed as a use of the higher intervals of the original key. Later in the same 1951 *Anthropology* solo just mentioned, bars 9–10 of the third alto chorus (1:24) are an example of a phrase repeated a semitone higher, thus clashing with the original chords, and a similar instance is the repetition of the riff of the 1952 *Lester Leaps In*, first of all in the original key and then (c. 2:15) a minor third higher. But this – like Parker's highly chromatic middle-eights on *Red Cross* (at 0:59) and *Shaw 'Nuff* (1:02) or his bi-tonal middle-eight on *Moose The Mooche* (1:03) – is something he used extremely sparingly after the mid-1940s.

Viewed in a purely melodic sense, the idea of repetition of an improvised phrase at a different pitch is a device probably derived from Parker's high-school acquaintance with European music. The first two bars of take A of *Embraceable You* (which also happen to be a quotation from another song), the opening phrase of the *Just Friends* solo, and the quotation from *Cocktails for Two* near the end of *Warming Up A Riff* are perhaps the best-known examples, but much subtler uses of repetition or of imitation (i.e. approximate repetition) are to be found in many improvisations, including take B of *Embraceable You*. The fact that take A has been analysed by Martin Williams, transcribed by Frank Tirro, and also analysed and transcribed by both Larry Koch and Henry Martin, may just mean that it's a suitable case for analysis. But there are some observations to be made about both of these October 1947 versions, two of the slowest ballad performances on disc up to that date. Although both are extremely lyrical and link up with Hawkins' and Young's tradition of ballad performances, one thing missing from take B is the affecting and rather pre-bebop moment where Charlie quietly backs Miles Davis' muted solo with a long-note counter-melody, but in common between the two takes is the use of several glancing allusions to the original Gershwin song. In take A these occur during bars 9–10 of the solo (0:43), bar 21 (1:26), more obliquely in bars 27–28 (1:50) and in bar 30 (1:59), while in take B they again occur at bars 9–10 (0:38, and very similar to the take A reference) and – more dramatically than in take A – at bars 27–28 (1:39).

This is striking, since the mood of the two solos varies considerably, with take A more redolent of European-style imitation – for instance, bars 1–2 (0:13) being transmuted up a fourth in bars 3–4; the transposed idea in bars 19–20 (1:17); the thrice-heard phrase in bars 23–24 (1:32); and the two linked "repetitions" in bars 28–29 (1:53). By contrast take B, the one originally released and recorded only minutes later, is more concerned with reminiscences of take A – so that take B's bar 5 (0:24) starts a half-beat earlier but is otherwise identical to bar 16 of take A (1:07); take B's bars 14–15 (0:54) contain a 'repetition' that imitates bar 22 of take A (1:29); while take B's internal imitation heard in bars 1, 2, 4 and 10 (0:12, 0:16, 0:21 and 0:40 respectively) is a development of the idea that opens bar 10 of take A (0:45). Although there are relatively few formulaic phrases here, the process involved clearly relates to Thomas Owens' theory concerning Parker's interchangeable use of short motives as his basic vocabulary – indeed, one familiar formula (the phrase in bar 5 of take B and bar 16 of take A mentioned above) is identified by Woideck in the originally issued *Billie's Bounce* (at 1:11), where its medium-tempo accompaniment is roughly twice as fast. But the relationship between take A and take B also lends some support to Henry Martin's thesis that the solos on both (and many other solos) are instinctively and intimately derived from the melody that Parker chose to improvise upon, implying that an improvisation on another item from the American songbook would come out very differently. Yet the fact of solos on the same material containing some of the same elements also needs to be seen in the context of a cultural tradition whereby, when a successful recorded improvisation has been released, the artist would try to reproduce it on live performances.

At any rate, if one allows that the blues form is at the opposite end of the harmonic spectrum from a sophisticated popular song (with *Rhythm* changes and a couple of jam session warhorses such as *Honeysuckle Rose* and *Lady Be Good* somewhere in the middle), it seems reasonable that blues solos will not be derived in the same way, unless the opening material of the head is particularly distinctive. So Martin's suggestion that the details of the famous take on the slow *Parker's Mood* relate directly to its two-bar introductory figure is less convincing, especially given that some of the same ideas appeared three years earlier (without this introduction) on the two takes of Red Norvo's *Slam Slam Blues*. Both *Parker's Mood* and Parker's contributions to *Slam Slam Blues* are full of discreet blues gestures – especially the "blue" inflection of the 3rd degree of the scale, and the use of fall-offs at the end of some 3rds and flat 3rds. But the whole is an artful, and feelingful, compromise between the relatively few direct references to the blues scale and the rest of the solo, which consists of great arcs of soaring diatonic melody. This should also point our attention towards the classical sense of melodic and rhythmic

Ex. 4: The "higher intervals" in the song *Cherokee* inspired Parker's melodic variations starting at bar 33 of his *Ko Ko* solo, using the 13th (marked x) and flat 13th (marked y) of F#7 and the 9th of Bmaj7 (marked z); an imaginary Lester Young solo on the same sequence shows his emphasis on the 9th of F#7 and the 6th of the B chord

Ex. 5: Melodic imitation employed motivically in Parker's improvisations, not only on take A of *Embraceable You* (phrase x) but also take B (phrase y)

balance that informs those beautiful instrumental "songs" such as the top-lines of *Confirmation* and *Quasimado*, both of which have in fact had words added by singer Sheila Jordan. The former has been described as a continuous, non-repeating melody, but in fact the first eight bars, the second eight and the last eight are extremely closely related, and it is instructive how one small difference necessitates another small difference which necessitates yet another small difference, in order to retain a perfect overall balance.

Exactly the same process is used in improvisation, where Parker's melodic sense reveals his absorption of all the best eighteenth- and nineteenth-century European composers, which is doubtless one reason for his subsequent feeling that he was repeating himself and for his interest in twentieth-century Europeans. Allied to his great harmonic expertise, it was also the reason why many younger jazzmen felt that the European aspects of jazz could never be more fully exploited than by Parker, and that it was time for something else. But what he perhaps did not have the confidence to realize was that his particular combination of European and African elements was more complex than any previously achieved, and that it was capable of infinite variation. The rhythmic subtlety which is crucial to *Confirmation* and *Quasimado* also gives life to, and is enlivened by, the melodic ambiguity of a theme like *Bird Feathers*, which in terms of pitch opens out almost like a pair of wings and then hovers around an unstated central note. Such a theme reminds us that, as well as the rhythmic variety within a phrase and the modification of the rate of harmonic changes, Parker also uses a melodic "macro-syncopation" of the length of phrases (a lack of which easily pinpoints those tunes attributed to but not in fact written by Parker, such as Benny Harris' *Ornithology* and Miles Davis' *Donna Lee*). Similarly during improvisations, which required control of the minutest rhythmic and harmonic details, Parker was able to mould huge blocks of sound of unequal weight and still impart a precise balance to the whole. In this way, his style would have been capable not only of infinite variation but of infinite extension, as hinted by various witnesses such as Barry Ulanov. Their statements that, towards the end of his career, Charlie was playing longer and longer solos should cause regret that so few recordings are extant from completely unfettered jam-session situations.

At the other extreme from jam-session playing, the studio quintet dates, especially in the late 1940s, reveal Charlie's ability to create varied ensemble statements, often based on a similar vocabulary to his improvisations but with a composerly concern for textures. Although the majority of the tunes are straightforward 32-bar or 12-bar choruses played in unison, there are interesting choices made as to whether the alto should be at exactly the same pitch as the trumpet or an octave below, as in *Dexterity* or *Barbados* – in all cases, either option would be possible, so this is an aesthetic matter – and whether his trumpeters should play with a mute or not. The most obvious exceptions to the unison statement are the two numbers recorded with Miles Davis, where the two horns have independent, interlocking lines, namely *Chasin' The Bird* and *Ah-Leu-Cha* – the latter (allegedly pronounced "Ah-lee-chay" and representing "Charlie" in dog Latin) was revived by Davis during his increasingly radical revision of bebop procedures in the second half of the 1950s. There are also pieces where trumpet and alto are voiced briefly in harmony, namely *The Hymn* and the introduction to *Klactoveeseedstene*, and, as well as the last-named, examples of items with arranged ensemble introductions also include *Charlie's Wig*, *Segment/Diverse* and *Shaw 'Nuff*. In the case of the latter, Gillespie apparently wrote the 32-bar *Rhythm*-changes theme (as mentioned in the notes to Chapter 3), whereas Charlie contributed the intro with its humorous, here-come-the-Indians rhythms that were also used in some musicians' versions of *Cherokee*.

Instances also occur of textural variation used for structural purposes, strikingly so when *The Hymn* bursts on our ears with four choruses of up-tempo blues improvisation before the alto-and-trumpet theme, which may be compared with the themeless up-tempo pieces described in Chapter 4 (*Merry-Go-Round*, *Klaunstance* and *Bird Gets The Worm*) that nevertheless have brief ensemble statements in their out-chorus. Also of interest is the adaptation of *Salt Peanuts* first heard in the December 12, 1948 broadcast version, whereby the interlude is followed by a brief imitative dialogue between Charlie and Miles Davis, of the kind Davis later undertook with John Coltrane. But there are further surprises when the *opening* chorus in both *Constellation* and *Another Hair-Do* also mixes unison ensemble phrases and bursts of improvisation in an exciting and only loosely programmed manner, as evidenced by the existing alternate takes. *Constellation*, too, is perhaps the only piece which, in the complicated timing of its brief head, capitalizes on the achievement of *Ko Ko*. That monumental track is memorable to most listeners for its glorious alto solo and the propulsive (and quite discreetly interactive) support of Max Roach, yet the shape of the piece is also unique. As noted in Chapter 3, the thirty-two bars of the introduction and coda is not related to the *Cherokee* chord sequence on which the main solo is based. Two pre-set alto-and-trumpet ensembles of eight bars each (one in octave unison, one in harmony) book-end two eight-bar solos by first Gillespie and then

Parker, implying a modal pedal-point that remains unstated, since the only accompaniment to the two horns comes from the drums.

Even today, this sounds overtly modernistic, and a direct influence on the future Ornette Coleman quartet – especially so when the closing reiteration of the same routine ends early, and deliberately up in the air. Although there is no chord sequence in this whole 32-bar section, it is possible that Parker heard a melodic relationship between the bluesy opening phrase of his piece and the opening phrase of the *Cherokee* melody and, if so, it could be seen as an abstruse example of using the upper intervals of the chords from which the original song was derived. It was indeed intriguing to note the response of Ornette when, at a famous 1965 London concert, a hostile audience member questioned Coleman's ability (viewed from a bebop perspective) by calling out during a moment of silence, "Now play *Cherokee!*" The next five notes heard from the alto mirrored the song's opening phrase, but concentrating on the lower intervals of the chords! Perhaps the audience member was right in one respect, and perhaps Ornette was right in going back to the roots, almost literally. In conclusion, it is probably fair to say, as Woideck and others have pointed out, that Parker opened up many possibilities which, in his last few years, he failed to pursue. But it might also be reasonable to be grateful for what he gave us, and to conclude that he had to leave something for people like Miles, Mingus, Coltrane and Ornette to explore.

Ex. 6a

Ex. 6b

Ex. 6c

Ex. 6: A comparison between (a) the opening of *Cherokee*; (b) the written opening of Parker's *Ko Ko*; and (c) part of Ornette Coleman's improvisation on *Silence*

In addition to the four books referred to in this chapter, there is also, if it can be located, an excellent essay by James Patrick accompanying the five-LP Savoy album of twenty-five years ago – sadly, when the essay was revised and reprinted for Savoy's eight-CD box, the musical illustrations were dropped. For those interested in pursuing the practical technicalities a little further, David Baker's *Charlie Parker: Alto Saxophone* (Shattinger, distributed by Hansen) has the advantage of longer musical examples and, while most of the volumes of music alone need to be approached with some caution, a veritable cornucopia of accurate transcriptions is contained in the *Charlie Parker Omnibook* (Atlantic Music Corporation).

8 confirmation

As we have seen, the mythology of Charlie Parker was already growing during his lifetime and it is hardly surprising that, given the combination of his musical abilities and his often scandalous behaviour, he attracted particular interest. In the hours and days after his death, the groundwork was laid for him to become an equally extraordinary figure posthumously. There is an eerie parallel to the incorrect forename that was given in the first printed recognition of his existence (see Chapter 1) with the possibly apocryphal story of his body lying unclaimed in the morgue under the name "John Parker," both instances arising no doubt from mishearing the relevant information. This confusion apparently began while Baroness Nica endeavoured to contact Chan, whose latest address she did not possess, rather than alerting the rumour mill. But word got out anyway, and Doris was the first to notify Addie, whose reaction was "I thought it wasn't nothing but an overdose of dope." Probably that was the reaction on the street too, but there were also conflicting and, of course, uncorroborated alternative theories – one implicating a fellow musician (allegedly Art Blakey) in a fist-fight that might have precipitated Charlie's death, and another suggesting that Charlie had been shot. It is easy to understand how either of these ideas could arise, relating to someone whose connections with the drug trade were so frequent and so well known, and the concept of a conspiracy to keep silent such details is undoubtedly appealing to certain fans.

This kind of theorizing often attaches to those taken in what should be the prime of their life, even if they may already have passed it artistically. As a result, the saxophonist's name has often been invoked in discussions of other similar figures, including singers as different as Billie Holiday, Edith Piaf or Elvis Presley, and the Welsh writer Dylan Thomas. Thomas died in the USA, just a few months before Charlie, earning him the Parker comparison in an essay by fellow poet Kenneth Rexroth, who was at least interested in jazz, and at this period it became common for beatnik writers such as Jack Kerouac and Allen Ginsberg to invoke the name of Parker. It is probably a backhanded tribute to Charlie's influence in the wider world that he is often compared to artists engaged in the use of language, which automatically gives them a much more direct line to the ears and emotions of the general public. A further tribute to his charisma, and perhaps to his symbolic status as an anti-authority figure, is the analogy drawn between him and the actor James Dean, whose death in a car accident six months after Charlie added much to the twenty-four-year-old's still embryonic fame. Similarly Marlon Brando, though born in 1923 and only departing from our midst in 2004, achieved a stylistic breakthrough in his mid-twenties that indirectly influenced everyone who followed and, as a result, continued to be revered even when he squandered his talent and his career. But a more resonant parallel may perhaps be that of Lenny Bruce, the satirist who addressed the hypocrisy of 1950s American society and fell foul of both hard drugs and the law.

It needs to be said that, while notions of victimhood have undoubtedly played their part in keeping alive Parker's reputation, it ultimately rests on the undying potency of his work. At least, the graffiti artists chose the appropriate nickname when, within days of his passing, they began writing on the walls of the New York subway: "Bird lives!" This was clearly also the message which insiders perceived when a favourite musicians' bar, Charlie's Tavern, soon became home to a pigeon that flew in from the streets, or when a feather floated from the ceiling of Carnegie Hall during an all-star memorial concert. The same message lay behind the comment of Mingus, as noted by Chan at the funeral, that the body in the coffin was not Charlie: "Later, I realized what he meant." This ceremony took place at Harlem's famous Abyssinian Baptist Church, home base of the preacher-turned-politician Adam Clayton Powell (husband of pianist-singer Hazel Scott), prior to the body being shipped to his mother in Kansas City. Chan's initial arrangements for a funeral had been overruled since, as a mere common-law wife, she was allowed a front-row seat in church but her wishes were legally subordinate to those of Doris, whose marriage was deemed still valid. (Ironically, in the 1960s this proved not to be the case, since the fact of her being wed in Mexico – and Charlie's possible reason for choosing that location – was that in fact his union with Gerri Scott had never been terminated.) A more immediate irony was that, like Doris when Charlie left her for Chan, Chan had no funds to call her own and, though the memorial concert was to benefit Charlie's two surviving children, she had to accept a backstage collection organized by Gerry Mulligan's wife Arlene.

If it is reasonable to describe both Chan and Doris to an extent as victims of Charlie's lifestyle, so also were some of his disciples. Sonny Rollins, almost exactly ten years younger than the altoist and often the recipient of his homilies about steering clear of hard drugs, was actually undergoing a course of treatment in the Federal Narcotics Hospital, Lexington (Kentucky) at the time Charlie died – and, although he cleaned up his act thereafter, he always regretted not having done so in time to tell Charlie about it. Miles Davis had kicked the habit the previous year but, when he heard of Charlie's death, he was being held temporarily at the New York state prison on Riker's Island for non-payment of alimony during the period of his addiction. Non-musician associates of Charlie's may also have paid a price, such as agent Billy Shaw whose premature death aged fifty-two from a heart attack only fifteen months after Charlie, was believed by Ross Russell to have been hastened by his tortuous relationship with the saxophonist. But another part of Charlie's legacy is undoubtedly the fact that so many younger African-American musicians saw his thwarted career as a reason for not limiting themselves to the role of entertainer. Among them, of course, was Miles, whose comeback was already under way and was confirmed for the jazz press by his appearance at the second Newport Jazz Festival in July 1955. Another was the clean-living Clifford Brown, whose playing sometimes sounds like a translation of pure Parker to the trumpet (and who tragically died in a car accident in 1956). It has to be significant, too, that a few of Brown's contemporaries, Gigi Gryce (briefly) and both Quincy Jones and Donald Byrd (at greater length), actually fulfilled Charlie's dream of studying composition in Paris under the renowned Nadia Boulanger.

In the popular imagination, at the time of his death the saxophonist's reputation had been reduced to Miles' description of "just another broke, weird, drunken nigger playing some strange music," and the popular press celebrated his death in exactly that vein. But, within the year, there was evidence of the beginnings of a serious appraisal of his music. *Metronome* magazine's *Jazz 1956* yearbook included a Parker history by Bill Coss and a transcription and commentary by clarinettist Tony Scott, and the same year saw the English-language publication of André Hodeir's essay (written before Charlie's death) in his book *Jazz: Its Evolution and Essence*. There was even interest on the part of television in the late 1950s, with a documentary by CBS-TV entitled *The Mythical Bird* on their Sunday morning slot *Camera Three*. And, by 1957, it was possible for writer Orrin Keepnews to talk of no fewer than four forthcoming books about Charlie. Chan was named as working on a memoir, which in fact took until 1993 to be published and then only in translation. Robert Reisner's suitably kaleidoscopic picture built up through interviews (a few of them previously printed in specialist magazines) appeared in 1962 as *Bird: The Legend Of Charlie Parker*, by which time the first Bird novel had been completed. This was *The Sound*, written by former record producer Ross Russell, while soon after (and unpredicted by Keepnews) a superior example of the novel form, *Night Song* by John A. Williams, surfaced and was later made into the film *Sweet Love, Bitter*, starring Dick Gregory as Charlie and with music by Mal Waldron featuring George Coleman on alto. The fourth, unnamed writer in Keepnews' list apparently never got beyond the planning stage, but the first book to cover the music in any detail was the English writer Max Harrison's pocket-size biography *Charlie Parker*, published in 1960 (later superseded by his chapter in Carl Woideck's *Charlie Parker Companion*).

Also in the late 1950s, the record industry started to reap the rewards which had not always been forthcoming during Charlie's lifetime. Following the example of the Dial material, whose alternate takes had already appeared prior to his death (before being sold off in mixed batches to several mail-order and budget labels), both Savoy and Norman Granz's Verve now began rediscovering previously unissued material. In the case of Verve, the consolidation of former singles and albums on Mercury, Clef and Norgran was supplemented by some extra whole takes from 1949 (the session with Kenny Dorham), 1950 (with Hank Jones, Dizzy Gillespie or Coleman Hawkins), 1951 (with Miles Davis or Red Rodney) and the final small-group dates, and these were assembled in fairly logical fashion on a series of albums called *The Charlie Parker Story* and *The Genius Of Charlie Parker*. Savoy, on the other hand, issued one by one a group of five LPs that included in piecemeal fashion some new complete takes and several performances called to a halt for various reasons, and thus including snatches of conversation by either producer or bandleader. In the case of the 1944 Tiny Grimes session, there were also three takes faded out after the alto improvisations, so that the reissue should not be burdened with further solos by Grimes. The last of these five LPs to appear included the entire *Now's The Time* date in performance order, and thereby set a precedent only followed up in the mid-1960s by the then UK licensee, which (with the encouragement and advice of critic Alun Morgan) reissued all the Savoy material chronologically.

This activity, though musically instructive, was perhaps a more academic exercise than the publication of the many live tracks that began to appear, and which give a different impression of Charlie's playing than either the studio dates or the staged jam sessions of Jazz At The Philharmonic. A couple were already in circulation before his death, namely the openly pirated set of Charlie guesting with Dizzy Gillespie and his rhythm-section at Carnegie Hall in 1947, and the famous 1953 Massey Hall concert that had been issued by Mingus's Debut label, after being turned down by Norman Granz. But, around 1957, Mingus also acquired Jimmy Knepper's copies of tapes made by himself, Joe Maini, Don Lanphere and others, that then appeared on albums titled *Bird At St. Nick's* (1950) and *Bird On 52nd Street* (whose July 1948 material consisted of second-generation copies of the already legendary Dean Benedetti archive). These two albums constituted the first to be issued from deliberately incomplete recordings that only preserved Charlie's playing and not that of other soloists, and the first to flout the convention that even live albums had to have halfway decent sound quality – the lack of which also bedevilled the Savoy label's first live discovery, *An Evening At Home*, strangely titled indeed since it was taken down in 1950 at Chicago's Pershing Ballroom. Sound quality was less of an issue with the first semi-official releases of off-air transcriptions by amateur engineer Boris Rose, who had often run off custom-made dubs for individual collectors, but in 1961 put out three albums of *Historical Recordings* on his Le Jazz Cool label. These airshots from the Royal Roost and the 1950 Birdland sets with Fats Navarro and Bud Powell were at least of broadcast standard (with the occasional off-mike piano solo removed) and were revelatory, in terms of Charlie's heights of invention during performances expected to be forgotten as soon as they were played.

Naturally, this excited the interest of the Charlie Parker estate, and Doris's then lawyer Aubrey Mayhew. Other live recordings were acquired and released for the first time by the newly founded Charlie Parker Records, such as the 1951 Christy's tapes heard on *The Happy Bird* and, on *Bird Is Free!*, part of the much appreciated 1952 Rockland Palace benefit concert. Even some of the classic Dial sides (which, thanks to the efforts of the budget labels, seemed to be passing rapidly into the public domain) were collected on a Parker Records album, and several new sessions were recorded, for instance by Duke Jordan, that included cover versions of Charlie's compositions. Possibly because of the slighter appeal of this new material, or through other examples of mismanagement, the Parker label didn't last long in this incarnation (it was subsequently bought by Audio Fidelity, which in the 1980s issued further Rockland Palace material, among other things). The prospect of the Dial recordings once again disappearing into a copyright-free limbo then inspired the UK-based collectors' label, Spotlite, to begin in 1970 assembling all the previously dispersed takes, with the covert cooperation of Ross Russell, then engaged in writing his 1973 biography *Bird Lives!* (which was unkindly said to contain as much fiction as his Parker novel). For these six chronological LPs of Dial material, Russell wrote new (unsigned) programme notes and discovered a couple of hitherto unknown takes, while primitive pitch-correction was undertaken by the present author. As a follow-up, Russell facilitated the first-ever release of the historic Jay McShann small-group recordings discussed in his book and which took place at station KFBI in Wichita.

Live-performance extensions of the music initially took the form of the pervasive hard-bop school in the second half of the 1950s. More specifically, the group led by Max Roach (initially with Clifford Brown until his demise) devoted one album to the Parker repertoire and occasionally used it on gigs, but concentrated more and more on original material, whereas Mingus, though valued for his own compositions, was regularly featuring Charlie's tunes on his personal appearances, sometimes in the form of a medley. Whereas Bud Powell often remained more faithful to bebop, though at a lower level of intensity than in his heyday, Dizzy Gillespie generally steered clear of it except in particular projects, such as one half of a 1963 album that recreated *Dizzy Atmosphere* and others with James Moody on saxophone. Both Gillespie and Powell lent their presence to a tenth anniversary Parker Memorial Concert at Carnegie Hall in March 1965 while, the previous summer, producer George Wein assembled perhaps the first specific tribute band (with Howard McGhee, J. J. Johnson, Sonny Stitt and Max Roach) which appeared at the Newport Festival and (with the substitution of Paris resident Kenny Clarke for Roach) toured various European festivals in autumn 1964. Before that, however, a conscious echo that reinforced the identification of Charlie with hard drugs was central to the off-Broadway play performed regularly from 1959–61 by the Living Theatre, *The Connection* by Jack Gelber. The script required an on-stage quartet "in the style of Charlie Parker" (using music written by pianist Freddie Redd and featuring Jackie McLean) while one of the fictional junkies, a would-be saxophonist, was called on to play a record listened to in respectful silence by the other actors. The original cast appeared in a 1961 film version directed by Shirley Clarke and including *Marmaduke*, in the alternate version (identified in the Discography as take -9) which ends with Charlie's voice saying to the producer "OK, play that back, please."

Although there was some continuity between the 1950s' beatniks and the 1960s' hippies, Charlie's reputation in the latter decade was probably at its lowest ebb. Bebop was being squeezed out, on the one side by avant-garde free jazz and on the other side by the pop industry's initially cautious embrace of alternative rock and folk – performers in these fields made the right noises politically, but their understanding of jazz was usually limited (except, interestingly, in England and other European countries). The other reason is, of course, that the espousal of hard drugs and the attendant anti-establishment mind-set was so eagerly taken up by young post-rock-and-roll musicians, just as it had been by so many incipient beboppers twenty years earlier. If you were into music primarily for sociological reasons, the jazz style forged in the 1940s seemed all but irrelevant and its current adherents far too well behaved to become counter-culture heroes. As for Charlie, and Billie Holiday or indeed Bud Powell (who died in 1966), the only role open for their personas at the time was as victims of racism, and occasional kind words from the emerging icons of free-jazz such as Cecil Taylor or Archie Shepp placed them in precisely that slot. On the other hand, Ornette Coleman often looks like the innovator with the clearest links to earlier styles – just as Charlie was in the beginning of bebop itself – and not only played the same instrument but used the musical materials Charlie had favoured. In his earliest recordings can be heard 12-bar blues, *I Got Rhythm*-like choruses, and other original 32-bar sequences such as *The Blessing*. There is even a live Coleman version, issued under the name of Paul Bley, of *Klactoveesedstene*, and Ornette was capable of passable (if brief) imitations of Charlie. So was his fellow altoist Eric Dolphy, and both of them referred to "Bird" in the titles of some of their early originals.

In the swings and roundabouts of fashionable favouritism, it is conventional to note that the first traditional jazz revival was partly brought about through the increased interest sparked by the popularity of swing, and partly because the advanced concepts of late swing and early bebop were one step too far for many listeners. That revival got under way in the early 1940s, some twenty-five to thirty years after the original style crystallized in the 1910s. It was therefore to be expected that a determined re-examination of early-to-mid-1940s jazz might take place in the early 1970s, just as the first wave of free jazz (with its still discernible links to what went before) was foundering and the seemingly alien excesses of early fusion came over the horizon. With the previously mentioned record reissues forming a backdrop, musicians in New York, Chicago, Los Angeles and Europe began reviving the repertoire and the improvising style of Charlie Parker. Trumpeter Red Rodney, who had lost many intervening years to imprisonment and Las Vegas showbands, made a symbolic re-emergence on the jazz scene in 1972, the year that saw the debuts of the West Coast group Supersax and the London-based Bebop Preservation Society. The latter quintet, run by pianist Bill LeSage, was the first retrospective project to harness one aspect of altoist Peter King's playing, while Supersax was more ambitious and perhaps less successful. Its lead alto and arranger Med Flory, taking his cue from what the Woody Herman band did with *Dark Shadows*, harmonized for five saxophones the heads and several of the solos from classic Parker records of the 1940s. But, despite their early live performances featuring creative improvisation by Tristano alumnus Warne Marsh, the rather bland, studio-honed ensemble sound and the equally conventional orchestration tended to undermine the vitality of the music.

Around the turn of the 1980s, developments on the visual front brought new insights into Charlie's life and performance. Some apparently silent-movie footage showing him in a studio setting came to light, which much later proved to be the long-lost video of Charlie miming to his pre-taped tracks for an abandoned Norman Granz project originally done in 1950. Similar research then uncovered what are still the only surviving images of the altoist playing live, in an ad-hoc 1952 television performance with Dizzy Gillespie. Each of these iconic documents confirmed the memories of those who had seen him in person that he stood impassively still while playing – without wasted motion or visual telegraphing of his musical punches, allowing his lightning-fast fingering to achieve its effects as effortlessly as any classically trained musician. While such discoveries brought the physicality of the altoist back to life in no uncertain manner, there was an air of slightly morbid sanctification in the book published in 1981 by Chan Parker and designer Francis Paudras (who had befriended Bud Powell during his French period and would later write a biographical volume about him). *To Bird With Love*, by contrast, had no narrative but a huge assemblage of photographs from Chan's archive, some of them well-known and some never previously seen, plus reproductions of contracts, handbills, business letters, personal letters, telegrams and handwritten notes. All of them were related to Charlie, and some touched on specific difficulties with agents and promoters, and with those closest to him. Beautifully produced, it looked rather like a headstone and weighed almost as much.

By the time this volume appeared, a miniature memorial to Charlie had been included in the 1978 ceremony that officially renamed the relevant block of 52nd Street as "Swing Street." As part of the celebrations, twelve paving-stones were created in imitation of the stars on Hollywood Boulevard, honouring musicians closely associated with "the Street," Charlie among them. (The reverence for jazz musicians being somewhat disproportionate to that for movie idols, and the pedestrian traffic being so much heavier than in Hollywood, little concern was expressed when, by the 1990s, the images were all worn smooth by footfalls, but it is rumoured that there is a plan to reinstate them at some point.) A prime mover of this event was Bruce Lundvall of CBS Records, which was then in one of its jazz phases and with its corporate offices located on 52nd Street, and one of the outcomes was that CBS then purchased many of Chan Parker's live tapes, only to find their release blocked by the Parker estate, now administered by his eldest son Leon. CBS did achieve the first legitimate issue – that is, with payment to musicians and heirs – of several off-air Boris Rose recordings, in the albums entitled *Summit Meeting At Birdland* (including the 1951 quintet with Gillespie and Powell), *One Night In Birdland* (with the Navarro–Powell group) and the equally Birdland-derived *Bird With Strings*. These, of course, were already familiar in bootleg versions to hardened record-collectors, but the discovery of the mid-1980s was that Bob Redcross' private 1943 recordings were still preserved in an attic, wrapped in a 1949 newspaper. The public availability of the hotel-room session with Gillespie and Oscar Pettiford, and the hitherto unsuspected discs of Charlie playing tenor along with commercial records, made the LP *Birth Of The Bebop* an appropriately titled revelation.

The mid-1980s also saw the publication of another previously unattainable artifact, known to exist from being pictured in the Parker–Paudras book. This was the acetate disc of Charlie playing unaccompanied in Kansas City around 1940 on a medley of *Honeysuckle Rose* and that nemesis of his teenage years *Body And Soul*, and sounding fully in command of his personal language. Though Spotlite had considered releasing this with a modern rhythm-section dubbed in, the performance appeared in its natural state as the opening track on the first LP of what eventually grew to be a twenty-five-volume set called *Bird's Eyes* from the Milan-based Philology label (named, not coincidentally, for the altoist Phil Woods who had married Chan Parker in the years following Charlie's death and subsequently separated). But, if the 1943 hotel-room discs were the Rosetta Stone of Ornithology and the 1940 solo acetate was its Holy Grail, then the Dead Sea Scrolls were the legendary Dean Benedetti recordings. Though Ross Russell had fantasized about these, and perhaps even discussed them with Jimmy Knepper, they were presumed lost until a phone-call to producer/disc-jockey Bob Porter, some thirty years after Dean's death in 1957. The result was that almost all of Benedetti's archive was purchased by the specialist mail-order label Mosaic Records, who assigned another producer/disc-jockey (Phil Schaap) deemed sufficiently obsessive to sort through a mass of incompletely documented, partly preserved Parker performances. The task took around two years but, on release, the material occupied seven CDs with tracks lasting anywhere from six minutes to two seconds, and very nearly all of it featuring Charlie, since the solos of other musicians were omitted at the time of recording. Though there are several possible ways of measuring the amount of Parker that has been released publicly, this injection boosted the total material by a considerable amount, so that maybe as much as seventy-five per cent of it now consists of live recordings. One could argue that the high proportion of live material conveys a more realistic picture of the artist's overall achievement, and certainly it is fair to say that even now, some fifteen years after the appearance of the Benedetti box, its contents and their implications have yet to be fully assimilated.

All of this activity was meat and drink for the specialists, of course, but there had been a recent dearth of explication for those who knew less and might be thirsting to know more. That changed in the second half of the 1980s, first of all with two almost contemporaneous documentary movies. One of the minor achievements of *Bird Now*, by Belgian director Marc Huraux, was to include original interviews not only with Dizzy Gillespie, Walter Bishop and Tommy Potter but with both Chan and Doris – one must presume that neither of them had been told the other was to appear. The US film *Celebrating Bird* was produced in conjunction with a short, large-format book of the same name by writer Gary Giddins, who earned a credit as co-director of the video. While Giddins' book and film make an excellent general introduction and contain interviews by Gillespie, Jay McShann, Roy Haynes and Rebecca Ruffin Parker, a volume first published in 1988 by musician-educator Larry Koch (*Yardbird Suite*) is an impressive attempt to combine the biographical, the discographical and the musicological in a meaningful manner. Already as early as the late 1970s, there was serious talk of a Charlie Parker biographical movie. Warner Brothers had taken the prescient step of optioning the rights to Ross Russell's book, with a draft script written by Ray Lafaro and a music director in Stewart Levine, producer of The Crusaders and others. The prospective star was Richard Pryor, whose previous musical role was as Diana Ross' pianist in the misconceived *Lady Sings The Blues*. Russell complained about the script (which he wanted to write himself) and may have been responsible for suggesting Chan as a consultant. Since a Hollywood biopic has to have a love interest, she was also in the frame for being one of the fictionalized characters but, when her agent refused the fairly minimal offer for her rights and threatened to sue if her name was used without her agreement, that version of the project was put firmly on ice.

Nearly ten years later, however, actor/director Clint Eastwood took an interest in the idea, after his Malpaso production company had helped finance Warners' *Round Midnight*, the film inspired by Francis Paudras' friendship with Bud Powell. A more intelligent Parker-specific script by writer Joel Oliansky was bought for Warners, and Eastwood (an amateur pianist and jazz fan of forty years' standing) made it a priority to bring Chan on side. With Forest Whitaker (previously seen in *Good Morning Vietnam*) playing the altoist and Diane Venora in the role of Chan, the final version of the narrative closely reflected her view of Charlie, alongside some input from fellow consultant Red Rodney, who became the other main white character. The portrayal of Parker was sombre and to some extent controversial, and so was the bold choice of soundtrack music. Using a mix of classic 1940s studio sides plus Chan's tapes of the Rockland Palace engagement and the 1951 session at Lennie Tristano's apartment, technical wizardry was employed to isolate the saxophone lines from their recorded accompaniment, and newly created stereo backings were added in an odd reversal of the overdubbing that Charlie himself had done in the Chicago hotel room. While possibly acceptable on paper (except for adding strings to the profound *Parker's Mood*), this process and the choice of source material means that the sound quality of the alto is limited and/or distorted compared to the rhythm-section sound, which is further compromised by the stiff, click-track-dictated drumming of John Guerin and the anachronistic style of Ron Carter. On screen, however, the acting and the staging brings sufficient suspension of disbelief for the viewer to experience the excitement of Charlie in the (simulated) flesh.

The fact that such re-recording is much easier with digital technology has led to any number of subsequent horrors unrelated to Parker, but it is worth noting that sampling of Charlie's work has been used quite often, though never in a particularly organic way. A later film soundtrack, for Spike Lee's *Mo' Better Blues*, has one of such instances in the number *Jazz Thing*, featuring Branford Marsalis and rapper Guru plus samples of Charlie and Symphony Sid. The use of such fragments in hip-hop records and in free-form radio shows has kept the sounds and the name of the altoist in the ears of a young generation. But the discovery of yet more new examples of Charlie's work, though continuing at a slower pace than hitherto, can still startle even the most blasé observer. It took until 1991, nearly fifty years after the fact, to uncover and release a slightly wobbly but otherwise vibrant airshot of the Jay McShann band playing for dancers at Harlem's Savoy Ballroom. Five years later, but a mere forty-six years after the fact, one of a series of Boston broadcasts revealed a particularly strong set with Joe Gordon, Roy Haynes, Mingus and the pianist Dick Twardzik while, as recently as 2004, the Town Hall recording discussed in Chapter 3 finally surfaced. Meanwhile, memoralizing Charlie's work through live music now includes an annual Charlie Parker Jazz Festival begun in 1993 and held around the date of his birthday in the East Village at Tompkins Square – the square looked out on from 151 Avenue B which was Charlie's last permanent New York address.

In the same year of 1993 Chan, who had been living in France more or less continuously since the late 1970s, finally saw her memoir published in a French translation but with the title that she had chosen years earlier, *My Life In E-flat*, E-flat being the "home key" of the alto saxophone. A year later in September 1994, her archive of memorabilia was auctioned at the London saleroom Christie's where, during the private viewing, the famous plastic saxophone was demonstrated in a brief but storming set by Peter King (by then a veteran of the occasional Parker-oriented jazz group led by Charlie Watts of The Rolling Stones). The instrument on which Charlie had performed regularly in the last years of his life – and which Clint Eastwood had borrowed while filming *Bird* – was bought on behalf of the municipality of Kansas City for £93,500, then roughly equivalent to $185,000, with a view to becoming the centrepiece for one of the country's only jazz museums. This planned sanitization of a murky local history may be what inspired film director Robert Altman's 1996 work *Kansas City*, a relatively linear (for him) story of the political corruption rife in what was also Altman's hometown during the 1930s. Because Altman is another music fan and had clearly read the right books, he counterpointed the main narrative with a recreation of the legendary jam sessions of Kansas City's nightclub district, using a band of contemporary players including pianist Geri Allen and the duelling saxophones of Joshua Redman and Craig Handy. In an oblique tribute, a black teenager named "Charlie Parker" is allowed to sit up in the balcony, while improbably nursing his alto saxophone and witnessing the happenings on the bandstand. Between the above two events, in September 1995 the US postal service included Charlie among ten black jazz artists immortalized on 32-cent postage stamps. In this activity, they were chronologically well behind the former French colony of Gabon which portrayed him on a postage stamp in 1984 while, also in 1995, Belgium included an outline of Charlie on a 200-franc banknote honouring Adolphe Sax, which is believed to be the only association of folding money with the image of a jazz musician.

If you had asked Charlie in 1955 about the likelihood of such events forty years down the line, he would have probably been sceptical, despite his earlier comment "But in 50 or 75 years, the contributions of present-day jazz will be taken as seriously as classical music." He was certainly vindicated by the appearance of three further technical treatises on his music published in 1995–96, respectively written by Thomas Owens, Carl Woideck and Henry Martin and discussed in the previous chapter. Yet he would doubtless have been incredulous at the idea that, in the 1990s, Kansas City would have a black mayor, Emanuel Cleaver, who would become the driving force behind the establishment of a municipal jazz museum. Located at 1616 East Vine St., in the area of "18th and Vine" once immortalized in song by Big Joe Turner, the permanent exhibit was opened in September 1997 along with the Negro Leagues Baseball Museum. Symbolically perhaps, the Negro leagues which had grown up around the country after the Civil War had been consolidated into a Negro National League founded at a meeting in Kansas City in 1920, the year Charlie was born. As well as providing a vital focus for black life in the ensuing decades, the League cultivated players who were often superior to their white counterparts, as was proved in the post-World War II period when first Jackie Robinson and then others were signed to previously all-white teams. As the integration of the national game gradually proceeded, this eventually spelled the death of the segregated black league. The parallel with jazz is not exact, of course, since baseball was originally created by white settlers in the States and jazz wasn't, but the way the baseball business developed in the twentieth century provides some food for musical thought.

The further municipal project was a statue of Charlie for the nearby plaza and, in an idea floated by the local Jazz Ambassadors society, a new grave in the same location. The sad and unsatisfactory saga of Charlie's burial site at the historically all-black Lincoln Cemetery, just outside the city boundary, begins with a vertical headstone that displayed the wrong death date, which was then stolen in the 1970s and advertised for sale. The horizontal slab that replaced it, matched by one for his mother buried alongside him in 1967, had the right dates but a picture of a tenor saxophone instead of an alto. The Jazz Ambassadors wanted to rectify that and Mayor Cleaver ran with the idea, requesting $25,000 from the city budget for the purpose, which the city council refused in May 1998 (some of them stating that the museum was sufficient). But the hard-to-find, weed-infested site at Lincoln Cemetery seemed inadequate for its occupant, and charitable money was found to commission the sculptor Robert Graham for a statue, with space for the re-burial at its base. Removal of Charlie's remains, however, required the consent of all family members, and those in favour included Doris (provided that Addie's body was also included), Chan and Kim, each of whom heard about the plan from the press rather than from the estate. Leon was quoted in May as saying he would consult his mother Rebecca when the details were "off the drawing board." With the work almost completed and the date of the unveiling set for March 27, 1999, at the start of February Leon refused permission. So a mini-festival went ahead, with live music and panel discussions including a wide spectrum of contributors from Oliver Todd (who employed Charlie in the mid-1930s) to Doris, Jay McShann, Max Roach, Milt Jackson, Billy Taylor, Bobby Watson and Peter King. And the ten-foot high statue, on its eight-foot high base bearing the carved inscription "Bird lives," was ceremonially erected with Cleaver and other dignitaries wearing African robes, but with Bird still outside the city limits.

Charlie himself might reasonably have said that statues and grave-stones are not for the living, any more than the historical plaques (not one, but two) that now adorn the façade of 151 Avenue B. But the advance of civil rights for minorities, and the honouring of jazz itself, have both come quite a way in the past fifty years. Since the year 2000, for instance, the Kansas-born altoist (and ex-Art Blakey sideman) Bobby Watson has been directing the jazz programme at Kansas City's Conservatory of Music, part of the University of Missouri-Kansas City. Had he been a dif-ferent personality, Charlie could have moved into academia in the 1970s, as did musicians such as Max Roach and Jackie McLean (both just a few years younger than Charlie). Like Dr John McLean, as he now is, Charlie could have only recently decided to slow down and could even have been the outgoing director handing over to Bobby Watson.

In retrospect, however, it seems all of a piece with the emotional qualities of his music that Charlie should have been a bright burning flame quickly snuffed out. This and other metaphors, all of which appear to have been used up by now, can seem unbearably sentimental, and yet they express a very real reaction on the part of everyone who responds to his music. The challenge is surely to realize that the flame continues to burn in our hearts, and to ensure that future generations of listeners are brought face to face with his achievement.

Now is the time.

discography

This listing is intended to include everything that has ever been made available publicly of Parker's playing. There is still material, mostly fragmentary, from sessions that are known to exist and have not been released, and these are not included.

Only the original issue number is shown and, in the case of studio sessions, this is usually a 78 rpm single. Material first released on vinyl, sometimes from those same sessions, has the issue number in italic, while material first released on CD has the number in bold. The figures and letters shown in brackets before the issue number refer the reader to the index of recent reissues at the end of this listing.

For reasons of space, if a batch of titles was released together for the first time on LP or CD, they are separated by "/" but, if a single performance contains a medley of two or more themes, the individual tunes are separated by ";"

Alternative titles for a single performance are usually shown in brackets after the correct title (if the new title has been used, deliberately or in error, for a subsequent release).

The abbreviations used are as follows:

(arr) arranger, (as) alto sax, (b) bass, (bgo) bongos, (bs) baritone sax, (bsn) bassoon, (cel) cello, (cga) congas, (cl) clarinet, (cond) conductor, (d) drums, (eng-h) english-horn, (f) flute, (fr-h) french-horn, (g) guitar, (mc) master of ceremonies, (mca) maraccas, (ob) oboe, (org) organ, (p) piano, (perc) percussion, (ss) soprano sax, (tap) tapdancing, (tb) trombone, (tbl) timbales, (tp) trumpet, (ts) tenor sax, (v) vocal, (vib) vibraphone, (vla) viola, (vln) violin, (vtb) valve-trombone, (*) incomplete recording (where shown alongside the issue number, this is known to be an incomplete version of a longer performance), (**) edited on the issue in question.

As well as consulting earlier printed discographies and relevant websites, I am grateful to Ira Gitler, Dan Morgenstern, Chris Sheridan, Alain Tercinet, the books of Lawrence Koch and Carl Woideck and especially to Malcolm Walker, who checked the draft and is working on the Parker discography to end all Parker discographies.

CHARLIE PARKER
CP (unacc. as)
Kansas City, c. 1940

Honeysuckle Rose; Body And Soul   (31) *Philology 214W5**

JAY McSHANN AND HIS ORCHESTRA
Prob. as for April 30, 1941
Trocadero Ballroom, Wichita, KS, poss. August 9, 1940

I Got Rhythm (Walkin' And Swingin')   (18) **Stash STCD-542**
Jumpin' At The Woodside*   unissued

Buddy Anderson, Orville Minor (tp), Bud Gould (tb, vln), CP (as), William J. Scott, Bob Mabane (ts), Jay McShann (p), Gene Ramey (b), Gus Johnson (d)
Station KFBI, Wichita, KS, November 30, 1940

I Found A New Baby / Body And Soul / Honeysuckle Rose / Lady Be Good / Coquette / Moten Swing / Blues (Wichita Blues)
                                                   (18) *Onyx ORI221*

Buddy Anderson, Orville Minor, Harold Bruce (tp), Taswell Baird (tb), CP, John Jackson (as), Bob Mabane, Harold Ferguson (ts), Jay McShann (p), Gene Ramey (b), Gus Johnson (d), Walter Brown (v)
Dallas, April 30, 1941

93730A   Swingmatism   (3,18) Decca 8570
93731A   Hootie Blues-vWB   (3,18) Decca 8559
93732A   Dexter Blues   (3,18) Decca 8583
Note: Horn sections not heard on other titles from this session

Orville Minor (tp), Taswell Baird (tb), poss. CP (as), Jay McShann (p), Gene Ramey (b), Gus Johnson (d), Walter Brown (v)
Chicago, November 18, 1941

93809A   One Woman's Man-vWB   (3,18) Decca 8607
Note: Although listed for the sake of completeness, it is possible that the altoist heard in the background is John Jackson

As for April 30, 1941 except Bob Merrill (tp) Fred Culliver (ts) replace Bruce and Ferguson; Lawrence Anderson (tb), James Coe (bs), Lucky Enois (g), Al Hibbler (v) added

Savoy Ballroom, NYC, February 13, 1942

St. Louis Mood* / I'm Forever Blowing Bubbles / Hootie Blues-vWB / Swingmatism

(18) **Stash STCD-542**

I Got It Bad-vAH / Love Don't Get You Nothin' But The Blues* (theme)

Stash STCD-542

Note: Some sources claim Doc West (d) replaces Johnson for this broadcast

Prob. Jimmy Forrest (ts) replaces Mabane and Coe; Doc West (d) replaces Johnson

NYC, July 2, 1942

70993A	Lonely Boy Blues-vWB	(3,19) Decca 4387
70994A	Get Me On Your Mind-vAH	(3,19) Decca 4418
70995A	The Jumpin' Blues-vWB	(3,19) Decca 4418
70996A	Sepian Bounce	(3,19) Decca 4387

CHARLIE PARKER

CP (as); unknown musicians poss. incl. George Treadwell, Vic Coulsen (tp), Ray Abrams (ts), Allen Tinney (p), Ebenezer Paul (b), 'Mole' (d), Clark Monroe (v)

Poss. Monroe's Uptown House, NYC, c. 1942

Cherokee   (18) Onyx ORI221*
I Remember You-vCM   unissued

Dizzy Gillespie (tp), CP (ts), Oscar Pettiford (b)

Room 405, Savoy Hotel, Chicago, February 15, 1943

Sweet Georgia Brown*   (19) Stash ST-260

Billy Eckstine-1, Shorty McConnell-2 (tp), CP (ts), unknown ts, Hurley Ramey (g), Bob Redcross (brushes)

Same location, February 28, 1943

	Three Guesses-1* / *Boogie Woogie*-2,3* / *Indiana*-2,3*		
		(19) *Stash ST-260*
	Yardin' With Yard-2,3* / *Body And Soul** / *Lady Be Good(?)**		
		(19) **Stash STCD-535**

CP (ts), overdubbing commercial records
Same location, c. February 1943

China Boy-3 / *Avalon*-4	(19) **Stash STCD-535**
Embraceable You-5	(19) *Stash ST-260*

3-Benny Goodman (cl), Teddy Wilson (p), Gene Krupa (d) from Victor 25644
4-As last plus Lionel Hampton (vib) from Victor 25533
5-Hazel Scott (p), J. C. Heard (d) from Decca 18341

CP (as), poss. Lucky Enois or Efferge Ware (g), 'Little Phil' Phillips (d)
Kansas City, poss. Autumn 1943

Cherokee / *My Heart Tells Me* / *Body And Soul**		
	(18) **Stash STCD-535**
I Found A New Baby	unissued

Note: A date of September 1941 has also been suggested for this Kansas City session

TINY GRIMES QUINTET

CP (as), Clyde Hart (p), Tiny Grimes (g, v), Jimmy Butts (b), Doc West (d)
NYC, September 15, 1944

S5710-1	*Tiny's Tempo*	(D) *Savoy MG12001*, SJL1129*
S5710-2	*Tiny's Tempo*	(D) *Savoy MG12001*, SJL1107*
S5710-3	*Tiny's Tempo*	(C,D) *Savoy 526*
S5711-1	*I'll Always Love You Just The Same*-vTG*	unissued
S5711-2	*I'll Always Love You Just The Same*-vTG	(D) *Savoy SJL2208*

S5711-3	I'll Always Love You Just The Same-vTG	(C,D) Savoy 526
S5712-1	Romance Without Finance-vTG	(D) Savoy SJL2208
S5712-2	Romance Without Finance-vTG*	(D) Savoy S5J5500
S5712-3	Romance Without Finance-vTG	(D) Savoy SJL1107
S5712-4	Romance Without Finance-vTG*	(D) Savoy S5J5500
S5712-5	Romance Without Finance-vTG	(C,D) Savoy 532
S5713-1	Red Cross	(D) Savoy MG12001*, SJL1107
S5713-2	Red Cross	(C,D) Savoy 532

Note: Before the false starts were released on S5J5500, matrix number S5712-5 was officially known as "S5712-3". Similar discrepancies occur in other Savoy and Mercury/Clef sessions, and in each case the revised numbering is used for the sake of clarity

CLYDE BERNHARDT AND HIS KANSAS CITY BUDDIES

Clyde Bernhardt (tb, v), CP (as), Jay McShann (p), unknown b and d
NYC, January 1945

| Lay Your Habits Down-vCB / Triflin' Woman Blues-vCB / So Good This Mornin'-vCB / Would You Do Me A Favor-vCB | (20,46) **Philology W849.2** |

Note: Gene Ramey (b) and Gus Johnson (d) have been suggested for this session, but seem unlikely to have participated

CLYDE HART ALL STARS

Dizzy Gillespie (tp), Trummy Young (tb, v), CP (as), Don Byas (ts), Clyde Hart (p), Mike Bryan (g), Al Hall (b), Specs Powell (d), Rubberlegs Williams (v)
NYC, January 4, 1945

W3301	What's The Matter Now-vRW	(20,46) Continental 6013
W3302	I Want Every Bit Of It-vRW	(20,46) Continental 6020
W3303	That's The Blues-vRW	(20,46) Continental 6013
W3304	4-F Blues-vRW	(20,46) Continental 6020
W3304 (alt.)	G.I. Blues-vRW	(20,46) Plymouth 100-38
W3305	Dream Of You-vTY	(20,46) Continental 6060

W3306   *Seventh Avenue*-vTY   (20,46) Continental 6005
W3307   *Sorta Kinda*-vTY   (20,46) Continental 6005
W3308   *Oh, Oh, My, My*-vTY   (20,46) Continental 6060

COOTIE WILLIAMS AND HIS ORCHESTRA

Money Johnson, Ermit Perry, George Treadwell, Cootie Williams (tp), Ed Burke, Bob Horton (tb), Frank Powell, CP (as), Lee Pope, Sam Taylor (ts), Ed deVerteuil (bs), Arnold Jarvis (p), Leroy Kirkland (g), Carl Pruitt (b), Vess Payne (d), Toni Warren (v)

Savoy Ballroom, NYC, February 12, 1945

'Round Midnight (theme) / *711* / *Do Nothin' Till You Hear From Me* / *Don't Blame Me* / *Perdido* / *Night Cap* / *Saturday Night Is The Loneliest Night In The Week*-vTW / *Floogie Boo*-1 / *St. Louis Blues**

(49) *One Night Stand 582*

1-Williams, CP, Taylor, Jarvis, Pruitt and Payne only

DIZZY GILLESPIE SEXTET

Dizzy Gillespie (tp), CP (as), Clyde Hart (p), Remo Palmier (g), Slam Stewart (b), Cozy Cole (d)

NYC, prob. February 28, 1945

G554-1   *Groovin' High*   (3a,20,D) Guild 1001
G556   *All The Things You Are*   (3a,20,D) Musicraft 488
G557   *Dizzy Atmosphere*   (3a,20,D) Musicraft 488

DIZZY GILLESPIE AND HIS ALL STAR QUINTET

Dizzy Gillespie (tp, v), CP (as), Al Haig (p), Curley Russell (b), Sid Catlett (d), Sarah Vaughan (v)

NYC, May 11, 1945

G565-A1   *Salt Peanuts*-vDG   (3a,20,D) Guild 1003
G566A-1   *Shaw 'Nuff*   (3a,20,D) Guild 1002
G567A-1   *Lover Man*-vSV   (3a,20,D) Guild 1002
G568A-1   *Hot House*   (3a,20,D) Guild 1003

SARAH VAUGHAN

Dizzy Gillespie (tp), CP (as), Flip Phillips (ts), Nat Jaffe-1, Tadd Dameron-2 (p), Bill DeArango (g), Curley Russell (b), Max Roach (d), Sarah Vaughan (v)

NYC, May 25, 1945

W3325	*What More Can A Woman Do?-1*	(21,46) Continental 6008
W3326	*I'd Rather Have A Memory-2*	(21,46) Continental 6008
W3327	*Mean To Me-1*	(21,46) Continental 6024

DIZZY GILLESPIE

Dizzy Gillespie (tp), CP (as), poss. Lucky Thompson (ts), unknown p, b, d

Lincoln Square, NYC, May 30, 1945

| | *Sweet Georgia Brown** | (A) *Stash ST-260* |

Note: This was described on its first release as being done in LA. c. February 1946

Dizzy Gillespie (tp), CP (as), Al Haig (p), Curley Russell (b), Stan Levey (d)

Academy of Music, Philadelphia, June 5, 1945

| | *Blue 'N Boogie* | (21,44) **Philology W847.2** |

RED NORVO AND HIS SELECTED SEXTET

Dizzy Gillespie (tp), CP (as), Flip Phillips (ts), Teddy Wilson (p), Red Norvo (vib), Slam Stewart (b), Specs Powell-1, J. C. Heard-2 (d)

NYC, June 6, 1945

T8-A	*Hallelujah-1*	(21,D) *Dial LP903*
T8-B	*Hallelujah-1*	(21,D) Dial 1045
T8-F	*Hallelujah-1*	(21,D) Comet T6
T9-B	*Get Happy-1*	(21,D) Dial 1035
T9-D	*Get Happy-1*	(21,D) Comet T7
T10-A	*Slam Slam Blues (Bird Blues)-2*	(21,D) Dial 1045
T10-B	*Slam Slam Blues-2*	(21,D) Comet T6

	Congo Blues-2*	(21,D) *Dial LP903*
T11-AA/-BB/-A	Congo Blues-2*	(21,D) *Dial LP903*
T11-B	Congo Blues-2	(21,D) *Dial 1035*
T11-C	Congo Blues-2	(21,D) *Comet T7*

DIZZY GILLESPIE QUINTET

Dizzy Gillespie (tp, vcl), CP (as), Don Byas (ts-1), Al Haig (p), Curley Russell (b), Max Roach, Sid Catlett-2 (d), Symphony Sid (mc)

Town Hall, NYC, June 22, 1945

| | Bebop-1 / Night In Tunisia / Groovin' High / Salt Peanuts-vDG / Hot House-2 / 52nd Street | |
| | Theme-2 | (56) **Uptown UPCD27.51** |

SIR CHARLES AND HIS ALL STARS

Buck Clayton (tp), CP (as), Dexter Gordon (ts), Sir Charles Thompson (p), Danny Barker (g), Jimmy Butts (b), J. C. Heard (d)

NYC, September 4, 1945

R1030	Takin' Off	(21) Apollo 757
R1031	If I Had You	(21) Apollo 757
R1032	20th Century Blues	(21) Apollo 759
R1033	The Street Beat	(21) Apollo 759

CHARLIE PARKER'S REE BOPPERS

Miles Davis (tp-1), Dizzy Gillespie (tp-2, p-3), CP (as), Sadik Hakim (Argonne Thornton) (p-4), Curley Russell (b), Max Roach (d)

NYC, November 26, 1945

S5850-1	Billie's Bounce-1,3	(D) *Savoy MG12079*
S5850-2	Billie's Bounce-1,3*	(D) *Savoy MG12079*
S5850-3	Billie's Bounce-1,3	(D) *Savoy MG12079*
S5849	Warming Up A Riff-3*	(4,C,D) Savoy 945
S5850-4	Billie's Bounce-1,3*	(D) *Savoy MG12079*
S5850-5	Billie's Bounce-1,3	(4,C,D) Savoy 573
S5851-1/-2	Now's The Time-1,3*	(D) *Savoy MG12079*

S5851-3	Now's The Time-1,3	(D) Savoy MG12079
S5851-4	Now's The Time-1,3	(4,C,D) Savoy 573
S5852-1	Thriving From A Riff-1,4	(D) Savoy MG12079
S5852-2	Thriving From A Riff-1,4*	(D) Savoy MG12079
S5852-3	Thriving From A Riff-1,4	(4,C,D) Savoy 903
	Meandering-3*	(D) Savoy MG12079
S5853-1	Ko Ko-2,4*	(D) Savoy MG12079
S5853-2	Ko Ko (Co-coa)-2,3	(4,C,D) Savoy 597

Note: On original issues, piano by both Gillespie and Hakim was credited to "Hen Gates," and Davis was incorrectly named as the trumpeter on *Ko Ko*

SLIM GAILLARD

Dizzy Gillespie (tp), CP (as), Jack McVea (ts), Dodo Marmarosa (p), Slim Gaillard (g, p-1, v), Bam Brown (b, v), Zutty Singleton (d)

LA, prob. December 29, 1945

BTJ38-?	Dizzy Boogie-1	(D) Polydor 545.107
BTJ38-2	Dizzy Boogie-1	(D) Bel-Tone 753
BTJ39-?	Flat Foot Floogie-vSG, BB	(D) Halo 50273
BTJ39-2	Flat Foot Floogie-vSG, BB	(D) Bel-Tone 758
BTJ40-2	Poppity Pop-vSG, BB	(D) Bel-Tone 753
BTJ41-RE	Slim's Jam	(D) Bel-Tone 761

Note: Speech by Gaillard (and briefly Gillespie and CP) heard on *Slim's Jam*, and Gillespie shown on original issues as "John Berks" for contractual reasons

DIZZY GILLESPIE AND HIS REBOP SIX

Dizzy Gillespie (tp, v), CP (as), Al Haig (p), Milt Jackson (vib-1), Ray Brown (b), Stan Levey (d), Bubbles Whitman (mc)

LA, December 29, 1945

JUB161	Groovin' High	(22) Main-Man BFWHCB617
JUB162	Shaw 'Nuff	(22) Spotlite SPJ123
JUB209	Dizzy Atmosphere-1	(22) Klacto MG102

Lucky Thompson (ts) added, Rudy Vallee, Harry "The Hipster" Gibson (mcs) replace Whitman

LA, January 24, 1946

      Salt Peanuts-1,vDG   (22,41) *Meexa Discox 1776*

Notes: The *Night In Tunisia* issued on **Philology W80.2** (and claimed as being from JUB163) is a fake, assembled from elements of a Dizzy Gillespie 1951 airshot and the CP broadcast of February 26, 1949. However, the *Groovin' High* on *Philology 214W18* (described as "probably 1945") is identical to the version above

JAZZ AT THE PHILHARMONIC

Dizzy Gillespie, Al Killian (tp), CP, Willie Smith (as), Lester Young, Charlie Ventura (ts), Mel Powell (p), Billy Hadnott (d), Lee Young (d)

Philharmonic Auditorium, LA, January 28, 1946

413/414	*Sweet Georgia Brown*	(60,H) Disc 2004

Howard McGhee (tp), Arnold Ross (p) replace Gillespie and Powell, Ventura out

Same location and date

D241/2	*Blues for Norman*	(60,H) Disc 2001
D243/4	*I Can't Get Started*	(60,H) Disc 2002
D245/6	*Lady Be Good*	(60,H) Disc 2005
D247/8	*After You've Gone*	(60,H) Disc 5100

Note: Gillespie shown on original issues as "John Birks" for contractual reasons

CHARLIE PARKER

Dizzy Gillespie (tp), CP, unknown p, Red Callender (b), poss. Doc West (d)

LA, February 3, 1946

      Lover Come Back To Me   (22) *Stash ST-260*

TEMPO JAZZMEN

Dizzy Gillespie (tp), CP (as), Lucky Thompson (ts), George Handy (p), Arv Garrison (g), Ray Brown (b), Stan Levey (d)

LA, February 5, 1946

D1000	*Diggin' Diz (Bongo Beep)*	(3a,D,F) Dial 1004

Note: Though reissued under Gillespie's name, his participation was originally credited to "Gabriel" for contractual reasons

CHARLIE PARKER QUINTET

Miles Davis (tp), CP (as), Joe Albany (p), Addison Farmer (b), Chuck Thompson (d)

Finale Club, LA, March 1946

Anthropology / Billie's Bounce / Blue 'N Boogie / All The Things You Are / Ornithology*

(22,45) Queen-Disc Q-017

CHARLIE PARKER SEPTET

Miles Davis (tp), CP (as), Lucky Thompson (ts), Dodo Marmarosa (p), Arv Garrison (g-1), Vic McMillan (b), Roy Porter (d)

LA, March 28, 1946

D1010-1	Moose The Mooche	(D,F) Dial DLP201
D1010-2	Moose The Mooche	(4,55,C,D,F) Dial 1003, 1004
D1010-3	Moose The Mooche	(D,F) Spotlite 101, 105
D1011-1	Yardbird Suite-1	(D,F) Dial DLP201
D1011-4	Yardbird Suite-1	(4,55,C,D,F) Dial 1003
D1012-1	Ornithology-1	(D,F) Dial DLP208
D1012-3	Bird Lore (Ornithology)-1	(D,F) Dial 1006
D1012-4	Ornithology-1	(4,55,C,D,F) Dial 1002
D1013-1	Famous Alto Break-1	(D,F) Dial DLP905*
D1013-4	Night In Tunisia-1	(D,F) Dial DLP201
D1013-5	Night In Tunisia-1	(4,55,C,D,F) Dial 1002

Note: Early issues of D1012-4 are titled Orinthology(!) on the labels

JAZZ AT THE PHILHARMONIC

Buck Clayton (tp), Willie Smith, CP (as), Lester Young, Coleman Hawkins (ts), Kenny Kersey (p), Irving Ashby (g), Billy Hadnott (b), Buddy Rich (d)

Embassy Theatre, LA, April 22, 1946

101/2/3/4	JATP Blues	(60,H) Clef 101/102
	I Got Rhythm	(60,H) Mercury MG35014

WILLIE SMITH/BENNY CARTER/CHARLIE PARKER

Willie Smith-1, Benny Carter-2, CP-3 (as), Nat King Cole (p), Oscar Moore (g), Johnny Miller (b), Buddy Rich (d)

LA, April–May 1946

JUB186   *Medley: Tea For Two-1; Body And Soul-2; Cherokee-3 / Ornithology*-3*

                 (22,45) *Spotlite SPJ123*

CHARLIE PARKER QUINTET

Howard McGhee (tp), CP (as), Jimmy Bunn (p), Bob Kesterton (b), Roy Porter (d)

LA, July 29, 1946

D1021-A	*Max Is Making Wax*	(4,55,C,D,F)	*Jazztone J1004*
D1022-A	*Lover Man*	(4,55,C,D,F)	*Dial 1007*
D1023-A	*The Gypsy*	(4,55,C,D,F)	*Dial 1043*
D1024-A	*Bebop*	(4,55,C,D,F)	*Dial 1007*

Note: D1024-A originally issued as Howard McGhee Quintet

CHARLIE PARKER

CP (as), Russ Freeman (p), Arnold Fishkind (b), Jimmy Pratt (d)

Chuck Copely's home, LA, February 1, 1947

D901/2	*Lullaby In Rhythm*	(D,F)	*Spotlite 107**
K903	*Home Cooking III*	(D,F)	*Dial LP905**
K904	*Home Cooking II*	(D,F)	*Dial LP905**
K905	*Home Cooking I*	(D,F)	*Dial LP905**
	Blues (Blues On The Sofa)(Kopely Plaza Blues)	(D,F)	**Philology W80.2***
	Yardbird Suite-1	(D,F)	*Spotlite 107**

1-Howard McGhee, Shorty Rogers, Melvyn Broiles (tp) added

CHARLIE PARKER QUARTET

CP (as), Erroll Garner (p), Red Callender (b), Doc West (d), Earl Coleman (v)

LA, February 19, 1947

D1051-C	This Is Always-vEC	(4,55,C,D,F) Dial 1015, 1019
D1051-D	This Is Always-vEC	(D) Dial LP202
D1052-A	Dark Shadows-vEC	(D) Dial LP202
D1052-B	Dark Shadows-vEC	(D) Dial LP901
D1052-C	Dark Shadows-vEC	(4,55,C,D,F) Dial 1014
D1052-D	Dark Shadows-vEC	(D) Spotlite 105, 102
D1053-A	Bird's Nest	(D) Dial 1014
D1053-B	Bird's Nest	(D) Dial LP905
D1053-C	Bird's Nest	(4,55,C,D,F) Dial 1014
D1054-A	Hot Blues (Blowtop Blues)	(D) Dial LP202
D1054-B	Blowtop Blues (Cool Blues)	(D) Dial LP901
D1054-C	Cool Blues	(4,55,C,D,F) Dial 1015
D1054-D	Cool Blues	(D) Dial LP901

CHARLIE PARKER'S NEW STARS

Howard McGhee (tp), CP (as), Wardell Gray (ts), Dodo Marmarosa (p), Barney Kessel (g), Red Callender (b), Don Lamond (d)

LA, February 26, 1947

D1071-A	Relaxin' At Camarillo	(D) Dial 1030
D1071-C	Relaxin' At Camarillo	(4,55,C,D,F) Dial 1012
D1071-D	Relaxin' At Camarillo	(D) Dial LP901
D1071-E	Relaxin' At Camarillo	(D) Dial LP202
D1072-A	Cheers	(D) Dial LP202
D1072-B	Cheers	(D) Spotlite 103
D1072-C	Cheers	(D) Spotlite 103

D1072-D	Cheers	(4,55,C,D,F) Dial 1013
D1073-A	*Carvin' The Bird*	(D) *Dial LP901*
D1073-B	*Carvin' The Bird*	(4,55,C,D,F) Dial 1013
D1074-A	*Stupendous*	(4,55,C,D,F) Dial 1022
D1074-B	*Stupendous*	(D) *Dial LP202*

HOWARD McGHEE QUINTET

Howard McGhee (tp), Charlie Parker (as), Hampton Hawes (p), Addison Farmer (b), Roy Porter (d)

Hi-de-Ho Club, LA, March 9, 1947

| | *Dee Dee's Dance* | (B) *Spotlite 107*￼* |

As last plus Earl Coleman, Danny Knight (v) on some tracks

Same location, March 1–13, 1947

| | *202 further incomplete items* | (B) **Mosaic MD7-129***, *MR10-129** |
| | *other incomplete items* | unissued |

CHARLIE PARKER ALL STARS

Miles Davis (tp), CP (as), Bud Powell (p), Tommy Potter (b), Max Roach (d)

NYC, May 8, 1947

S3420-1	*Donna Lee**	(D) *Savoy S5J5500*
S3420-2/-3	*Donna Lee*	(D) *Savoy MG12001*
S3420-4	*Donna Lee*	(D) *Savoy MG12009*
S3420-5	*Donna Lee*	(4,C,D) *Savoy 652*
S3421-1	*Chasin' The Bird*	(D) *Savoy MG12001*
S3421-2	*Chasin' The Bird**	(D) *Savoy S5J5500*
S3421-3	*Chasin' The Bird*	(D) *Savoy MG12009*
S3421-4	*Chasin' The Bird*	(4,C,D) *Savoy 977*
S3422-1	*Cheryl*	(D) *Savoy MG12001*

S3422-2	Cheryl	(4,C,D) Savoy 952
S3423-1	Buzzy	(D) *Savoy MG12009*
S3423-2	Buzzy*	(D) *Savoy MG12001*
S3423-3	Buzzy	(D) *Savoy MG12001*
S3423-4	Buzzy*	(D) *Savoy MG12000*
S3423-5	Buzzy	(4,C,D) Savoy 652

MILES DAVIS ALL STARS

Miles Davis (tp), CP (ts), John Lewis (p), Nelson Boyd (b), Max Roach (d)

NYC, August 14, 1947

S3440-1	Milestones*	(D) *Savoy S5J5500*
S3340-2	Milestones	(D) *Savoy MG12009*
S3340-3	Milestones	(C,D) Savoy 934
S3441-1	Little Willie Leaps*	(D) *Savoy MG12001*
S3441-2	Little Willie Leaps	(D) *Savoy MG12001*
S3441-3	Little Willie Leaps (Wailing Willie)	(C,D) Savoy 977
S3442-1	Half Nelson	(D) *Savoy MG12001*
S3442-2	Half Nelson	(C,D) Savoy 951
S3443-1	Sippin' At Bells*	(D) *Savoy MG12009*
S3443-2	Sippin' At Bells	(C,D) Savoy 934
S3443-3	Sippin' At Bells*	(D) *Savoy S5J5500*
S3443-4	Sippin' At Bells	(D) *Savoy MG12001*

ALLEN EAGER-CHARLIE PARKER

CP, Allen Eager (as, ts), Bud Powell (p), Specs Goldberg (b), Max Roach or Morty Yoss (d)

NYC, September 1947

Swapping Horns / All The Things You Are / Original Horns

(57) **Uptown UPCD27-49**

BARRY ULANOV'S ALL STAR MODERN JAZZ MUSICIANS

Dizzy Gillespie (tp), CP (as), John LaPorta (cl), Lennie Tristano (p), Billy Bauer (g), Ray Brown (b), Max Roach (d), Barry Ulanov, Bruce Elliott (mcs)

NYC, September 13, 1947

Ko Ko (theme) / Hot House / I Surrender Dear–1 / Fine And Dandy

(23,44) *Spotlite 107*

NYC, September 20, 1947

Ko Ko (theme) / Sunny Side Of The Street / How Deep Is The Ocean / 52nd Street Theme (theme)

(23,44) *Spotlite 107*

Tiger Rag (23,44) Steiner Davis 49

1–Gillespie, CP and LaPorta out

"A NITE AT CARNEGIE HALL"

Dizzy Gillespie (tp), CP (as), John Lewis (p), Al McKibbon (b), Joe Harris (d)

Carnegie Hall, NYC, September 29, 1947

13000/1	*Night In Tunisia*	(23,43a) Black Deuce (unnumbered)
13002	*Dizzy Atmosphere*	(23,43a) Black Deuce
13003/4	*Groovin' High*	(23,43a) Black Deuce
13005	*Confirmation (Riff Warmer)*	(23,43a) Black Deuce*, *Natural Organic 7000*
	Ko Ko	(23,43a) *Natural Organic 7000*

CHARLIE PARKER QUINTET

Miles Davis (tp), CP (as), Duke Jordan (p), Tommy Potter (b), Max Roach (d)

NYC, October 28, 1947

D1101A	*Dexterity*	(D,F) *Dial LP203*
D1101B	*Dexterity*	(5,55,C,D,F) Dial 1032
D1102A	*Bongo Bop (Blues)*	(5,55,C,D,F) Dial 1024
D1102B	*Bongo Bop (Parker's Blues)*	(D,F) Dial 1024
D1103A	*Prezology (Dewey Square)*	(D,F) Dial 1056*

D1103B	Dewey Square	(D,F) *Dial LP203*
D1103C	Dewey Square	(5,55,C,D,F) Dial 1019
D1104A	The Hymn (Superman)	(5,55,C,D,F) Dial 1056
D1104B	Superman	(D,F) *Dial LP212*
D1105A	Bird Of Paradise (All The Things You Are)	(D,F) Dial 1032
D1105B	Bird Of Paradise	(D,F) Dial 1032
D1105C	Bird Of Paradise	(5,55,C,D,F) Dial 1032
D1106A	Embraceable You	(D,F) Dial 1024
D1106B	Embraceable You	(5,55,C,D,F) Dial 1024

NYC, November 4, 1947

D1111C	Bird Feathers (Schnourphology)	(5,55,C,D,F) Dial 1058
D1112A	Klactoveedsedstene	(5,55,C,D,F) Dial 1040
D1112B	Klactoveedsedstene	(D,F) *Dial LP904*
D1113B	Scrapple From The Apple	(D,F) *Dial LP203*
D1113C	Scrapple From The Apple	(5,55,C,D,F) Dial 1021
D1114A	My Old Flame	(5,55,C,D,F) Dial 1058
D1115A	Out Of Nowhere	(D,F) *Dial LP207*
D1115B	Out Of Nowhere	(D,F) *Dial LP904*
D1115C	Out Of Nowhere	(5,55,C,D,F) *Spotlite 105*
D1116A	Don't Blame Me	(5,55,C,D,F) Dial 1021

BARRY ULANOV AND HIS ALL STAR METRONOME JAZZMEN

Fats Navarro (tp), CP (as), Allen Eager (ts), John LaPorta (cl), Lennie Tristano (p), Billy Bauer (g), Tommy Potter (b), Buddy Rich (d), Sarah Vaughan (v), Barry Ulanov, Bruce Elliott (mcs)

NYC, November 8, 1947

| | 52nd Street Theme (theme) / Donna Lee-3,4 / Fats Flats-3,4 / Groovin' High / Ko Ko; Anthropology | |
| | (23,44) *Spotlite 108* | |

Everything I Have Is Yours-1,2,3,4,vSV / *Tea For Two*-1,2,3 / *Don't Blame Me*-1,2,3,4,5

(23) *Spotlite 108*

1-Navarro out, 2-CP out, 3-Eager out, 4-LaPorta out, 5-Roach out

CHARLIE PARKER WITH THE NEAL HEFTI ORCHESTRA

CP (as) with Al Porcino, Ray Wetzel, Doug Mettome (tp), Bill Harris, Bart Varsalona (tb), Vincent Jacobs (fr-h), Murray Williams, Sonny Salad (as), Flip Phillips, Pete Mondello (ts), John LaPorta (cl), Sam Caplan, Harry Katzman, Gene Orloff, Ziggy Smirnoff, Sid Harris, Manny Fiedler (vln), Fred Ruzilla, Nat Nathanson (vla), Joe Benaventi (cel), Tony Aless (p), Curley Russell (b), Shelly Manne (d), Diego Iborra (cga, bgo), Neal Hefti (arr, cond)

NYC, December 1947

| 2071-5 | *Repetition* | (61,C,H) Jazz Scene (unnumbered) |

CHARLIE PARKER

CP (as), Hank Jones (p), Ray Brown (b), Shelly Manne (d)

NYC, December 1947

| 2081-5 | *The Bird* | (62,C,H,J) Jazz Scene (unnumbered) |

CHARLIE PARKER SEXTET

As October 28 plus J. J. Johnson (tb)

NYC, December 17, 1947

D1151B	*Giant Swing (Drifting On A Reed)*	(5,55,C,D,F) Dial 1056
D1151D	*Drifting On A Reed*	(D,F) *Dial LP904*
D1151E	*Drifting On A Reed (Air Conditioning)*	(D,F) Dial 1043
D1152A	*Quasimado*	(D,F) *Dial LP203*
D1152B	*Quasimado (Trade Winds)*	(5,55,C,D,F) Dial 1015
D1153B	*Charlie's Wig*	(D,F) *Dial LP905*
D1153D	*Bongo Bop (Charlie's Wig)*	(D,F) *Dial LP203*

D1153E	Charlie's Wig	(5,55,C,D,F) Dial 1040
D1154B	Dexterity (Bird Feathers)	(5,55,C,D,F) Dial LP904
D1154C	Bird Feathers (Bongo Beep)	(D,F) Dial LP207
D1155ABX	Crazeology II	(D,F) Dial 1034**
D1155C	Crazeology	(5,55,C,D,F) Dial LP905
D1155D	Crazeology	(D,F) Dial 1034,1055
D1156A	How Deep Is The Ocean	(5,55,C,D,F) Dial 1055
D1156B	How Deep Is The Ocean	(D,F) Dial LP211

CHARLIE PARKER ALL STARS
As last except Johnson out
Detroit, December 21, 1947

D830-1/-2	Another Hair-Do*	(D) Savoy MG12000
D830-3	Another Hair-Do*	(D) Savoy S5J5500
D830-4	Another Hair-Do	(5,C,D) Savoy 961
D831-1	Bluebird	(D) Savoy MG12000
D831-2	Bluebird*	(D) Savoy S5J5500
D831-3	Bluebird	(5,C,D) Savoy 961
D832-1	Klaunsen's Vansen's (Klaunstance)	(5,C,D) Savoy 967
D833-1	Bird Gets The Worm	(D) Savoy MG12000
D833-2	Bird Gets The Worm*	(D) Savoy S5J5500
D833-3	Bird Gets The Worm	(5,C,D) Savoy 952

New Savoy Ballroom, Chicago, January 3, 1948
The Chase / Big Foot (Drifting On A Reed)   (41) **Philology W844.2**

CHARLIE PARKER QUINTET
As last plus Kenny Hagood (v)
Three Deuces, NYC, March 31, 1948

52nd Street Theme (3 versions)* / Big Foot / Dizzy Atmosphere / My Old Flame* / Half Nelson* / All The Things You Are-vKH*
(B) Spotlite SPJ141

Onyx Club, NYC, July 6-11, 1948

52nd Street Theme** / Shaw 'Nuff** / Out Of Nowhere (2 versions)** / Hot House** / This Time The Dream's On Me (2 versions)** / Night In Tunisia* / My Old Flame** / 52nd Street Theme (2 versions)* / The Way You Look Tonight** / Chasin' The Bird* / Dizzy Atmosphere** / How High The Moon**
(10,26,B) Jazz Workshop JWS501

As last but Earl Coleman, Kenny Hagood, Carmen McRae (v) added, Thelonious Monk (p-1) replaces Jordan
Same location and dates

Cheryl (2 versions)* / These Foolish Things* / Groovin' High (2 versions)* / Little Willie Leaps (2 versions)* / Night And Day-vEC* / The Way You Look Tonight* / Out Of Nowhere (2 versions)* / How High The Moon (3 versions)* / Chasin' the Bird* / Don't Blame Me* / Tico Tico* / Indiana; Donna Lee* / I'm In The Mood For Love* / This Time The Dream's On Me* / Yesterdays; 52nd Street Theme* / What Price Love-vCM* / All The Things You Are-vKH* / Well You Needn't-1* / Big Foot* / I Can't Get Started* / Spotlite; 52nd Street Theme* / September Song* / The Hymn* / 52nd Street Theme-2* / Half Nelson-2
(10,B) **Mosaic MD7-129**, MD10-129

52nd Street Theme (4 versions)* / Bird Lore* / Blues (Set closing blues)*
(B) **Mosaic MD7-129**, MD10-129

2-CP out

CHARLIE PARKER ALL STARS
As last except Tadd Dameron (p), Curley Russell (b) replace Jordan and Potter
Royal Roost, NYC, September 4, 1948

52nd Street Theme (E) Savoy MG12186
Ko Ko (E) Le Jazz Cool LJC101

As last except John Lewis (p) replaces Dameron

NYC, September 18, 1948

B900-1	*Barbados*	(D) *Savoy MG12000*
B900-2	*Barbados**	(D) *Savoy MG12009*
B900-3	*Barbados*	(D) *Savoy MG12009*
B900-4	*Barbados*	(6,C,D) Savoy 936
B901-1	*Ah-Leu-Cha**	(D) *Savoy MG12000*
B901-2	*Ah-Leu-Cha*	(6,C,D) Savoy 939
B902-1	*Constellation**	(D) *Savoy S5J5500*
B902-2	*Constellation*	(D) *Savoy MG12000*
B902-3	*Constellation**	(D) *Savoy MG12000*
B902-4	*Constellation**	(D) *Savoy MG12009*
B902-5	*Constellation*	(6,C,D) Savoy 939
B903-1	*Parker's Mood-1**	(D) *Savoy S5J5500*
B903-2	*Parker's Mood-1*	(D) *Savoy MG12000*
B903-3	*Parker's Mood-1**	(D) *Savoy S5J5500*
B903-4	*Parker's Mood-1**	(D) *Savoy MG12009*
B903-5	*Parker's Mood-1*	(6,C,D) Savoy 936

NYC, September 24, 1948

B908-1	*Perhaps*	(D) *Savoy MG12014*
B908-2	*Perhaps**	(D) *Savoy MG12009*
B908-3	*Perhaps*	(D) *Savoy MG12009*
B908-4	*Perhaps**	(D) *Savoy S5J5500*
B908-5	*Perhaps**	(D) *Savoy MG12000*
B908-6	*Perhaps*	(D) *Savoy MG12000*
B908-7	*Perhaps*	(6,C,D) Savoy 938

B909-1	Marmaduke*	(D) Savoy SJ5500
B909-2	Marmaduke*	(D) Savoy MG12000
B909-3/-4	Marmaduke*	(D) Savoy SJ5500
B909-5	Marmaduke	(D) Savoy MG12000
B909-6	Marmaduke*	(D) Savoy SJL1129
B909-7/-8	Marmaduke*	(D) Savoy MG12001
B909-9	Marmaduke	(D) Savoy MG12001
B909-10	Marmaduke*	(D) Savoy SJ5500
B909-11	Marmaduke*	(D) Savoy MG12009
B909-12	Marmaduke	(6,C,D) Savoy 938
B910-1	Steeplechase*	(D) Savoy SJ5500
B910-2	Steeplechase	(6,C,D) Savoy 937
B911-1	Merry-Go-Round	(D) Savoy MG12000
B911-2	Merry-Go-Round	(6,C,D) Savoy 937

1-Davis out

CHARLIE PARKER WITH THE DIZZY GILLESPIE ORCHESTRA

CP (as) with Dizzy Gillespie, Dave Burns, Willie Cook, Elmon Wright (tp), Andy Duryea, Jesse Tarrant (tb), John Brown, Ernie Henry (as), Joe Gayles, James Moody (ts), Cecil Payne (bs), James Foreman Jr. (p), Nelson Boyd (b), Teddy Stewart (d), Chano Pozo (cga)
Pershing Ballroom, Chicago, September 26, 1948

Things To Come* / Oo-Bop-Sh'bam* / Yesterdays* / Night In Tunisia* / Round Midnight* / Good Bait(?)* / Hot House(?)* / Manteca* / Algo Bueno* / Lover Man*

(40) **Stash STB-2500**

unknown blues* / Don't Blame Me* / I Can't Get Started* / Groovin' High* / Ool-Ya-Koo* / All The Things You Are* / unknown ballad*-1 / Cool Breeze*

(40) **Philology W843.2**

1-Miles Davis (tp) replaces CP

CHARLIE PARKER QUINTET

As September 18 except unknown p replaces Lewis

Waukegan, IL, c. Autumn 1948

Dexterity* / The Way You Look Tonight* / Barbados* / All The Things You Are* / Embraceable You* / Ornithology* / 52nd Street Theme*

(31) *Philology* 214W18

I Can't Get Started* / Diggin' Diz*

(33) *Philology* 214W29

Poss. Argyle Lounge, Chicago, c. Autumn 1948

The Way You Look Tonight / Night In Tunisia / Groovin' High

(45) *Philology* 214W29

My Old Flame / How High The Moon / Big Foot / Slow Boat To China (2 versions) / *All Of Me*-1 / *Cheryl / Home Sweet Home / Wee* (2 versions) / *Little Willie Leaps / Dizzy Atmosphere* (2 versions) / *Bebop* (2 versions) / *52nd Street Theme* (2 versions) / *All The Things You Are / Barbados / Salt Peanuts / Embraceable You*

(41) **Philology W844.2**

Half Nelson-2* / *Slow Boat To China; 52nd Street Theme**

Stash STB-2500

1-unknown v added; 2-CP out

Note: Recordings above issued on Philology LPs and Stash CD were ascribed to November 1947 and March 1948, but Koch points out that *Slow Boat* and *Barbados* were not in CP's repertoire before Autumn 1948, so this may apply to the entire batch

As last

Three Deuces, NYC, Autumn 1948

How High The Moon* / 52nd Street Theme*

(31) *Philology* 214W5

Note: Dating these two items is dubious; see also note to the c. June 1950 William Henry apartment sessions

CHARLIE PARKER ALL STARS

Miles Davis (tp), CP (as, v), Al Haig (p), Tommy Potter (b), Max Roach (d), Symphony Sid (mc)

Royal Roost, NYC, December 11, 1948

Groovin' High	(E) *Le Jazz Cool LJC101***
Big Foot	(E) *Le Jazz Cool LJC102*
Ornithology	(E) *Le Jazz Cool LJC101***
Slow Boat To China	(E) *ESP ESP-BIRD-1*

Art Ford (mc) replaces Sid

Royal Roost, NYC, December 12, 1948

Hot House	(E) *Le Jazz Cool LJC101***, *LJC103*
Salt Peanuts*-vCP*	(E) *Le Jazz Cool LJC102*

Symphony Sid (mc) replaces Ford

Royal Roost, NYC, December 18, 1948

Chasin' The Bird	(E) *Meexa Discox 1776*
Out Of Nowhere	(E) *Le Jazz Cool LJC102*
How High The Moon	(E) *Le Jazz Cool LJC102*

CHARLIE PARKER WITH MACHITO AND HIS ORCHESTRA

CP (as) with Mario Bauzá, Paquito Davilla, Bob Woodlen (tp), Gene Johnson, Freddie Skerritt (as), José Madera (ts), Leslie Johnakins (bs), René Hernandez (p), Roberto Rodriguez (b), José Mangual (bgo), Luis Miranda (cga), Ubaldo Nieto (tbl), Machito (mca), band v

NYC, December 20, 1948

2155-2	No Noise Pt.2	(6,63,C,H) *Mercury/Clef 11012*
2157-1	Mango Mangue*-v*	(6,63,C,H) *Mercury/Clef 11017*

Note: CP replaced by Flip Phillips (ts) on *No Noise Pt.1* (2154-9) and *Bucabu* (2156)

CHARLIE PARKER ALL STARS
As December 11 except Kenny Dorham (tp) replaces Davis
Royal Roost, NYC, December 25, 1948

Half Nelson / Little Willie Leaps	(E) *Okiedoke (unnumbered)*
White Christmas	(E) *Le Jazz Cool LJC101***

As last except Joe Harris (d) replaces Roach
Royal Roost, NYC, January 1, 1949

Bebop / Ornithology / Groovin' High / East Of The Sun	(E) *ESP ESP-BIRD-2*
Slow Boat To China	(E) *Le Jazz Cool LJC103*
Cheryl	(E) *Le Jazz Cool LJC102***

Conte Candoli (tp), Bennie Green (tb), Charlie Ventura, Flip Phillips (ts), Curley Russell (b), Shelly Manne, Ed Shaughnessy (d) added
Same location and date

How High The Moon	(E) *Savoy SJL2260*

CHARLIE PARKER WITH MACHITO AND HIS ORCHESTRA
As December 20
NYC, January 1949

2171-1	Okey Dokie (Okiedoke)	(5a,63,C,H) Mercury/Clef 11017

Note: CP replaced by Flip Phillips (ts) on *Caravan* (2170-2), *Tanga* (2172-3/4) and *Flying Home* (2173-9)

METRONOME ALL STARS
Dizzy Gillespie, Fats Navarro, Miles Davis (tp), J.J. Johnson, Kai Winding (tb), CP (as), Charlie Ventura (ts), Ernie Caceres (bs), Buddy DeFranco (cl), Lennie Tristano (p, arr-1), Billy Bauer (g), Eddie Safranski (b), Shelly Manne (d), Pete Rugolo (cond, arr-2)
NYC, January 3, 1949

D9-VB-0021-1	Overtime-2	(53) Victor 20-3361
D9-VC-1000-2	Overtime-2	(53) *Victor EPBT3046, LPT3046*

D9-VB-0022-1   Victory Ball-1,3   (53) Victor 20-3361
D9-VB-0022-2   Victory Ball-1,3   (41) Camden CAL339
D9-VC-1001-3   Victory Ball-1   (53) Victor EPBT3046, LPT3046
3-Navarro, Davis, Johnson and Caceres out

CHARLIE PARKER ALL STARS
As January 1
Royal Roost, NYC, January 15, 1949
    Scrapple From The Apple / Bebop / Hot House   (E) Le Jazz Cool LJC103

Max Roach (d) replaces Harris
Royal Roost, NYC, January 22, 1949
    Oop Bop Sh'bam-vCP   (E) Le Jazz Cool LJC103
    Scrapple From The Apple / Salt Peanuts-vCP   (E) Grotto 495

Royal Roost, NYC, January 29, 1949
    Groovin' High   (E) Savoy SJL2260

Royal Roost, NYC, February 5, 1949
    Scrapple From The Apple / Barbados / Salt Peanuts-vCP   (E) Le Jazz Cool LJC103

JAZZ AT THE PHILHARMONIC
Fats Navarro (tp), Tommy Turk (tb), CP, Sonny Criss (as), Flip Phillips (ts), Hank Jones (p), Ray Brown (b), Shelly Manne (d)
Carnegie Hall, NYC, February 11, 1949
    Leap Here / Indiana / Lover Come Back To Me   (30) **Pablo PACD5311**

CP (as) with Machito and his Orchestra
Same location and date

No Noise / Mango Mangue   unissued

Note: Date is mistakenly given as November 2, 1949 on the Pablo album

CHARLIE PARKER ALL STARS
As January 22
Royal Roost, NYC, February 12, 1949

Scrapple From The Apple / Bebop   (E) *Savoy SJL1108*
Barbados   (E) *Savoy MG12179*

Royal Roost, NYC, February 19, 1949

Groovin' High / Confirmation / Salt Peanuts–vCP   (E) *Savoy SJL1108*

METRONOME AWARD SHOW OF 1949
Shorty Sherock (tp-1), unknown tb-2, Sidney Bechet (ss-3), CP (as), Joe Bushkin (p), Chubby Jackson (b), George Wettling (d), Teddy Hale (tap-4), unknown others

Station WPIX, NYC, February 21, 1949

Now's The Time / Lover–4 / I Can't Get Started–1 / Jam Session*–1,2,3   (48) **Stash ST-CD-21**

Note: Speech by CP, Chubby Jackson and Charles Delaunay heard

CHARLIE PARKER ALL STARS
As February 12 plus Lucky Thompson (ts), Milt Jackson (vib), Dave Lambert, Buddy Stewart (v)
Royal Roost, NYC, February 26, 1949

Half Nelson / Night In Tunisia / Scrapple From The Apple   (E) *Savoy MG12179*

Deedle–vDL,BS,1,2   (E) *Grotto 495*
What's This?–DL,BS,1,2   (E) *S.C.A.M. JPG3*

ADVENTURES IN JAZZ
Miles Davis, Max Kaminsky (tp), Kai Winding, Will Bradley (tb), Joe Marsala (cl), CP (as), Mike Coluccio, Joe Sullivan-1 (p), Specs Powell, Max Roach (d), unknown ts, g, b, William B. Williams (mc)
CBS-TV, NYC, March 4, 1949

Anthropology-1 / Jam Blues; Big Foot*	(48) Stash ST-CD-21

CHARLIE PARKER ALL STARS
As February 26
Royal Roost, NYC, March 5, 1949

Cheryl / Anthropology	(E) S.C.A.M. JPG3
Hurry Home-vBS	(E) Savoy SJL1173
Deedle-vDL,BS,1,2 / Royal Roost Bop-vDL,BS,1,2	(E) Grotto 495

As last but Lambert and Stewart out, Rudi Blesh (mc) replaces Sid
Waldorf Astoria Hotel, NYC, March 5, 1949

Barbados-2 / Anthropology	(43) Jazz Showcase 5003

Symphony Sid (mc) replaces Blesh
Royal Roost, NYC, March 12, 1949

Cheryl / Slow Boat To China-1 / Chasin' The Bird	(E) Savoy MG12179
1-Thompson out, 2-Jackson out	

CHARLIE PARKER AND HIS ORCHESTRA
As February 26 except Tommy Turk (tb), Carlos Vidal (bgo) replace Thompson and Jackson
NYC, c. Spring 1949

292	Cardboard	(6,62,C,H,J) Norgran MGN1035
293	Visa	(6,62,C,H,J) Mercury/Clef 11022
Turk and Vidal out		

NYC, May 5, 1949

294-3	Segment	(6,64,C,H,J) Verve MGV8009
295-2	Passport	(6,64,C,H,J) Mercury/Clef 11022
295-5	Passport	(6,64,C,H,J) Verve MGV8000
296	Diverse	(6,64,H) Verve MGV8009

Note: Despite the confusion over titles, 294-3 and 296 are alternate takes of the same tune, while 295-2 and 295-5 are two different tunes; on reissue (J), 295-5 is described as Passport — I Got Rhythm

CHARLIE PARKER QUINTET
As last
Salle Pleyel, Paris, May 8 / 9 / 14 / 15, 1949

(ST3014) Ham And Haig Vogue V5012*
Salt Peanuts-vCP / Barbados* / 52nd Street Theme / Out Of Nowhere
(37,A) Bird in Paris CP3

Salt Peanuts-vCP / 52nd Street Theme / Out Of Nowhere / Scrapple From The Apple / Allen's Alley*
(38,A) Bird in Paris CP3

Out Of Nowhere / Night In Tunisia / Moose The Mooche / I Got Rhythm / 52nd Street Theme / Hot House
(A) **Jazz Up / New Sound Planet JUTBCD3002**

Note: Ham And Haig was issued under the name of Max Roach, and is a version of Hot House beginning after CP's solo

Théâtre Colisée, Roubaix, May 12, 1949
Ornithology* / Out Of Nowhere* (2 versions) / Cheryl / 52nd Street Theme* (2 versions) / Lover Man* / Groovin' High* / Half Nelson*
(38,A) **Philology W622.2**

JAM SESSION
Hot Lips Page, Miles Davis, Bill Coleman, Aimé Barelli (tp), Russell Moore (tb), Sidney Bechet, Pierre Braslavsky (ss), CP (as), Don Byas, James Moody (ts), Hubert Rostaing (cl), Al Haig (p), Hazy Osterwald (vib), Toots Thielemans (g), Tommy Potter (b), Max Roach (d)
Salle Pleyel, Paris, May 15, 1949
Farewell Blues (Jam Blues)
(39) Bird in Paris CP3*

JAZZ AT THE PHILHARMONIC

Roy Eldridge (tp), CP (as), Coleman Hawkins (ts), Hank Jones (p), Eddie Safranski (b), Buddy Rich (d)

Carnegie Hall, NYC, June 19, 1949

*Bean and The Boys (Lover Come Back To Me)**	(36) **Philology W120.2**
Stuffy	(34) *Bird Box (unnumbered)*

Roy Eldridge (tp), Tommy Turk (tb), CP (as), Lester Young, Flip Phillips (ts), Hank Jones (p), Ray Brown (b), Buddy Rich (d), Ella Fitzgerald (v)

Carnegie Hall, NYC, September 18, 1949

382/3/4	*The Opener*	(65,H) Mercury/Clef 11054/5/6
385/6/7	*Lester Leaps In*	(65,H) Mercury/Clef 11056/5/4
	Embraceable You	(65,H) *Mercury MG35013*
	The Closer	(65,H) *Mercury MG35013*
	*Ow!-*vEF	(65,H) *Verve (Jap) 817 151-1*
	*Flying Home-*vEF	(65,H) *Verve 815 147*
	*How High The Moon-*vEF / *Perdido-*vEF	(65,H) *Verve* **837 141-2**

CHARLIE PARKER QUINTET

As May 5

Three Deuces, NYC, poss. Autumn 1949

Big Foot / 52nd Street Theme	*Philology 214 W5*
Ornithology	*Philology 214 W19*

Note: The dating of these items by Philology is extremely dubious

Red Rodney (tp), Roy Haynes (d) replace Dorham and Roach

Pershing Hotel, Chicago, November 1949

*I Cover The Waterfront** / *Confirmation** / *Now's The Time** / *Big Foot** / *Perdido** / *Smoke Gets In Your Eyes; Ruby My Dear** / *Wee**	
	(32) *Philology 214 W12*
*Hot House** / *Cheryl** / *I Can't Get Started** / *Groovin' High**	
	(32) *Philology 214 W15*

How High The Moon / Cool Blues / Stardust (Embraceable You)-1 / All The Things You Are

(41) **Philology W844-2**

(41) **Philology W844-2**

New Savoy Ballroom, Chicago, late 1949

Billie's Bounce-2

1-unknown v added, 2-unknown ts added

Note: Nine of the 11 performances first issued on *Philology 214W12* and *214W15* are presented in two versions each, of different length and recording quality

CHARLIE PARKER WITH STRINGS

CP (as), Mitch Miller (ob, eng-h), Bronislaw Gimpel, Max Hollander, Milton Lamask (vln), Frank Brieff (vla), Frank Miller (cel), Meyer Rosen (harp), Stan Freeman (p), Ray Brown (b), Buddy Rich (d), Jimmy Carroll (arr, cond)

NYC, November 30, 1949

319-5	*Just Friends*	(6,61,C,H,J)	Mercury/Clef 11036
320-3	*Everything Happens To Me*	(6,61,C,H,J)	Mercury/Clef 11037
321-3	*April In Paris*	(6,61,C,H,J)	Mercury/Clef 11038
322-2	*Summertime*	(6,61,C,H,J)	Mercury/Clef 11038
323-2	*I Didn't Know What Time It Was*	(6,61,C,H,J)	Mercury/Clef 11037
324-3	*If I Should Lose You*	(6,61,C,H,J)	Mercury/Clef 11036

CHARLIE PARKER

Red Rodney (tp), CP (as), Al Haig (p), Tommy Potter (b), Roy Haynes (d)

Carnegie Hall, NYC, December 24, 1949

Ornithology / Cheryl / KoKo / Bird Of Paradise (Bird's Perch) / Now's The Time

(25) *Hot Club de Lyon (unnumbered)*

Miles Davis (tp) replaces Rodney

Hotel Diplomat, NYC, poss. c. 1949–50

Billie's Bounce* / Caravan* / Big Foot   (39) *Stash ST-260*

Cool Blues / April In Paris / Ornithology / 52nd Street Theme

(41) **Philology W844.2**

Note: The above tracks may be from Davis's tenure in the regular quintet, for instance on March 26, 1948 when CP appeared at the Hotel Diplomat

As December 24 plus J. J. Johnson (tb)
Birdland, NYC, February 14, 1950

Anthropology; Allen's Alley / Visa; 52nd Street Theme	(33) *J For Jazz JFJ802*
Dizzy Atmosphere / *Yesterdays; 52nd Street Theme*	(33) *Chazzer 2001*
What's New; Ruby My Dear / Little Willie Leaps / I Can't Get Started / *Wahoo*	
	(33) *Chazzer 2004*
Hot House / Out Of Nowhere / Slow Boat To China / Night In Tunisia	

(33) **Philology W19/29.2**

Johnson out
St. Nicholas Arena, NYC, February 18, 1950

I Didn't Know What Time It Was** / Ornithology** / Embraceable You** / Visa** / I Cover The Waterfront** / Scrapple From The Apple**
/ Star Eyes; 52nd Street Theme** / Confirmation** / Out Of Nowhere** / Hot House** / What's New** / Now's The time** / Smoke Gets
In Your Eyes; 52nd Street Theme** (11,27) *Jazz Workshop JWS500*
52nd Street Theme (4 versions)** / *Wahoo** / I Can't Get Started* / Anthropology* / Groovin' High** / Cheryl***

(11,47) *Zim ZIM1007*

CP (as), Hank Jones (p), Ray Brown (b), Buddy Rich (d)
NYC, March–April 1950

371-4	*Star Eyes*	(7,C,H,J) *Norgran MGN1035*
372-12	*Blues (fast)*	(7,C,H,J) *Verve MGV8009*
373-2	*I'm In The Mood For Love*	(7,C,H,J) *Verve MGV8009*

As last except Bernie Leighton (p) replaces Jones
NYC, c. 1950

	I Can't Get Started	(36) *Parktec 4627-1*

Note: Poss. from around the July 5 session with the same rhythm-section

Poss. Jon Nielson (tp), CP, poss. Joe Maini or Charlie Kennedy (as), unknown p, b, Freddie Gruber (d)
Prob. NYC, c. 1950

Groovin' High / The Great Lie / unknown blues / How High The Moon

(47) **Philology W850.2**

Note: The tentative dating is from Koch, and is more plausible than "1952–53" offered by Philology

GENE ROLAND ORCHESTRA

Marty Bell, Don Ferrara, Don Joseph, Jon Nielson, Al Porcino, Sonny Rich, Red Rodney, Bill Verlin (tp), Eddie Bert, Porky Cohen, Jimmy Knepper, Paul Selden (tb), Frank Orchard (vtb), CP, Joe Maini (as), Al Cohn, Don Lanphere, Tommy Mackagon, Zoot Sims (ts), Bob Newman, Marty Flax (bs), Harry Biss (p), Sam Herman (g), Buddy Jones (b), Phil Arabia, Freddie Gruber, Don Manning (d), Gene Roland (arr, cond)
NYC, April 3, 1950

It's A Wonderful World / *Just You, Just Me* / *unknown title* / *Stardust**

(42) *Spotlite SPJ141**

Limehouse Blues / *Down Home Blues* / *East Side West Side**

(42) **Philology W845.2**

CHARLIE PARKER

CP, John Maher, Marshall Stearns, Chan Richardson (speech)
NYC, poss. May 1, 1950

Interview

(34) *Meexa Discox 1776*

Fats Navarro (tp), CP (as), Bud Powell (p), Curley Russell (b), Art Blakey (d)
Unknown venue, poss. Bronx, NYC, prob. May 15–16, 1950

*Round Midnight-1 / Move** / *Ornithology / Cool Blues; 52nd Street Theme-2**

(9,A) *Le Jazz Cool LJC101*

*Wahoo** / *The Street Beat (Rifftide)*

(9,A) *Le Jazz Cool LJC102*

Conception (Poobah)-2,3

(A) *Alto AL701*

Little Willie Leaps; 52nd Street Theme / Embraceable You-2,4

(9,A) *Meexa Discox 1776*

I'll Remember April; 52nd Street Theme   (9,A) Grotto 495
This Time The Dream's On Me-1 / Dizzy Atmosphere / Night In Tunisia-5 / Out Of Nowhere
                                     (9,A) Columbia JG34808

1-Navarro out, 2-Walter Bishop (p) replaces Powell, 3-Miles Davis (tp), J. J. Johnson (tb), Brew Moore (ts) added, 4-Little Jimmy Scott (v) added, 5-CP out

CP (as) with poss. Machito and his Orchestra
NYC, May 19, 1950

Reminiscing At Twilight (Bongo Ballad) (Mambo Fortunado) / Lament For The Congo (Bird's Mambo)
                                     (49) Ozone 4

CP (as), Charlie Rouse (ts), Buddy DeFranco (cl), poss. Dick Hyman (p), unknown g, Tommy Potter (b), Max Roach (d)
Birdland, NYC, May 23, 1950

Lover Come Back To Me; 52nd Street Theme   (A) Parktec 4627-1

Note: The pianist is certainly not Erroll Garner, who is sometimes mentioned. An alternative personnel (including Hyman, Brew Moore (ts), Tony Scott (cl), poss. Chuck Wayne or Mundell Lowe (g), Leonard Gaskin (b), Irv Kluger or Ed Shaugnessy (d) and dated as from Café Society, June 1950) has also been posited for this track

CHARLIE PARKER QUINTET
As February 18 except Kenny Dorham (tp) replaces Rodney
Café Society, NYC, June 1950

52nd Street Theme (2 versions) / Just Friends (2 versions) / April In Paris (2 versions) / Night In Tunisia
                                     (14a) Grotto 495
Moose The Mooche; 52nd Street Theme-1   (14a) Bombasi 11235
What's New; It's The Talk Of The Town   (14a) **Philology W120.2**
Bewitched; Summertime / I Cover The Waterfront; Gone With The Wind / Easy To Love; 52nd Street Theme / 52nd Street Theme / Just Friends / April In Paris
52nd Street Theme-1 / Just Friends-1 / April In Paris-1   (14a) Klacto MG101

(A) **Jazz Up/New Sound Planet JUTBCD3004**

(A) **Jazz Up/New Sound Planet JUTBCD3004**

52nd Street Theme-2 / *Just Friends*-2 / *April In Paris*-2

1-Tony Scott (cl) added, 2-Brew Moore (ts) added

JAM SESSION
Norma Carson, Jon Eardley (tp), Jimmy Knepper (tb), CP, Joe Maini (as), Bob Newman, Gers Yowell (ts), John Williams (p), Buddy Jones (b), Phil Brown-1, Frank Isola-2, Buzzy Bridgeford-3 (d)
William Henry apartment, NYC, c. June 1950

Little Willie Leaps-1 / *All The Things You Are*-2 / *Bernie's Tune*-3 / *Donna Lee*-1 / *Out Of Nowhere*-2 / *Half Nelson*-1 / *Fine And Dandy*-1

(45) *Zim ZM1006***

poss. Jon Nielson (tp), Jimmy Knepper (tb), CP, Joe Maini (as), Don Lanphere (ts), Al Haig (p), unknown b, Frank Isola (d)
Same location and period

Half Nelson / *Cherokee* / *Scrapple From The Apple* / *Star Eyes*

(45) *Zim ZM1006***

Note: *Donna Lee* on Philology 214W18 (described as "probably 1945") is identical to the version above. The versions of *Indiana* (actually *Donna Lee*), *Out Of Nowhere*, *Fine And Dandy* and *All The Things You Are* heard on *Philology 214W5* – where they run far too slow – are described as "Autumn 1948" yet they are the same versions as above

CHARLIE PARKER AND HIS ORCHESTRA
Dizzy Gillespie (tp), CP (as), Thelonious Monk (p), Curley Russell (b), Buddy Rich (d)
NYC, June 6, 1950

410-4	*Bloomdido*	(7,66,H,J) Mercury/Clef 11058
411-3	*An Oscar For Treadwell*	(66,H) *Verve MGV8006*
411-4	*An Oscar For Treadwell*	(7,66,H,J) Mercury/Clef 11082
412-3	*Mohawk*	(66,H) *Verve MGV8006*

412-6	*Mohawk*	(7,66,H,J) Mercury/Clef 11082
413-1	*My Melancholy Baby*	(66,H) **Verve 521 436-2**
413-2	*My Melancholy Baby**	(H) **Verve 521 436-2**
413-3	*My Melancholy Baby*	(7,66,H,J) Mercury/Clef 11058
414-1/-2/-3/-4	*Leap Frog**	(66,H) **Verve 837 141-2**
414-5	*Leap Frog*	(66,H) **Verve 831 133-2**
414-6/-7	*Leap Frog**	(66,H) **Verve 837 141-2**
414-8	*Leap Frog*	(66,H) **Verve 837 141-2**
414-9	*Leap Frog*	(66,H) *Verve MGV8006*
414-10	*Leap Frog**	(66,H) **Verve 837 141-2**
414-11	*Leap Frog*	(7,66,H,J) Mercury/Clef 11076
415-1/-2/-3	*Relaxin' With Lee**	(66,H) **Verve 831 133-2**
415-4	*Relaxin' With Lee*	(66,H) *Verve MGV8006*
415-5	*Relaxin' With Lee**	(66,H) **Verve 831 133-2**
415-6	*Relaxin' With Lee*	(7,66,H,J) Mercury/Clef 11076

Note: Before the comprehensive release of unissued material, 413-3, 414-9, 414-11, 415-4 and 415-6 were known respectively as "413-2," "414-4," "414-6," "415-2" and "415-3"

CHARLIE PARKER WITH STRINGS

CP (as), Joseph Singer (fr-h), Edwin Brown (ob), Sam Caplan, Howard Kay, Sam Rand, Harry Melnikoff, Zelly Smirnoff (vln), Isadore Zir (vla), Maurice Brown (cel), Verley Mills (harp), Bernie Leighton (p), Ray Brown (b), Buddy Rich (d), Joe Lippman (arr, cond)

NYC, July 5, 1950

442-5	*Dancing In The Dark*	(7,61,67,C,H,J) Mercury/Clef 11068
443-2	*Out Of Nowhere*	(7,61,C,H,J) Mercury/Clef 11070
444-1	*Laura*	(H) **Verve 837 141-2**
444-3	*Laura*	(7,61,67,C,H,J) Mercury/Clef 11068

445-4	East Of The Sun	(7,61,C,H,J) Mercury/Clef 11070
446-2	They Can't Take That Away From Me	(7,61,C,H,J) Mercury/Clef 11071
447-4	Easy To Love	(7,61,69,C,H,J) Mercury/Clef 11072
448-2	I'm In The Mood For Love	(7,61,C,H,J) Mercury/Clef 11071
448-3	I'm In The Mood For Love	(H) **Verve 837 141-2**
449-1/-2	I'll Remember April	(H) **Verve 837 141-2**
449-3	I'll Remember April	(7,61,C,H,J) Mercury/Clef 11072

Prob. similar to September 16 except Billy Taylor (p) instead of Haig

Apollo Theatre, NYC, August 17–23, 1950

	Easy To Love	(37) S.C.A.M. JPG4
	Repetition / April In Paris / What Is This Thing Called Love	
		(37) Saga ERO8006
	Repetition (3 versions) / April In Paris (3 versions) / Easy To Love (3 versions) / What Is This Thing Called Love (3 versions)	
		(37) **Philology W200.2**

Sarah Vaughan (vcl), CP (as), unknown big-band
Same location and date

| | I Cried For You* | (36) **Philology W120.2** |

CHARLIE PARKER QUINTET As February 18 except unknown tb replaces Rodney
New Brunswick, NJ, August 28, 1950

| | Hot House / I May Be Wrong / Indiana-1 / 'S Wonderful-1 / Parker's Mood | |
| | | (24) Stash ST-280 |

1-unknown tp added

CHARLIE PARKER WITH STRINGS

CP (as), Tommy Mace (ob), Sam Caplan, Stan Karpenia, Teddy Blume (vln), Dave Uchitel (vla), Bill Bundy (cel), Wallace McManus (harp), Al Haig (p), Tommy Potter (b), Roy Haynes (d), Jimmy Mundy-1, Gerry Mulligan-2 (arr)

Carnegie Hall, NYC, September 16, 1950

Repetition / What Is This Thing Called Love / April In Paris / Easy To Love-1 /

Rocker (I'll Remember April) -2   (7,61,H) *Norgran MGJC3502*

CHARLIE PARKER

CP (as), Coleman Hawkins (ts)-1, Hank Jones (p), Ray Brown (b), Buddy Rich (d)

NYC, c. September 1950

Celebrity / Ballade-1   (7,62,H) *Verve MGV8002*

CP (as), Von Freeman (ts), Chris Anderson (p), George Freeman (g), Leroy Jackson (b), Bruz Freeman (d), unknown v

Pershing Ballroom, Chicago, October 23, 1950

Indiana / I Can't Get Started / Anthropology / Out Of Nowhere / Get Happy / Hot House / Embraceable You-v / Body And Soul-v / Cool Blues / Stardust-v / All The Things You Are / Billie's Bounce / Pennies From Heaven

(12) *Zim ZM1003***

There's A Small Hotel / These Foolish Things* / Keen And Peachy* / Hot House*

(12) *Savoy MG12152*

Bird, Bass And Out* / Goodbye*   (12) *Savoy SJL1132*

As last but unknown tb added

Poss. same location and date

Pennies From Heaven   **Stash STB-2500***

CP (as), Milton DeLugg (acc-1), unknown studio band, Ray Malone (tap-2), Buddy Lester (vcl, mc), Jerry Lester (mc)

Channel 5 TV, NYC, October 31, 1950

Anthropology / Donna Lee-2 / Blues (theme)-1,vBL / Almost Like Being In Love-vBL

(48) **Philology W851.2**

Rolf Ericson (tp), CP (as), Gosta Theselius (p-1, ts-2), Thore Jederby (b), Jack Norén (d)
Amiralen Dance Hall, Malmö, November 22, 1950
Anthropology-1 / *Cheers*-1 / *Lover Man* / *Cool Blues*-1

(13) *Oktav OKTLP164*

As last
Folkets Park, Halsingborg, November 24, 1950
Anthropology-1 / *Scrapple From The Apple*-1 / *Embraceable You*-1 / *Cool Blues*-1 / *Star Eyes*-1,3 / *All The Things You Are*-1 / *Strike Up The Band*-1

(13) *Sonet SLP27*

Rowland Greenberg (tp), Lennart Nilsson (p) added
Same location and date
Body And Soul-2** / *Fine And Dandy*-2 / *How High The Moon*-2

(13) *Sonet SLP27*

3-Ericson out

CP (as) with prob. Roger Guérin, Georges Jouvin, Pierre Fassin, Yves Alouette (tp), André Paquinet, Maurice Gladieu, Charles Huss (tb), Robert Merchez, Roger Simon (as), Jacques Tess, Marcel Pomes (ts), Honoré Truc (bs), Robert Cambier (p), Henri Karen (b), Pierre Lotéguy (d), unknown perc. Maurice Moufflard (cond)
ORTF Studios, Paris, late November 1950
Lady Bird

(39) *Bird in Paris CP3*

Red Rodney (tp), CP (as), Kenny Drew (p), Curley Russell (b), Art Blakey (d), Symphony Sid (mc)
Birdland, NYC, December 1950
Anthropology / *Embraceable You* / *Cheryl* / *Salt Peanuts*-vCP / *Jumpin' With Symphony Sid* (theme)

(36) **Royal Jazz RJD506**

MACHITO AND HIS ORCHESTRA

As December 20, 1948 plus Harry Edison, Allen Stewart (tp), Flip Phillips (ts), Sol Rabinowitz (bs), Buddy Rich (d), Chino Pozo (cga), Chico O'Farrill (arr, cond)

NYC, December 21, 1950

557-4	Canción	(63,H) Clef MGC505
558-2	Mambo	(63,H) Clef MGC505
559	Rumba Abierta	(63,H) Clef MGC505
560-2	6/8	(63,H) Clef MGC505
561-3	Jazz	(63,H) Clef MGC505

CHARLIE PARKER AND HIS ORCHESTRA

Miles Davis (tp), CP (as), Walter Bishop (p), Teddy Kotick (b), Max Roach (d)

NYC, January 17, 1951

489-2	Au Privave	(64,H) Verve MGV8010
489-3	Au Privave	(64,C,H,J) Mercury/Clef 11087
490-3	She Rote	(64,H) Verve MGV8010
490-5	She Rote	(64,C,H,J) Clef 11101
491-1	K.C. Blues	(64,C,H,J) Clef 11101
492-2	Star Eyes	(64,C,H,J) Mercury/Clef 11087

CHARLIE PARKER AND HIS JAZZERS

As last except Roy Haynes (d), José Mangual (bga), Luis Miranda (cga) replace Davis and Roach

NYC, March 12, 1951

540-6	My Little Suede Shoes	(63,C,H,J) Mercury/Clef 11093
541-2	Un Poquito De Tu Amor	(63,C,H,J) Mercury/Clef 11092
542-9	Tico Tico	(63,C,H,J) Mercury/Clef 11091
543-3	Fiesta	(63,C,H,J) Norgran MGN1035
544-2/-6	Why Do I Love You	(H) Verve MGV8008
544-7	Why Do I Love You	(63,C,H,J) Clef MGC646

CHARLIE PARKER WITH STRINGS
Prob. as last except unknown ob, strings and harp replace Mangual and Miranda, Symphony Sid (mc)
Birdland, NYC, March 22, 1951

    Easy To Love   (44,G) **Stardust (unnumbered)**
    Rocker / Jumpin' With Symphony Sid (theme)   (44.G) *Meexa Discox 1776*

Birdland, NYC, March 24, 1951

    Jumpin' With Symphony Sid (theme) / Just Friends / Everything Happens To Me / East Of The Sun / Laura / Dancing In The Dark /
    Jumpin' With Symphony Sid (theme)   (G) *Columbia JC34832*

CHARLIE PARKER/DIZZY GILLESPIE
Dizzy Gillespie (tp), CP (as), Bud Powell (p), Tommy Potter (b), Roy Haynes (d), Symphony Sid (mc)
Birdland, NYC, March 31, 1951

    Blue 'N Boogie / Anthropology / 'Round Midnight / Night In Tunisia / Jumpin' With Symphony Sid (theme)
                                       (G) *Temple M555*

Billy Taylor (p) replaces Powell
Similar location and date

JC26   *How High The Moon / Hot House / Embraceable You*
                                (A) *Klacto MG102*

CHARLIE PARKER
CP, Leonard Feather (speech)
Voice Of America recording, c. Spring 1951

JC26   *Interview*   (36) *Philology 214W29*

As March 24
Birdland, NYC, April 7, 1951

Laura   (G) Okiedoke (unnumbered)
What Is This Thing Called Love / Repetition / They Can't Take That Away From Me / Easy To love
                                                 (G) Columbia JC34832

Howard McGhee (tp), CP (as), Wardell Gray, Bill Wellington-1 (ts), Nat Pierce (p), Jack Lawlor (b), Joe McDonald (d)
Christy's, Framingham, MA, April 12, 1951

Scrapple From The Apple / Lullaby In Rhythm (I May Be Wrong)-1* / Happy Bird Blues*
                                                 (8) Charlie Parker PLP404

Poss. Bennie Harris (tp), CP (as), Walter Bishop (p), Teddy Kotick (b), Roy Haynes (d)
Christy's, Framingham, MA, poss. April 21, 1951

Wahoo (Perdido)* / Out Of Nowhere* / Ornithology* / Lady Bird; Half Nelson* / Little Willie Leaps* / Star Eyes*
                                                 (35) **Philology W80.2**

52nd Street Theme* (2 versions) / I Can't Get Started*
                                                 (43) **Philology W846.2**

The Way You Look Tonight / 52nd Street Theme / Groovin' High
                                                 unissued

CHARLIE PARKER QUINTET
Benny Harris or Red Rodney (tp), CP (as), Walter Bishop (p), Teddy Kotick (b), Roy Haynes (d)
Eastern Parkway Ballroom, Brooklyn, June 23, 1951

Embraceable You / Steeplechase / 52nd Street Theme / Now's The Time / Be My Love; April In Paris / Dance Of The Infidels; 52nd Street Theme /
This Time The Dream's On Me   (31) Philology 214W19
Ornithology   (31) **Philology W5/18.2**
Cool Blues / Wee   (34) **Philology W57.2**
52nd Street Theme (2 versions) / Don't Blame Me / Night In Tunisia / All The Things You Are
                                                 (43) **Philology W846.2**

Veterans' Hospital, Philadelphia, June 1951

Cool Blues* / Out Of Nowhere* / This Is Always-1* / Now's The Time* / Scrapple From The Apple*	(33) *Philology 214W29*
Thrivin' On A Riff / Blue 'N Boogie	unissued

1-unknown v (prob. not Sarah Vaughan) added

WOODY HERMAN AND HIS ORCHESTRA WITH CHARLIE PARKER

CP (as) with Roy Caton, Don Fagerquist, Johnny Macombe, Doug Mettome (tp), Jerry Dorn, Urbie Green, Fred Lewis (tb), Dick Hafer, Bill Perkins, Kenny Pinson (ts), Sam Staff (bs), Dave McKenna (p), Red Wooten (b), Sonny Igoe (d), band v

Municipal Arena, Kansas City, July 22, 1951

You Go To My Head / Leo The Lion (The Lion) / Cuban Holiday (Cubop Holiday) / The Nearness Of You / Lemon Drop-v / The Goof And I (Sonny Speaks) / Laura / Four Brothers	(50) *MainMan BFWHCB617*
Leo The Lion / More Moon	(50) *Alamac QSR2442*

CHARLIE PARKER

CP (as), Lennie Tristano (p), Kenny Clarke (brushes)
Lennie Tristano's home, NYC, August 1951

All Of Me / I Can't Believe That You're In Love With Me	(31) *Philology 214W18*

CHARLIE PARKER QUINTET

Red Rodney (tp), CP (as), John Lewis (p), Ray Brown (b), Kenny Clarke (d)
NYC, August 8, 1951

609-4	*Blues For Alice*	(64,C,H,J) *Clef MGC646*
610-4	*Si Si*	(64,C,H,J) *Mercury/Clef 11103*
611-3	*Swedish Schnapps*	(64,H) *Verve MGV8010*
611-4	*Swedish Schnapps*	(64,C,H,J) *Mercury/Clef 11103*

612-1 Back Home Blues (64,H) Verve MGV8010
612-2 Back Home Blues (64,C,H,J) Mercury/Clef 11095
613-2 Lover Man (64,C,H,J) Mercury/Clef 11095

CHARLIE PARKER WITH STRINGS
CP (as) with Chris Griffin, Al Porcino, Bernie Privin (tp), Will Bradley, Bill Harris (tb), Toots Mondello, Murray Williams (as), Hank Ross, Art Drellinger (ts), Stan Webb (bs), unknown strings, Verley Mills (harp), Lou Stein (p), Art Ryerson (g), Bob Haggart (b), Don Lamond (d), Joe Lippman (arr, cond)
NYC, January 22, 1952
675-2 Temptation (67,H,J) Mercury/Clef 11088
676-3 Lover (67,H,J) Mercury/Clef 11089
677-4 Autumn In New York (67,H,J) Mercury/Clef 11088
678-4 Stella By Starlight (67,H,J) Mercury/Clef 11089

CHARLIE PARKER QUINTET
Benny Harris (tp), CP (as), Walter Bishop (p), Teddy Kotick (b), Max Roach (d), Luis Miranda (cga)
NYC, January 23, 1952
679-4 Mama Inez (63,H,J) Mercury/Clef 11092
680-3 La Cucaracha (63,H,J) Mercury/Clef 11093
681-5 Estrellita (63,H,J) Mercury/Clef 11094
682-3 Begin The Beguine-1 (63,69,H,J) Mercury/Clef 11094
683-1 La Paloma (63,H,J) Mercury/Clef 11091
1-Harris out

CHARLIE PARKER/DIZZY GILLESPIE
Dizzy Gillespie (tp), CP (as), Dick Hyman (p), Sandy Block (b), Charlie Smith (d), Earl Wilson, Leonard Feather (mcs)
Channel 5 TV, NYC, February 24, 1952
Hot House (48) *Phoenix LP12*

CHARLIE PARKER BIG BAND

CP (as) with Jimmy Maxwell, Carl Poole, Al Porcino, Bernie Privin (tp), Bill Harris, Lou McGarity, Bart Varsalona (tb), Harry Terrill, Murray Williams (as), Flip Phillips, Hank Ross (ts), Danny Bank (bs), Oscar Peterson (p), Freddie Green (g), Ray Brown (b), Don Lamond (d), Joe Lippman (arr, cond)

NYC, March 25, 1952

756-5	Night And Day	(67,69,H,J) Mercury/Clef 11096
757-4	Almost Like Being In Love	(67,H,J) Mercury/Clef 11102
758-1	I Can't Get Started	(67,H,J) Mercury/Clef 11096
759-5	What Is This Thing Called Love	(67,69,H,J) Mercury/Clef 11102

JERRY JEROME ALL STARS

CP (as), Teddy Wilson (p), Eddie Safranski (b), Don Lamond (d)

Loew's Valencia Theatre, Brooklyn, March 25, 1952

| JC35 | Cool Blues | (35) Jazz Showcase 5003 |

Dick Cary (p) replaces Wilson, Bill Harris (tb), Buddy DeFranco (cl) added
Same location and date

| | Ornithology | (35) **Royal Jazz RJD505** |

JAM SESSION

Charlie Shavers (tp), Benny Carter, Johnny Hodges, CP (as), Flip Phillips, Ben Webster (ts), Oscar Peterson (p), Barney Kessel (g), Ray Brown (b), J. C. Heard (d)

LA, June 5, 1952

802-2	Jam Blues	(68) Clef MGC601
803-3	What Is This Thing Called Love	(68) Clef MGC602
804-2	Ballad Medley	(68) Clef MGC601
805-2	Funky Blues	(68) Clef MGC602**

Note: CP's solo feature on Ballad Medley is Dearly Beloved

CHARLIE PARKER

Chet Baker (tp), CP, Sonny Criss (as), Donn Trenner, Russ Freeman (p), Harry Babasin (b), Lawrence Marable (d)
Trade Winds Club, Inglewood, CA, June 16, 1952

The Squirrel / Irresistible You (They Didn't Believe Me) / Indiana; Donna Lee / Liza

(14) *Jazz Showcase 5007*

CP, Frank Morgan (as), Don Wilkerson (ts), Amos Trice (p), Dave Bryant (b), Lawrence Marable (d)
Zorthian's Ranch, Altadena, CA, July 14, 1952

Hot House / Embraceable You   (35) **Royal Jazz RJD505**

Night In Tunisia / Ornithology   **Royal Jazz RJD505**

Note: Issues of the above session give an incorrect date, location and personnel (including Teddy Edwards (ts) and Roy Haynes (d))

CHARLIE PARKER

CP (as), Duke Jordan (p), Charles Mingus (b), Phil Brown (d), Bob Garrity (mc)
Birdland, NYC, September 20, 1952

Ornithology / 52nd Street Theme   (14a,36) *Mark MG101*

Note: Some issues of this broadcast are reproduced much too fast

CP (as), unknown ob and strings-1, Walter Bishop (p), Mundell Lowe (g), Teddy Kotick (b), Max Roach (d)
Rockland Palace Ballroom, NYC, September 26, 1952

Rocker-1 / Moose The Mooche* / My Little Suede Shoes-1 / Sly Mongoose / Laura-1 / Star Eyes* / This Time The Dream's On Me / Cool Blues /
Lester Leaps In   (17) *Charlie Parker PLP401*

Just Friends-1 / I'll Remember April-1 / Easy To Love-1* / What Is This Thing Called Love-1 / I Didn't Know What Time It Was-1 /
Repetition-1 / East Of The Sun-1 / April In Paris-1 / Out Of Nowhere-1 / Rocker-1 / Sly Mongoose**

(17) *Charlie Parker CP(2)502*

East Of The Sun-1 / What Is This Thing Called Love-1 / Stardust-1 / Ornithology-1 / Easy to Love-1 / Just Friends-1 / Dancing In The Dark-1 /
Gold Rush-1 / Don't Blame Me / Repetition-1 / Everything Happens To Me-1*

(17) **Jazz Classics JZCL6010**

Note: Two different recorded sources preserved parts of this material, and the source of PLP401 suffered from serious pitch fluctuation, corrected on later issues; the version of *Lester Leaps In* on (17) uses both sources to create a stereo effect. Woideck notes that the two versions of *Sly Mongoose*, heard separately on (17), are edited together on *CP(2)502*

Earl Swope (tb), CP (as), Bill Shanahan (p), Charlie Byrd (g), Mert Oliver (b), Don Lamond (d), unknown cga
Howard Theatre, Washington, DC, October 18, 1952

Scrapple From The Apple / Out Of Nowhere / Now's The Time-1

(1) *VGM VGM0009*

Cool Blues / 52nd Street Theme* VGM VGM0009

1-Charlie Walp (tp), Kai Winding, Rob Swope (tb), Zoot Sims (ts) added

CP (as), John Lewis (p), Milt Jackson (vib), Percy Heath (b), Kenny Clarke (d)
Birdland, NYC, November 1, 1952

How High The Moon / Embraceable You / 52nd Street Theme

(14a) *Mark MG101*

CP (as), unknown ob, strings and harp, Walter Bishop (p), Walter Yost (b), Roy Haynes (d), Candido (cga-1)
Carnegie Hall, NYC, November 14, 1952

(1st concert) Just Friends / Easy To Love / Repetition-1 / Strings Theme

(31,A) *Philology 214W5*

(2nd concert) Just Friends / Easy To Love / Repetition-1 / Strings Theme / Night In Tunisia-1,2 / 52nd Street Theme-1,2

(A) *FDC1005/6*

2-Dizzy Gillespie (tp) replaces ob, strings and harp

Note: Billie Holiday was one of the artists on this concert (with Buster Harding (p), Tony Scott (cl)) but her *Tenderly* on **Philology W80.2**, claimed as including CP and Dizzy Gillespie, bears no trace of either of them

CHARLIE PARKER
Joe Gordon (tp), CP (as), Dick Twardzik (p), Charles Mingus (b), Roy Haynes (d), Symphony Sid (mc)
Hi-Hat Club, Boston, December 14, 1952

Ornithology / Cool Blues / Groovin' High / Don't Blame Me / Scrapple From The Apple / Cheryl / Jumpin' With Symphony Sid*

(58) **Uptown UPCD27.42**

Prob. as above plus poss. Bill Wellington (ts)
Christy's, Framingham, MA, c. December 1952
I'll Remember April**   (8) *Charlie Parker PLP404*

CP (as), Hank Jones (p), Teddy Kotick (b), Max Roach (d)
NYC, December 30, 1952

1118-3	*The Song Is You (I Hear Music)*	(62,H,J) *Clef 89144*
1119-7	*Laird Baird*	(62,H,J) *Clef 89144*
1120-2	*Kim*	(62,H) *Verve MGV8005*
1120-4	*Kim*	(62,H,J) *Clef 89129*
1121-2	*Cosmic Rays*	(62,H,J) *Clef 89129*
1121-5	*Cosmic Rays*	(62,H) *Verve MGV8005*

MILES DAVIS
Miles Davis (tp), Sonny Rollins, CP (ts), Walter Bishop (p), Percy Heath (b), Philly Joe Jones (d)
NYC, January 30, 1953

450	*Compulsion*	(28) *Prestige PRLP7044*
451-1	*Serpent's Tooth*	(28) *Prestige PRLP7044*
451-2	*Serpent's Tooth*	(28) *Prestige PRLP7044*
452	*'Round Midnight*	(28) *Prestige PRLP7044*

Note: Though first released after CP's death, he was credited as "Charlie Chan" for contractual reasons

CHARLIE PARKER
CP (as), Brew Moore (ts-1), Paul Bley (p), Dick Garcia (g), Neil Michaud (b), Ted Paskert (d)
CBFT-TV, Montréal, February 5, 1953
Cool Blues / Bernie's Tune-1,2 / Don't Blame Me / Wahoo-1
                                    (59) *Jazz Showcase 5003*

2-CP out

Valdo Williams (p), Hal Gaylor (b), Billy Graham (d) replace Moore, Bley, Michaud and Paskert
Chez Paree, Montréal, February 7, 1953
Ornithology   (59) *Jazz Showcase 5003*
Cool Blues   (59) **Uptown UPCD27.36**

Steep Wade (p), Bob Rudd (b), Bob Malloy (d) replace Williams, Gaylor and Graham
Same location and date
Embraceable You   (59) *Jazz Showcase 5003*
Moose The Mooche / Now's The Time   (59) **Uptown UPCD27.36**

CP (as) with the Harris-Jackson Herd: Bill Harris (tb), Charlie Mariano (as), Harry Johnson (ts), Sonny Truitt (p), Chubby Jackson (b), Morey Feld (d), band v, Bob Garrity (mc)
Band Box, NYC, February 16, 1953
Your Father's Moustache-v   (36) *Queen-Disc Q-002*

CP (as) with "The Orchestra": Ed Leddy, Marky Markowitz, Charlie Walp, Bob Carey (tp), Earl Swope, Rob Swope, Don Spiker (tb), Jim Riley (as), Angelo Tompros, Jim Parker, Ben Lary (ts), Jack Nimitz (bs), Jack Holliday (p, arr), Mert Oliver (b), Joe Timer (d, arr), Bill Potts, Gerry Mulligan, Al Cohn, Johnny Mandel (arr)
Club Kavakos, Washington, DC, February 22, 1953
Fine And Dandy / These Foolish Things / Light Green / Thou Swell / Willis / Don't Blame Me** / Something To Remember You By; Blue Room / Roundhouse   (1) *Musician E1-60019*

CP (as), Jack Holliday (p), Frank Skeete (b), Max Roach (d)
Howard Theatre, Washington, DC, March 8, 1953
Ornithology / Out Of Nowhere / Cool Blues / Anthropology
                                               (1) *VGM VGM0009*

CP (as), Red Garland (p), Bernie Griggs (b), Roy Haynes (d), John McLellan (mc)
Storyville Club, Boston, March 10, 1953

Moose The Mooche / I'll Walk Alone / Ornithology / Out Of Nowhere*

(2) *Blue Note BT85108*

CP (as), Milt Buckner (org), Bernie McKay (g), Cornelius Thomas (d), Leonard Feather (mc)
Band Box, NYC, March 23, 1953

Groovin' High

(48) *Queen-Disc Q-002*

CP (as), Walter Bishop (p), Kenny O'Brien (b), Roy Haynes (d), Leonard Feather, unknown (not Bob Garrity) (mcs)
Band Box, NYC, March 30, 1953

Caravan (theme) / Star Eyes / Ornithology / Diggin' Diz / Embraceable You

(48) *Klacto MG100*

CP (as), John Lewis (p), Curley Russell (b), Kenny Clarke (d), Candido (cga-1), Bob Garrity (mc)
Birdland, NYC, May 9, 1953

Cool Blues / Star Eyes / Moose The Mooche / Lullaby Of Birdland (theme) / Broadway-1 / Lullaby Of Birdland (theme)-1

(14a) *Klacto MG100*

THE QUINTET OF THE YEAR
Dizzy Gillespie (tp, v), CP (as), Bud Powell (p), Charles Mingus (b), Max Roach (d)
Massey Hall, Toronto, May 15, 1953

Perdido* / Salt Peanuts-vDG / All The Things You Are; 52nd Street Theme

(29) *Debut DLP2*

Wee* / Hot House / Night In Tunisia

(29) *Debut DLP4*

Note: CP originally credited as "Charlie Chan" for contractual reasons. The performances of *Perdido* and *Wee* heard on **Debut 12-DCD-4402-2** are not complete, but simulate complete versions by repeating edited portions of the existing recording

DIZZY GILLESPIE QUINTET WITH CHARLIE PARKER
Dizzy Gillespie, Miles Davis-1 (tp), CP (as), Sahib Shihab (bs), Wade Legge (p), Lou Hackney (b), Al Jones (d), Joe Carroll (v)
Birdland, NYC, May 23, 1953

The Bluest Blues-1,vJC / On The Sunny Side Of The Street-vJC

(14a) *Klacto MG102*

CHARLIE PARKER AND HIS ORCHESTRA
Junior Collins (fr-h), Charlie Parker (as), Al Block (f), Hal McKusick (cl), Tommy Mace (ob), Manny Thaler (bsn), Tony Aless (p), Charles Mingus (b), Max Roach (d), Dave Lambert Singers (incl. Annie Ross, Dave Lambert, Jerry Parker, Butch Birdsall) (v), Gil Evans (arr, cond)
NYC, May 25, 1953

1238-1/-2	*In The Still Of The Night**	(67,H) **Verve 837 141-2**
1238-3	*In The Still Of The Night*	(67,H) **Verve 837 141-2**
1238-4	*In The Still Of The Night**	(67,H) **Verve 837 141-2**
1238-5	*In The Still Of The Night*	(67,H) **Verve 837 141-2**
1238-6	*In The Still Of The Night*	(67,H) **Verve 837 141-2**
1238-7	*In The Still Of The Night*	(67,69,H,J) Clef 11100
1239-1/-2	*Old Folks**	(67,H) **Verve 837 141-2**
1239-3	*Old Folks*	(67,H) **Verve 837 141-2**
1239-4/-5	*Old Folks**	(67,H) **Verve 837 141-2**
1239-6	*Old Folks*	(67,H) **Verve 837 141-2**
1239-7	*Old Folks**	(67,H) **Verve 837 141-2**
1239-8	*Old Folks*	(67,H) **Verve 837 141-2**
1239-9	*Old Folks*	(67,H,J) Clef 11100
1240-9	*If I Love Again*	(67,H,J) *Verve MGV8009*

BUD POWELL TRIO WITH CHARLIE PARKER

CP (as), Bud Powell (p), Charles Mingus (b), Art Taylor (d), Candido (cga-1), Bob Garrity (mc)

Birdland, NYC, May 30, 1953

Moose The Mooche-1 / Cheryl-1   (14a) *Queen-Disc Q-002*

Max Roach (d) replaces Taylor

Same location and period

Dance Of The Infidels   (14a) *Parktec 4627-1*

Note: Some issues of this track are reproduced much too fast

CHARLIE PARKER

CP, John McLellan (speech)

Station WHDH, Boston, June 13, 1953

Interview   (2) **Blue Note CDP7 85108-2***

Herb Pomeroy (tp), CP (as), Dean Erle (p), Bernie Griggs (b), Bill Grant (d), Symphony Sid (mc)

Hi-Hat Club, Boston, June 14, 1953

Cool Blues / Scrapple From The Apple / Laura

Cheryl / Ornithology / 52nd Street Theme   (15) **Fresh Sound FSCD-1006**
     (15) *Phoenix LP10**

Hi-Hat Club, Boston, prob. June 1953

Cool Blues / Out Of Nowhere / My Funny Valentine / Ornithology

     (16) **Fresh Sound FSCD-1007**

Benny Harris (tp), CP (as), Al Haig (p), Charles Mingus (b), Art Taylor (d)

The Open Door, NYC, July 26, 1953

Out Of Nowhere / Star Eyes / Cool Blues / East Of The Sun / The Song Is You / 52nd Street Theme / Ornithology / Scrapple From The Apple /

My Old Flame / My Little Suede Shoes   (51) **Philology W854-2**

I Remember You / All The Things You Are / Just You, Just Me* / I'll Remember April / Hot House / 52nd Street Theme / I Cover The Waterfront / This Time The Dream's On Me / I'll Remember April; 52nd Street Theme*-1

(52) **Philology W855.2**

1-Bud Powell (p) is heard very briefly at the end of this track

CHARLIE PARKER QUARTET
CP (as), Al Haig (p), Percy Heath (b), Max Roach (d)
NYC, July 30, 1953

1246-1	Chi Chi	(62,H) *Verve MGV8005*
1246-2	Chi Chi*	(62,H) **Verve 837 141-2**
1246-3	Chi Chi	(62,H) *Verve MGV8005*
1246-4	Chi Chi	(62,H) **Verve 825 671-2**
1246-5	Chi Chi*	(62,H) **Verve 837 141-2**
1246-6	Chi Chi	(62,H,J) Clef 89138
1247-3	I Remember You	(62,H,J) Clef 89138
1248-1	Now's The Time	(62,H,J) *Clef MGC517*
1249-1/-2	Confirmation*	(62,H) **Verve 837 141-2**
1249-3	Confirmation	(62,H,J) *Clef MGC517*

CHARLIE PARKER
Herb Pomeroy (tp), CP (as), Sir Charles Thompson (p), Jimmy Woode (b), Kenny Clarke (d), John McLellan (mc)
Storyville Club, Boston, September 22, 1953
Now's The Time / Don't Blame Me / Dancing On The Ceiling* / Cool Blues / Groovin' High
(2) Blue Note BT85108

Chet Baker (tp), CP (as), Jimmy Rowles (p), Carson Smith (b), Shelly Manne (d)
University of Oregon, Eugene, OR, November 5, 1953
How High The Moon* / Barbados* / Cool Blues*   (14, 24) Stash ST-260

CP, Paul Desmond, John McLellan (speech)
Station WHDH, Boston, January 1954
Interview

(35) **Philology W80.2**

Herbie Williams (tp), CP (as), Rollins Griffith (p), Jimmy Woode (b), Marquis Foster (d), Symphony Sid (mc)
Hi-Hat Club, Boston, January 18, 1954
Ornithology / Out Of Nowhere / Cool Blues / Scrapple From The Apple*

(35) **Uptown UPCD27.42**

George Solano (d) replaces Foster, Jay Migliori (ts) added
Hi-Hat Club, Boston, January 23, 1954
Now's The Time / Out Of Nowhere / My Little Suede Shoes / Jumpin' With Symphony Sid (theme)

(16) *Fresh Sound FSR303*

As January 18
Hi-Hat Club, Boston, January 24, 1954
Cool Blues / My Little Suede Shoes* / Ornithology / Out Of Nowhere / Jumpin' With Symphony Sid (theme)

(16) *Phoenix LP12*

Hi-Hat Club, Boston, January 1954
Ornithology / My Little Suede Shoes / Now's The Time / Groovin' High

(15) *Phoenix LP10*

CHARLIE PARKER WITH STAN KENTON AND HIS ORCHESTRA
CP (as) with Sam Noto, Vic Minichelli, Buddy Childers, Stu Williamson, Don Smith (tp), Milt Gold, Joe Ciavardone, Frank Rosolino, George Roberts (tb), Charlie Mariano, Dave Schildkraut (as), Mike Cicchetti, Bill Perkins (ts), Tony Ferina (bs), Stan Kenton (p), Bob Lesher (g), Don Bagley (b), Stan Levey (d), Joe Lippman-1, Bill Holman-2 (arr)
Civic Auditorium, Portland, OR, February 25, 1954
Night And Day-1 / My Funny Valentine-2 / Cherokee-2

(35) *Jazz Supreme JS703*

CHARLIE PARKER QUINTET

CP (as), Walter Bishop (p), Jerome Darr (g-1), Teddy Kotick (b), Roy Haynes (d)

NYC, March 31, 1954

1531-2	I Get A Kick Out Of You	(H) Verve MGV8007
1531-7	I Get A Kick Out Of You-1	(69,H,J) Verve MGV8007
1532-1	Just One Of Those Things-1	(69,H,J) Verve MGV8007
1533-2	My Heart Belongs To Daddy-1	(69,H,J) Verve MGV8007
1534-1	I've Got You Under My Skin	(69,H,J) Verve MGV8007

CHARLIE PARKER

CP (as), unknown ob and strings, Walter Bishop (p), Teddy Kotick or Tommy Potter (b), Roy Haynes (d)

Birdland, NYC, August 27, 1954

| | What Is This Thing Called Love / Repetition / Easy To Love / East Of The Sun | |
| | | (14a) Spook Jazz SPJ6604 |

CP (as), John Lewis (p), Percy Heath (b), Kenny Clarke (d)

Carnegie Hall, NYC, September 25, 1954

| | The Song Is You / My Funny Valentine / Cool Blues | (54) Roulette RE127 |

CHARLIE PARKER QUINTET

CP (as), Walter Bishop (p), Billy Bauer (g), Teddy Kotick (b), Art Taylor (d)

NYC, December 10, 1954

2115-4	Love For Sale	(H) Verve MGV8007
2115-5	Love For Sale	(69,H,J) Verve MGV8001
2116-2	I Love Paris	(69,H,J) Verve MGV8007
2116-3	I Love Paris	(H) Verve MGV8001

CHARLIE PARKER

CP (as, speech), Dick Meldonian (speech)
Dick Meldonian's home, NYC, c. 1954
    Musical Discussion

(43) **Philology W846.2**

POSTSCRIPT – The "BIRD" soundtrack

CP (as, rec. November 26, 1945) overdubbed by Red Rodney (tp), Charles McPherson (as), Walter Davis Jr (p), Ron Carter (b), John Guerin (d)
Los Angeles, 1987
(S5851-4)   *Now's The Time*

As last except Jon Faddis (tp) replaces Rodney
Same location and period
(S5853-2)   *Ko Ko*

CP (as, rec. September 24, 1948) overdubbed by unknown strings, Barry Harris (p), Chuck Berghofer (b), John Guerin (d), Lennie Niehaus (arr, cond)
Same location and period
(B903-5)   *Parker's Mood*

As last except CP (as, rec. November 30, 1949), Tom Boyd (ob) added
Same location and period
(321-3)   *April In Paris*

CP (as), Art Blakey (d, both rec. May 17–21, 1950) overdubbed by Jon Faddis (tp), Charles McPherson (as), Charlie Shoemake (vib), Walter Davis Jr (p), Ron Carter (b), John Guerin (d)
Same location and period
    Ornithology

CP (as, rec. August 1951) overdubbed by Monty Alexander (p), Ray Brown (b), John Guerin (d)

Same location and period
All Of Me / I Can't Believe That You're In Love With Me

As last except CP (as, rec. September 26, 1952)
Same location and period
Lester Leaps In / This Time The Dream's On Me

As last except overdubbed by Walter Davis (p), Ron Carter (b), John Guerin (d)
Same location and period
Cool Blues

As last except overdubbed by unknown strings, Tom Boyd (ob), Barry Harris (p), Chuck Berghofer (b), John Guerin (d), Lennie Niehaus (arr, cond)
Same location and period
Laura

All on (X) *Columbia CK44299*

INDEX TO DISCOGRAPHY

Recently available CDs are shown here; though some may technically be unavailable (and that number will of course grow), they should all be traceable through specialist retailers. Basic recommended albums are those printed in bold type; box sets larger than a double CD are shown separately at the end of this list and, in the foregoing discography, it is often just the tracks which are only to be found on a box set that are cross-referenced to this index. Items which have not been available on CD are not shown here.

(1) **Blue Note 5 22626 2: The Washington Concerts**
(2) Blue Note 7 85108 2: At Storyville
(3) Classics 740: Jay McShann 1941-43
(3a) Classics 935: Dizzy Gillespie 1945–46
(4) **Classics 980: Charlie Parker 1945–47**
(5) **Classics 1000: Charlie Parker 1947**
(6) **Classics 1103: Charlie Parker 1948–49**
(7) Classics 1222: Charlie Parker 1950

notes

introduction

(p. 1) *sound of the record on the radio...* BBC Light Programme, prob. December 24, 1955. The announcer who read a script prepared for him was David Jacobs, later famous for his connection with pop and middle-of-the-road music.

(p. 2) *any other musician ever...* Another contender is guitarist Charlie Christian, whose career was so short that all his official recorded work was done within a two-year span, but whose alternate takes and live recordings add considerably to his total output.

(p. 3) *"If you come on a band tense..."* Quoted by Gene Ramey, *Melody Maker*, May 28, 1955 (reprinted in Woideck, *Companion*, pp. 135–39).

(p. 4) *he was fond of reading...* Interview by Robert Reisner, *Jazz Review*, September–October 1960.

(p. 4) *"He studied the workings..."; "But Bird was always able..."* Chan Richardson Parker, p. 40; p. 56. (All page refs. are to the English edition.)

(p. 5) *"He rejected the Church..."* Reisner, p. 139. There is also a comment by Chan Richardson Parker (pp. 40–41) that he became briefly interested in Reichian therapy.

(p. 5) *he described as his "judges"...* Reisner, p. 40. The movie in question was undoubtedly Jean Cocteau's *Orphée* (1949), an updating of the Greek myth about the musician Orpheus.

(p. 5) *"Poverty and want angered him..."* Reisner, p. 73 (see also p. 128).

(p. 5) *"They just came to see..."* Reisner, p. 206.

(p. 6) *"I've seen a well-known musician..."* *Playboy*, November 1960. There is no indication that Gillespie was referring directly to Parker, but aspects of his performance when drinking make him an obvious example of the phenomenon described.

(p. 6) *"Charlie had no childhood..."* Reisner, p. 170.

(p. 7) *"His thing was like..."* Taylor, p. 233.

(p. 7)   *"He had a great resentment..."* Ellington, p. 107.

(p. 7)   *"I don't let anyone..."* Ahmed Basheer interview in Reisner, p. 41.

(p. 7)   *"If I saved my money..."* *Jazz Review*, September–October 1960.

(p. 7)   *"Bread is your only friend..."* Reisner, p. 14.

(p. 7)   *"Life has many changes..."* Interview by the author, BBC Radio London, August 10, 1972 (partially used on the soundtrack of *Triumph Of The Underdog*, dir. Don McGlynn, 1997).

(p. 7)   *"[Bird] put something else..."* Interview by Mike Dean, BBC TV, August 1972.

1 body and soul

(p. 9)   *Charlie's birth certificate... ; passport...* These are, respectively, reproduced in Reisner, p. 161 and simulated in Parker and Paudras, p. 1.

(p. 9)   *her first daughter-in-law...* Giddins, p. 26.

(p. 9)   *she herself was interviewed...* *Jazz Review*, September–October 1960.

(p. 9)   *she was not more than about 17...* Russell, p. 32; Koch, p. 7; and the first edition of this present book.

(p. 10)   *he stated repeatedly...* Interview by Marshall Stearns and John Maher, prob. May 1 1950 (transcribed in Woideck, *Companion*, pp. 91–109 and Vail, pp. 74–77).

(p. 10)   *"older than his mother..."* *Jazz Review*, September–October 1960. Presumably the confusion experienced by Russell and later authors about Addie's age derives solely from this ironic remark.

(p. 10)   *two years older than Charlie...* *Jazz Review*, September–October 1960.

(p. 10)   *Charles Parker Sr's own father...* Reisner, p. 124.

(p. 10)   *bringing in the regular money...* Addie said of the Kansas City, Kansas period that Charlie "was raised at a Catholic day school because I was working all the time" (*Jazz Review*, September–October 1960).

(p. 10)   *any more than he drank...* Giddins, p. 25.

(p. 11)   *when he was seven years old...* Interview by Mike Levin and John S. Wilson, *Down Beat*, September 9, 1949 (transcribed in Woideck, *Companion*, pp. 69–79 and partially reproduced in Vail, p. 66).

(p. 11)   *at the Kansas City, Kansas school...* Giddins, p. 28.

(p. 11)   *Charles Sr.'s presence...* Giddins (p. 26) speculates that the father had already left the household, as opposed to being merely absent for most of the time. However, although Addie's estimates of date and age are not always reliable, she said (*Jazz Review*, September–October 1960) that "His father and I had been separated eight years" by the time of Charles Sr.'s death in late 1939.

(p. 11)   *raised alongside Charlie...* Addie referred to their joint upbringing (*Jazz Review*, September–October 1960) with the words "John never knew the difference because I treated them both equally."

(p. 11)   *a dining-car waiter...* Stearns and Maher, op. cit. According to Charlie, "He was a waiter on this train. Santa Fe. Runs from Kansas City to Chicago. Los Angeles and back. Florida and back. Texas and back," which sounds like the same locomotive immortalized in the 1940s song *The Atchison, Topeka and the Santa Fe*. Concerning his actual work, it is of course possible that he was first a chef and then transferred to being a waiter.

(p. 12)   *"As far as I can gather..."* Reisner, p. 172.

(p. 12)   *"We were the little cats..."* Gillespie, p. 214.

(p. 12)   *"Charlie discovered jazz..."* Levin and Wilson, op. cit.

(p. 12)   *one of the most popular saxophonists...* Private recordings from June 1950, released as *The Apartment Sessions*, include a moment where Parker plays the 1920s novelty tune *Dizzy Fingers* and then describes himself as "Rudy Wiedoeft." There is a fleeting reference to the same figuration in the February 12, 1949 broadcast version of *Barbados*.

(p. 13)   *"I wasn't ready for it then... Coop, coop!"* Stearns and Maher, op. cit.

(p. 13)   *The graduation ceremony...* The programme, reproduced in Giddins (p. 38), also featured readings of African-American poets including Langston Hughes, Claude McKay, Countee Cullen and Phyllis Wheatley, with the choir performing spirituals and an excerpt from the *Negro Choral Symphony* by Major N. Clark Smith, the school's distinguished former music director.

(p. 13)   *"his inseparable friend..."* *Jazz Review*, September–October 1960.

(p. 13)   *"just beautiful..."*; *"but I finished paying..."* *Jazz Review*, September–October 1960.

(p. 14)   *supervision by his half-brother...* Referring to this period, clubowner Tutty Clarkin said (Reisner, p. 68) that "The only way I could keep Charlie straight was to tell him his mother and half-brother were coming out."

(p. 14)   *used to smuggle Charlie...* Russell, p. 52.

(p. 14)   *passed him the marijuana...* Reisner, p. 69.

(p. 14) *"Pres would sit on the bandstand..."* Quoted by Chan Richardson Parker, p. 22.

(p. 16) *"I tried playing..."* Reisner, p. 23, seemingly paraphrased from Addie Parker interview, *Jazz Review*, September–October 1960.

(p. 16) *"I'd learned to play..."* Stearns and Maher, op. cit.

(p. 17) *"I was doing alright..."* Levin and Wilson, op. cit.

(p. 17) *One of Parker's favourite cross-references... Dawn On The Desert*, shown in Owens' book as Figure 16 of Charlie's preferred formulas, is heard for instance between 0:41 and 0:50 on the 1953 recording of *Perdido*. (The timings refer to the track as originally released, not to the artificially extended version issued in 1990 where the quotation falls between 1:13 and 1:22.)

(p. 17) *"I put quite a bit of study..."* Interview by John McLellan and Paul Desmond, broadcast, WHDH, January 1954 (transcribed in Woideck, *Companion*, pp. 121–31).

(p. 18) *"just the way he did..."* Giddins, p. 45.

(p. 18) *found his mother in bed...* Reisner, p. 71.

(p. 18) *proposed to her on July 24...* The date comes from Rebecca's interview with Giddins (p. 43), but differs from Stanley Crouch who apparently interviewed her earlier (*New Republic*, February 27, 1989, reprinted in Woideck, *Companion*, pp. 251–62). He quotes Charlie's proposal as being on "the night that Joe Louis lost to Max Schmeling," which was in fact June 19, 1936. No one, so far, has suggested that he proposed because Louis lost.

(p. 19) *"It fell with a deafening sound..."* Melody Maker, May 28, 1955.

(p. 19) *"I broke three ribs..."* Stearns and Maher, op. cit.

(p. 19) *"Jas. Parker, 1516 Olive St. ..."* Woideck, *Music and Life*, p. 9.

(p. 20) *The promoter who had hired...* Levin and Wilson, op. cit.

(p. 20) *"He called me upstairs..."* Interview by Gary Giddins and Kendrick Simmons, *Celebrating Bird* (Sony Video Software, 1987).

(p. 20) *"I don't know if you can..."* Woideck, *Music and Life*, p. 10.

(p. 20) *"It all came from..."; "I didn't know..."* Interview by Leonard Feather, *Metronome*, August 1947 (in Woideck, *Companion*, pp. 61–65).

(p. 20) *stating that he was fifteen...* It's perhaps worth underlining that he remained fifteen until late August 1936, which would put less than a year between his first involvement and the further rite of passage marked by injecting himself in front of his wife.

(p. 20) *"He'd come to sessions..."* *Down Beat*, January 26, 1967, reprinted in Morgenstern, p. 250. Brookmeyer added that, presumably in the late 1940s, "Bird used to write to him about coming to New York. 'Those bebop drummers are driving me crazy,' he said in one letter. But Phil never left town."

(p. 20) *described as Charlie's supplier...* Reisner, p. 67.

(p. 21) *saxophone exercise book by Klosé...* Woideck (*Music and Life*, p. 136) identifies the record as the 1951 *K.C. Blues*, where the quotation appears at 2:46, and notes that the phrase occurs in several live recordings such as the March 8, 1947 version of *Wee* (at 0:58).

(p. 21) *"Naturally it wasn't done with mirrors..."* Interview by McLellan and Desmond, op. cit.

(p. 21) *until he could repeat them...* Gene Ramey interview in Dance, p. 274.

(p. 21) *he could still do so...* Lee Konitz and Dave Brubeck interview, *Northwest Review*, Spring 1958.

(p. 21) *"When I first knew Bird..."*; *"When Bird was sixteen..."* Interview by Jean Stein van den Heuvel in Reisner, pp. 67–68.

2 the jumpin' blues

(p. 22) *three different versions...* McShann has also given three different versions of his own birth year – 1909 appears in publications dating from the '50s, 1914 is the year implied by Ross Russell's interview with the pianist, and 1916 appears in more recent references. Some of the material in the present chapter was first published in my article on McShann in *Musica Jazz*, February 2002.

(p. 22) *"After I got through..."* Dance, p. 251.

(p. 22) *"We were, you know..."* Sidran, p. 17.

(p. 23) *"I was in a rhythm-section..."* Russell, p. 93.

(p. 23) *"I heard a broadcast..."* Interview by Gary Giddins and Kendrick Simmons, *Celebrating Bird* (Sony Video Software, 1987).

(p. 23) *"He'd improved a good bit..."* Interview by Don Gazzaway, *Jazz Review*, December 1959–February 1960.

(p. 23) *He also described himself...* *Jazz Review*, December 1959–February 1960.

(p. 23) *records on which Smith played...* Smith's solos on *Baby Look At You* and *Cherry Red*, from a 1939 session led by Johnson, are transcribed in Schuller, p. 797. The track *Jump For Joy* from the same session, rejected initially because of its inconclusive ending and/or the recording balance, was released for the first time in 2001 on the Hot Lips Page reissue *Jump For Joy!* (Columbia 503282 2).

(p. 23)   *only thing on record remotely like...* There are a couple of tantalizing references to other possible (and unidentified) influences on Charlie, in the Don Byas interview by Taylor (p. 53) and in Gillespie with Gene Lees (*Down Beat*, May 25, 1961, reprinted in Woideck, *Companion*, pp. 161–67).

The text of the latter includes the sentences: "You see, Charlie Parker had a Buster Smith background. And, of course, there was Old Yard – an old alto man – in Kansas City." I believe this to be an error of transcription, and that Gillespie most likely said: "That, of course, was Old Yard." His own book (footnote, p. 151) makes it clear that he believed "Old Yardbird" to be the nickname of Buster Smith.

(p. 24)   *"In my band, we'd split solos..."* Jazz Review, December 1959–February 1960.

(p. 24)   *in September 1938...* Woideck (*Music and Life*, p. 14) and Koch (p. 17) give "1938" and "early 1938" for Smith's move, but the date shown here is taken from the painstaking research of Chilton (p. 307).

(p. 24)   *"That is when I realized..."* Reisner, p. 147.

(p. 24)   *Whether or not Charlie...* Stearns and Maher (op. cit.) speculated that Marshall Stearns would have heard Charlie as a member of McShann's seven-piece band in K.C. "in about '40," adding that he "came out with George Avakian." But the recollection of Avakian (e-mail to the author, July 18, 2004) is that the trip took place in summer 1939 and that Parker was not in the band, its most impressive saxophonist being William Scott.

(p. 25)   *"Once in Kansas City..."* Reisner, p. 41.

(p. 25)   *"His mother, who didn't approve..."* Levin and Wilson, op. cit.

(p. 25)   *psychiatric tests while in Kansas City...* Letter dated February 7, 1947, reproduced in Parker and Paudras, p. 72 and quoted in Russell, pp. 236–38.

(p. 25)   *"A guy comes up..."; "According to what..."* Interview by Max Jones, *Melody Maker*, September 11, 1954, reprinted in Jones, p. 234. The reference to the saxophone's bell is frequently misquoted as "blew the hell off that thing," which makes little sense.

(p. 26)   *"I was off at the Woodside..."* Interview by Chris Goddard, NEA Jazz Oral History Project, January 13, 1981 (in Woideck, *Companion*, pp. 142–51).

(p. 26)   *This was where Coleman Hawkins...* Danny Barker, notes to *Chu* (1967 reissue), Epic EE22008.

(p. 26) *for $9.00 a week plus meals...* Levin and Wilson, op. cit. This represented quite a reasonable metropolitan wage, when compared with the musicians' salaries in Kansas City clubs of $1.25 per eight-hour shift, as described in the same article.

(p. 26) *owned by bandleader Andy Kirk...* Dahl, p. 105. As confirmed in the Buster Smith interview quoted in the previous paragraph, this seems more accurate than Russell's account taken from Reisner (p. 107), which has John Williams being the owner. Dahl, however, claims Kirk's restaurant only opened in 1940.

(p. 27) *"Lot of guitar players..."* Gitler, *Swing to Bop*, p. 70. Fleet's interview confirms that these sessions took place in 1939.

(p. 27) *"I kept thinking..."; "At the time..."* Levin and Wilson, op. cit., paraphrased in Shapiro and Hentoff, p. 342.

(p. 28) *"dissipation"* Metronome, August 1947 (in Woideck, *Companion*, pp. 61–65).

(p. 28) *at the start of 1940...* This conventional dating relies on various McShann interviews, but Russell implied that the Leonard stint and Charlie's joining the enlarged McShann band took place in early 1939. The rationale for this is based on a note of Russell's interview with Leonard, referring to a cheque dated January 10, 1939 (see discussion in Woideck, *Music and Life*, p. 14, 18 and 245). The present author, having tried (and failed) to convince himself that this chronology is plausible, is reduced to noting that a cheque made out in early January 1940 could have been mistakenly filled out as "1939" – and that the mistake may be responsible for it residing in Leonard's files decades later.

(p. 29) *"the first Kansas City outfit..."* Down Beat, November 1, 1939, quoted in McCarthy, p. 151.

(p. 29) *"We went into Chicago..."* Sidran, p. 16. Gene Ramey also mentioned this intended session, dating it to September 1939, when interviewed and translated by Francois Postif, *Jazz Hot*, March 1962 (reprinted in *Les Grands Interviews de Jazz Hot*, Paris: L'Instant, 1989).

(p. 29) *"He was an* interested *cat..."* Dance, p. 252.

(p. 29) *Soon, the band was to be heard...* Details in this paragraph from *Down Beat* (various issues), summarized in McCarthy, pp. 151–52.

(p. 30) *"These transcriptions..."* Schuller, p. 794. Long thought to have been made for use as radio transcriptions, the tracks are now believed to be recordings solely for the interest of the musicians and their local fans. It's a pity that Schuller goes on (footnote, p. 795) to endorse the claim of Benny Harris (Reisner, p. 107) that Gillespie was unaware of Charlie until introduced to him by Harris, around the time Charlie joined Earl Hines. As we shall see, this is a considerable exaggeration.

(p. 31)   *"If you listen..."* Dance, p. 275.

(p. 31)   *less than forty-five minutes' rehearsal...* Gene Ramey, *Melody Maker*, May 28, 1955. Jay McShann notes (Dance, p. 252) that "So long as we were playing from a written arrangement, I had John [Jackson] phrase it, but when it was a 'head' tune, then Bird phrased it. He set most of the riffs on the heads, too. Bird didn't have the tone John had, but he had so much feeling."

(p. 31)   *"Everything had a musical significance..."* ibid.

(p. 32)   *His longest surviving solo...* Veteran bandleader Don Radman fronted McShann's outfit for a couple of gigs, and was impressed by a four-chorus Parker solo on *The Whistler And His Dog*, according to Frank Driggs in Hentoff and McCarthy (p. 229).

(p. 32)   *"He used to tell me..."* Gitler, *Swing to Bop*, pp. 66–67.

(p. 32)   *"Bird started blowing..."* Dance, pp. 276–77.

(p. 32)   *"The jazz set forth..."* Metronome, March 1942.

(p. 33)   *while he was visiting Kansas City...* According to Shipton (p. 69), this was almost certainly on June 24, 1940, while the McShann band were playing a summer season at Fairyland Park in KC.

(p. 33)   *"He played in the same style..."* Reisner, p. 149.

(p. 33)   *"He wanted me to hear..."* Giddins, p. 12.

(p. 33)   *"Well, the first time..."; "I don't remember..."* McLellan and Desmond, op. cit.

(p. 33)   *"I don't know..."* Levin and Wilson, op. cit.

(p. 33)   *"Bird's ability and authority..."* Keepnews, p. 93.

(p. 34)   *"I began to listen..."* Feather, p. 15.

(p. 34)   *one writer believes...* McCarthy, p. 152.

(p. 34)   *"Bird would blow..."* Dance, p. 253.

(p. 35)   *at the end of 1942...* Shipton (p. 106) suggests the date may be in early 1943, though clearly both Parker and Gillespie had joined the band by the time of the Chicago session referred to below.

(p. 35)   *"The audition took place..."* John Rowland, notes to Charlie Parker Records CP503.

(p. 36)   *no records were made...* Information on the band's repertoire from George Hoefer, *Down Beat*, April 25, 1963.

(p. 36)   *"My contribution and Charlie Parker's..."* Interview by the author, BBC Radio London, prob. March 1, 1980.

(p. 36)   *"I think that was where..."* Reisner, p. 111.

(p. 36)   *"makes no sense..." Down Beat*, June 17, 1965, reprinted in Morgenstern, p. 194.

(p. 36)   *"We were together all the time..."* Gillespie, p. 176.

(p. 37)   *"I saw him again..."* Reisner, p. 180.

(p. 37)   *Charlie already knew...* Woideck (*Music and Life*, p. 28) mentions this claim, along with other material contradicted by Rebecca's earlier interviews.

(p. 37)   *"a very beautiful girl..."* Taylor, p. 273.

(p. 37)   *"When I met him..."* Reisner, p. 25.

(p. 38)   *in a Washington jail* Gillespie, p. 394.

(p. 38)   *the same West Virginia reformatory...* Reisner, p. 237; Russell, p. 370.

3 now's the time

(p. 39)   *another musician who wound up...* Reisner, p. 67.

(p. 39)   *"I heard the records..."* Reisner, p. 216. Doubt has been cast on the accuracy of Stitt's recollection (and especially his account of Charlie's reaction to him), since elsewhere he said that he first heard Charlie in Washington, DC; this hardly makes it impossible that he first introduced himself in Kansas City and, certainly, he did sound a lot like Parker by the time he began to record.

(p. 40)   *had still not transferred...* Shipton, p. 120.

(p. 41)   *"Diz made an arrangement..."* Eckstine interview in Gillespie, p. 190.

(p. 41)   *"The uniformed side..."* Chan Richardson Parker, p. 14.

(p. 42)   *"You cur!..."* Gillespie with Gene Lees, *Down Beat*, May 25, 1961 (in Woideck, *Companion*, pp. 161–67).

(p. 42)   *"Tadd Dameron..."* Reisner, p. 51.

(p. 42)   *"driving force..." Down Beat*, October 1, 1944.

(p. 42)   *"The whole band..."* Davis, p. vii. Krin Gabbard has pointed out (Criss Cross conference, Nottingham University, June 18–20, 2004) that the transcript of co-author Quincy Troupe's interviews shows Miles using slightly different words: "The whole band would just like have an orgasm everytime [sic] Bird would do something, you know... Sarah sounded like Bird and Diz. I mean they would look at her like another horn, you know. And she used to sing *You Are My First Love* and Bird had a solo. You should have heard that shit!! [Troupe: I know I should have.] Bird had a solo for about sixteen bars, no about eight bars, but the things he used to do in them eight bars man, they left everybody else" (transcript held by New York Public Library, Schomberg Institute).

(p. 43)   *"That horn ain't supposed..." Melody Maker*, September 11, 1954, reprinted in Jones, p. 235.

(p. 44)   *"Herman Lubinsky..."* Stearns and Maher, op. cit.

(p. 44)   *"I think that the music..."* Feather, p. 15.

(p. 44)   *Charlie himself had played...* The dates at the Spotlite belong chronologically around here, rather than the obviously incorrect "spring of 1944" quoted by Levin and Wilson (op. cit.); Stan Levey said that "This was Bird's first gig as leader, and it was also the first time I really had a chance to hear him play" (interview by John Tynan, *Down Beat*, March 20, 1958). Rather than being hired as a leader, Charlie was added to an existing rhythm-section of Levey, Curley Russell and pianist Joe Albany.

(p. 45)   *"The beat in a bop band..."* Levin and Wilson, op. cit.

(p. 45)   *"The critics tried to stop Bird..."* Interview by Mike Dean, BBC TV, August 1972.

(p. 46)   *"He was writing a lot..."* Reisner, p. 181.

(p. 46)   *"I had been putting down..."; " 'Not now,' I said..."* Reisner, p. 94.

(p. 46)   *Groovin' High...* This is one piece specifically described by Charlie as "first devised by the two of us years ago" (broadcast, WABC, March 23, 1953).

(p. 46)   *Shaw 'Nuff...* Gillespie later said that, while he himself wrote the 32-bar theme, Parker was responsible for the exotic introduction and ending – even specifying the drum part for Sid Catlett (interview by Phil Schaap, WKCR-FM, June 15, 1984).

(p. 46)   *Dizzy Atmosphere...* Despite the comments relating to the swing feel of both the intro and the head, the "shout chorus" following the bass solo is delightfully varied and quintessentially boppish. Its B-section begins with a direct quotation (at the same pitch) from a B-section in Duke Ellington's *Cotton Tail* – a number that shows Duke prefiguring bebop. Woideck (*Music and Life*, p. 101) has noted this same quotation in Charlie's 1943 hotel-room recording *Three Guesses*.

(p. 46)   *solo improvisation by Charlie Christian...* Asked about this seeming derivation, Gillespie said "It sounds very reasonable, because Charlie and I used to jam at Minton's all the time, so our licks sort of crossed one another sometimes... I wouldn't be surprised if that had been [borrowed], but I was unaware of that" (interview by the author, BBC Radio London, August 10, 1976).

(p. 46)   *Anthropology* (a.k.a. *Thriving From A Riff*)... Both initial recordings (that by Charlie as *Thriving...* and by Dizzy under the more common title) are jointly credited to "Parker, Gillespie," and both are played virtually identically. A minor mystery surrounds the version arranged by Gil Evans for Claude Thornhill in 1947, in that the second A-section uses a slight variant at bars 11–13; it is unknown if this originates from a lead-sheet later simplified in performance by the two principals, or whether there is some other explanation.

(p. 47)   *"forced to add his name..."* Levin and Wilson, op. cit.

(p. 47)   *would certainly not have been published...* As we shall see, Charlie cared little about the potential income from publishing, and it was already pointed out by Levin and Wilson (op. cit.) that he sold the rights to his originals from the *Now's The Time* date outright to Savoy. But, whereas such a company would simply register them and earn the royalties without making them available in print, the Gillespie–Parker material was actually published by Leeds Music in folio form.

(p. 47)   *"It's exciting and has plenty..."* *Down Beat*, December 10, 1945.

(p. 47)   *"Charley's solos almost never failed..."* *Metronome*, June 1945.

(p. 48)   *"Charlie Parker and I..."* Interview by the author, BBC Radio London, August 10, 1976. Max Roach (in Gillespie, p. 233) recalled being part of a line-up of himself, Charlie, Dizzy and African drummers at the Hotel Diplomat: "We just played the things we were playing on 52nd Street, *Woody'n You, Tunisia*, things like that."

(p. 48)   *Miles' apartment...* Davis, p. 48. Chan Richardson Parker (p. 22) describes Miles and Charlie living on different floors of a building at 149th St. and Amsterdam Avenue, during an unspecified period probably in early 1945. Incidentally, Chan's book refers to Doris Sydnor consistently as "Doris Green," and notes that she herself was born Beverly Dolores Berg. Her letter of February 7, 1947 (Russell, p. 236; Parker and Paudras, p. 72) says of Doris at this earlier period: "There was a girl who gave him the money to keep straight in N.Y.... She really loves Bird, and would do anything for him, but I doubt that she'd deny him anything he wanted."

(p. 48)   *"I didn't know anything..."* Reisner, pp. 174–77. Doris gave Levin and Wilson (op. cit.) the specific date of November 18, 1945 for when she and Charlie "were married," so perhaps this is when he moved into her apartment.

(p. 49)   *also played briefly at Minton's...* Davis, p. 62.

(p. 49)   *It seems likely...* see Gillespie (pp. 230–31) and Ray Brown in Shipton (p. 151).

(p. 49)   *"We were all back there..."* Gillespie, p. 235.

(p. 49)   *"All these people..."* Davis, p. 66.

(p. 49)   *apparently composed on the day...* Sadik Hakim (Argonne Thornton), *Jazz Review*, February 1959.

(p. 49)   *more traditional, riff-based... Now's The Time*, though it has typical "bebop" phrase-endings in bars 5–6, may be based on something already familiar. Indeed, it's not a million miles from the riffs set by the McShann sax-section behind Walter Brown on *The Jumpin' Blues*, or indeed they could be elaborated from the same source. Note too that, during the closing jam-session of the Paris Jazz Fair, Charlie leads the assembled horns in a new, rhythmically altered version of the same riff.

(p. 49)   *incorporates a note-for-note copy...* Interview by the author, *The Wire*, November 1989.

(p. 49)   *The masterpiece of the session... Ko Ko* has been spelled in slightly different ways, including sometimes with a hyphen – which more properly belongs to Duke Ellington's minor-key blues of 1940. No one has ever explained why two of the most intense three-minute marvels of recorded jazz should bear virtually the same title.

(p. 49)   *Gillespie took over trumpet duties...* In his book Gillespie (p. 299) confirms that "We, Bird and I, had been playing *Ko Ko* together, and he [Miles] didn't know the introduction." Davis corroborates this (ibid., p. 234) in conversation with Gillespie, who refers obliquely to Parker's authorship. The full quotation is: "Boy, when this music is solidified with the contributions of all those guys, and they show those notes that Charlie Parker wrote, the notes that guys who play don't even hear. Boy, you talk about perfect! Perfect melody with chords. It's just perfect, man, the lines that he wrote." The account in Haydon (p. 119), based on his interviews with Max Roach, describes the intro as being "of Charlie Parker's devising" and "written at Roach's request."

(p. 50)   *Charlie was a more important soloist...* Levin and Wilson include (op. cit.) the following comment: "'There's only one man really plays bop,' one New York reed musician said recently. 'That's Charlie Parker. All the others who say they're playing bop are only trying to imitate him.'"

(p. 50)   *"Only Charlie Parker..." Down Beat*, April 22, 1946. The short review in *Metronome* (March 1946) also criticizes Parker, Roach and Davis: "Worst of all, the trumpeter is a young Dizzy disciple who succeeds only in imitating all the faults of his mentor and none of the virtues."

(p. 50)   *"started slowly but it built..."* Interview by Bob Porter, notes to Savoy S5J5500.

(p. 51)   *organizing Harry The Hipster...* Gibson's unpublished manuscript *Bird Lives*, held at University of Texas, quoted by Woideck, *Music and Life*, p. 32.

(p. 51)   *"They were late..."* Lyons, p. 18.

(p. 52)   *"That was the way..."* Interview by John Shaw, *Jazz Journal*, March 1979.

(p. 52)   *"I think Charlie Parker..."* Interview by the author, BBC Radio London, December 21, 1976.

(p. 52)   *gave them to the band members...* Russell, p. 206; Stan Levey interview by Alun Morgan, *Jazz Monthly*, September 1961.

(p. 52)   *Handy's tune* Diggin' Diz... In view of the chaotic proliferation of tune-titles on Dial recordings (see the relevant sessions of the Discography), it may be worth noting that Charlie was adamant this piece had another title. Interviewed by Leonard Feather (broadcast, WABC, March 30, 1953) he said of the piece "It's a satire on the [Richard Rodgers] tune *Lover*. That's right, *Dynamo A* and *Dynamo B*." These two titles ended up being used for Gillespie's subsequent Dial session without Parker.

(p. 53)   *"When Bird left New York..."* Davis, p. 78.

(p. 53)   *"some chick who was writing..."* Reisner, p. 87.

(p. 54)   *"Howard was constantly..."* Davis, p. 80.

(p. 54)   *"I know the time..."* Letter dated February 7, 1947, reproduced in Parker and Paudras, p. 72 and quoted in Russell, pp. 236–38.

(p. 54)   *created a scene in the lobby...* Howard McGhee (interviewed by Ira Gitler, NEA Jazz Oral History Project, November 23, 1982, reprinted in Woideck, *Companion*, pp. 151–61) was told that Charlie came from his room to the lobby, wearing no pants of any kind. McGhee explicitly contradicts the idea that, on this occasion, Charlie set fire to his room – as stated (in Reisner, p. 98) by writer Elliot Grennard, who had attended the record session and later wrote a short story inspired by it.

4 parker's mood

(p. 55)   *"What made it worst..."* *Metronome*, August 1947 (in Woideck, *Companion*, pp. 61–65).

(p. 55)   *"whose help he recalls..."* *Metronome*, August 1947 (in Woideck, *Companion*, pp. 61–65).

(p. 55)   *"Ross got him a lawyer..."* Chan Richardson Parker, p. 27.

(p. 56)   *"wouldn't let him out..."* Russell, p. 234.

(p. 56)   *"Nothing but a leech..."* Davis, p. 79.

(p. 56)   *"clear-eyed..."; "But what horrified everybody..."* Davis, pp. 91 and 83.

(p. 56)   *His mother was aware...* Jazz Review, September–October 1960.

(p. 56)   *"According to Bird,..."* Chan Richardson Parker, p. 31. Her statement to a physician at Bellevue Hospital in 1954, on the other hand, mentioned sulphuric acid (see Reisner, p. 42).

(p. 56) *"He began to juice..."* Letter dated March 25, 1947, reproduced in Parker and Paudras, p. 73.

(p. 57) *"These guys were so enthusiastic..."* Interview by the author, November 2, 1980 in Priestley, p. 28.

(p. 57) *"Who didn't that was searching..."* Letter to the author, c. 1981.

(p. 58) *"Bird was up on stage..."* Davis, p. 90.

(p. 59) *authorship was contradicted...* James Patrick demonstrated (notes to Savoy S5J5500) that Charlie's contracts usually provided for the record company to purchase rights to all the original compositions he recorded. Thus, if one happened to be written by a sideman, it was still likely to be credited to the bandleader. The same thing occurred with the Miles Davis session in the next paragraph, where John Lewis's composition *Milestones* was shown as by Davis.

The derivation of *Donna Lee*'s opening phrase from Navarro was first pointed out by Douglas Parker's essay, *"Donna Lee* and the Ironies of Bebop," in Oliphant.

(p. 59) *"He told Max and me..."* Davis, p. 104.

(p. 59) *Parker playing tenor...* Davis's autobiography is silent on the reasons for this change of texture. But the suggestion sometimes made, that this was a producer's decision to avoid Charlie's presence being recognized, is undercut by the personnel being listed on the record labels.

(p. 59) *contributed his composition...* The authorship of *Milestones* was first noted by Giddins (p. 108) and confirmed in Lewis' interview with the author, *Jazzwise*, December 1999–January 2000.

(p. 59) *"Miles was tight with John Lewis..."* Reisner, p. 125.

(p. 60) *"He'd come on the stage..."* Haydon, p. 24.

(p. 60) *"Bird used to make me play..."* Down Beat, April 6, 1967.

(p. 61) *"We went to his room..."* Reisner, pp. 191–92.

(p. 61) *becoming incapable of playing...* Reisner, p. 126.

(p. 61) *observed him using heroin...* Russell, p. 249.

(p. 62) *"Wherever we would be..."* Reisner, p. 126.

(p. 63) *"Bird was very businesslike..."* Interview by Bob Porter, notes to Savoy S5J5500.

(p. 63) *"On sessions involving Charlie..."* Notes to Spotlite SPJ-CD4-101.

(p. 64) *"On recording dates..."* Reisner, p. 183.

(p. 64) *"He would tell..."* Haydon, p. 123.

(p. 64) *beginning without a theme-statement...* These pieces are "themeless" in the sense of having no opening ensemble passage outlining the chord-sequence to be improvised upon, but they each have brief gestures from alto and trumpet in unison to close the track (and, in the case of *Bird Of Paradise*, the unison introduction coined by Gillespie).

Of the closing statements, that at the end of *Bird Gets The Worm* is later used in a similar manner on Clifford Brown tracks based on *Cherokee*, while the one at the end of *Klaunstance* is also heard on the Benedetti/Onyx Club *Way You Look Tonight* (and on Sonny Rollins' 1954 version of the latter). It is not, however, the original Jerome Kern melody but a paraphrase popular during this period, and probably not authored by Parker.

(p. 65) *"see, when Bird went off..."; "Bird never talked about music..."* Davis, pp. 91 and 93.

(p. 65) *"Musicians were constantly..."* Davis, p. 94.

(p. 66) *audiences could sing along...* Dizzy Gillespie (with Gene Lees, *Down Beat*, May 25, 1961, reprinted in Woideck, *Companion*, pp. 161–67) says that "He'd play a phrase, and people might never have heard it before. But he'd start it, and people would finish it with him, humming. It would be so lyrical and simple that it just seemed the most natural thing to play." Ira Gitler (notes to Savoy 92911) mentions observing the same phenomenon at Chicago's Pershing Ballroom in the late 1940s.

(p. 67) *"Because of some of his irresponsible acts..."* Reisner, p. 195.

(p. 67) *funded by Billy Shaw...* Davis, p. 96.

(p. 67) *The consequence, recalled...* Davis, p. 97; Reisner, p. 126.

(p. 68) *returning to LA...* Reisner, pp. 170 and 184; Haydon, p. 30. This is clearly a genuine conflict between different observers' memories, even just a few years after the events concerned. However, as an incidental example of the kind of misinformation that now proliferates on the Internet, I offer the following: "Later that year [1947], Parker and his band toured across the country with a Philharmonic orchestra, which lasted until the start of 1948" (Lauren Peterson © 1999 *The Jazzine*).

(p. 69) *"I really had no strong desire..."* Reisner, p. 170.

(p. 69) *"The one he was gonna get rid..."* Gillespie, p. 400.

(p. 69) *the money to pay for the...* Reisner, p. 172.

(p. 69) *"Any musician who says..."* Levin and Wilson, op. cit.

(p. 69) *"Bird always said he hated..."* Davis, p. 110.

(p. 70) *"There was Bird..."* Haydon, p. 123.

(p. 70) *according to Sid's recollection...* Reisner, p. 218.

5 celebrity

(p. 71) *"Bird knew the limitations..."* Reisner, p. 126.

(p. 71) *a former jazz disc-jockey...* Spencer Leigh, obituary of Bill Randle, *The Independent*, July 20, 2004. Randle, interviewed in the Bjorn and Gallert book on Detroit, hosted jazz shows in the mid-1940s but later became famous in Cleveland for his involvement with rock-and-roll.

(p. 72) *"The band had a tremendous beat..."* Down Beat, July 1, 1949.

(p. 72) *"The reception in France..."* Reisner, p. 183.

(p. 72) *"Bird described the language..."* Down Beat, July 15, 1949.

(p. 73) *"When my turn came around..."* Dankworth, p. 65.

(p. 73) *"exemplified his belief..."* Giddins, p. 108.

(p. 73) *"I'm very glad to have met..."* Russell, p. 271.

(p. 73) *"Bird had also met..."* Chan Richardson Parker, p. 28.

(p. 73) *he actually took saxophone lessons...* Ellington, p. 88.

(p. 73) *For the future, he'd like...* Levin and Wilson, op. cit.

(p. 73) *had gone so far as to write...* Woideck, *Music and Life*, p. 249. The statement he quotes by Francis Paudras presumably derives ultimately from Chan.

(p. 74) *"I had three copies of..."* Interview by Bob Porter, notes to Savoy S5J5500.

(p. 74) *"I remember that..."* Down Beat, July 2004.

(p. 74) *described Parker improvising...* Notes to Columbia KC31039.

(p. 74) *also used to hang around...* Jazz Review, February 1960.

(p. 74) *an apparent uncertainty...* When the track runs out of steam without an instruction to end, Charlie plays a well-known riff used by Gillespie as the theme of *Emanon*.

(p. 74) *"You just try to align..."* Interview by the author, notes to Verve 539 757-2.

(p. 75) *"I asked for strings..."* Interview by Nat Hentoff, broadcast, WMEX, c. December 1952, edited for publication in *Down Beat*, January 28, 1953.

(p. 75) *"You is a prime example..."* Down Beat, January 28, 1949. Surprisingly, Barry Ulanov's review in *Metronome* (February 1949) claimed the track "achieves its only distinction in Miles' departure from the cloying melody."

(p. 75)   *apparently liked Joe Lippman's writing...* Interview by Nat Hentoff, op. cit.

(p. 76)   *"Mama, I'm going to the top..."* Jazz Review, September–October 1960.

(p. 76)   *his biggest and his third biggest-selling...* Bill Kirchner from research by Phil Schaap, notes to Verve 559 835-2.

(p. 76)   *"It turned out..."* Gitler, *Swing to Bop*, p. 294.

(p. 76)   *"He felt that we were greater..."* Interview by Phil Schaap, notes to Verve 837 141-2.

(p. 76)   *"I'm sure if Bird were given..."* Letter dated February 7, 1947, reproduced in Parker and Paudras, p. 72 and quoted in Russell, pp. 236–38.

(p. 76)   *"had yielded to Capitol's blandishments..."* E-mail to the author, July 18, 2004.

(p. 77)   *could fatally dilute the impact...* It's possible too that Charlie was upset about the R&B simplification of his *Now's The Time*, in Paul Williams's 1949 hit *The Huckle-Buck* (also recorded for Savoy, to whom Charlie had sold rights in the former tune, and credited to ex-big-band arranger Andy Gibson).

However, as previously noted, it may derive from some more public-domain riff. Annotating a reissue compilation (Ace CDCHD819), R&B disc-jockey and producer Stuart Colman writes: "*The Huckle-Buck* had been an entity for more than two decades prior to the Williams Orchestra getting hip to the song's novelty value."

(p. 77)   *"Some guys said..."* Levin and Wilson, op. cit.

(p. 77)   *"Dizzy was with the big band... The successful musician..."* Reisner, pp. 219–20.

(p. 77)   *"It is possible that..."* Reisner, p. 191.

(p. 77)   *"I think Dizzy's clowning..."* Interview by Nick St. George for Heavy Entertainment/BBC Radio 2, recorded February 18, 2003. There is an implied contradiction between Dankworth's statement here and his book (p. 51), where he describes Charlie at the Three Deuces commenting musically on the progress of two ladies towards the powder room. But, as with Gene Ramey's similar observation, this concerns humour aimed at fellow musicians, and not as a way of communicating with the public.

(p. 78)   *"only element of the Birdland show..."* Down Beat, October 21, 1949.

(p. 78)   *"I said 'Wow!'..."* Porter Crutcher interview in Bjorn and Gallert, p. 103.

(p. 79)   *"Red told me that..."* Reisner, p. 183.

(p. 80)   *smooth-talking 1950-disc-jockey...* Broadcasts from Café Society, June 1950.

(p. 80)   *"After the [Tatum] show, the quintet..."* Gitler, *Swing to Bop*, pp. 295–96.

(p. 81)   *choice of Buddy Rich...* Ross Russell made an implied side-swipe about this production decision some years later, saying "It might be as out of place to have a very able drummer, like, let's say Buddy Rich, on a date with Parker as to have someone like [New Orleans-style player] Baby Dodds" (interview by Martin Williams in Reisner, p. 197).

(p. 81)   *"I said to him..."* Interview by the author, notes to *Jazz Masters 57*, Verve 529 900-2.

(p. 81)   *"I was in no physical condition..."* Reisner, p. 170.

(p. 81)   *"Once when Doris was sick..."* Reisner, p. 164.

(p. 82)   *"To date the string backing..."* *Down Beat*, August 25, 1950.

(p. 82)   *Charlie's reputation...* Contract reproduced in Parker and Paudras, p. 260 and quoted in Vail, p. 80.

(p. 83)   *"in wig and trombone..."* Script reproduced in Vail, p. 87.

(p. 83)   *"He kicked his habit..."; had not been able to collect...* Chan Richardson Parker, pp. 30–31.

(p. 83)   *"The doctor told me..."* Leonard Feather, *Down Beat*, April 20, 1955. The health crisis proved to be real, yet the report in *Melody Maker* (December 9, 1950, unsigned but doubtless written by their Paris correspondent Henry Kahn) had another theory: "Suffice it to say that he felt he must return to seek shelter under the wing of his agent from a pending brush with the law."

    Without further details, it's hard to trust this any more than the following rumour: "Some cat went to the club where Henri [Renaud?] works and told Henri that you and Klook were both fags and were making it together here in Paris" (Annie Ross, letter to Charlie and Chan, December 13, 1950, in Vail, p. 95).

(p. 83)   *announced as winning for the first time...* *Down Beat*, December 29, 1950.

(p. 83)   *"made fun of Bird's conducting..."* E-mail to the author, August 2, 2004. Morgenstern also notes that, after the set, there were "Diz apologies and a hug."

(p. 84)   *rhythm-and-blues alto king...* A popular ex-sideman of Lionel Hampton's proto-rhythm-and-blues big-band, Bostic was widely admired by jazz musicians and especially fellow saxophonists for his technical mastery. Despite the deliberately simplistic style of his hit records, he was espoused by the anti-bebop wing of the French establishment (in the person of Hugues Panassié) as being a "true" jazzman, and therefore superior to the bebop of Parker.

(p. 84)　*a week at the Apollo Theatre...* Contract reproduced in Parker and Paudras, p. 359. These authors' clumsy attempt to remedy the poor print quality has resulted in the addition by hand of "AUG" and the changing of the year to "1954," despite the space for five letters in the typescript before "13th." It will be noted that, just two lines below, the original shows clearly the legend "REHEARSAL APRIL 12th, 1951." This engagement is correctly shown in Vail (p. 100) and is confirmed elsewhere, but his phantom listing of similar information for August 12 and 13, 1954 (Vail, p. 162, also accepted by Koch, p. 239) was based on Parker and Paudras' misinformation.

(p. 84)　*"Bird helped my morale..."* Interview by Nat Hentoff, *Down Beat*, April 7, 1954.

(p. 00)　Si Si *and* Blues For Alice... The titles seem to be accidentally reversed, since the written trumpet part for the latter melody is headed *Si Si* (reproduced in Parker and Paudras, p. 196).

(p. 85)　*"He took me into a listening booth..."* Chan Richardson Parker, p. 27.

(p. 85)　*Cab Calloway complained...* Ebony, February 1951.

(p. 85)　*named no specific individuals...* Woideck, *Music and Life*, p. 44.

(p. 86)　*appeared in court...* Chan Richardson Parker, p. 36.

(p. 86)　*"Your agency tells me..."* Telegram reproduced in Parker and Paudras, p. 222 and Vail, p. 103.

(p. 86)　*one of his frequent threats...* Correspondence from Shaw Artists in Parker and Paudras, p. 192 and Vail, p. 86.

(p. 86)　*"I guess you heard..."* Interview by Leonard Feather, Voice Of America, c. Spring 1951.

(p. 86)　*Around the end of the year...* The timing of this visit, tentatively established in the first edition of the present book, rests solely on Addie Parker's reference to "driving a great big 1952 Cadillac," with the clear implication that this was a very new vehicle. My supposition has been accepted by fellow authors, Koch (pp. 250–51) and Vail (p. 106).

(p. 87)　*"I always had $150...";* usually in the audience...; *"pushed dope..."* Jazz Review, September–October 1960.

(p. 87)　*"We got word somehow..."* Reisner, p. 68.

6　i remember you

(p. 88)　*"A piano player..."* Reisner, pp. 88–89.

(p. 88)　*"Through the years..."* Interview by John Robert Brown in *Libretto*, no. 2004:2, Spring 2004.

(p. 88)   *a weekly salary of $50.00...* Woideck, *Music and Life*, p. 45.

(p. 89)   *unexpectedly playing...* Taylor, p. 233.

(p. 89)   *such uncommon vehicles as... She Rote* was once incorrectly described (by Bill Simon, notes to Verve MGV8010) as being based on *Out Of Nowhere*. *Cardboard*, on the other hand, is unusual in using two somewhat different chord-sequences: the head derives from *Don't Take Your Love From Me*, whereas the solos are based on something closer to *Me And My Shadow*.

(p. 89)   *Red Rodney told the story...* Rodney was the source of this uplifting sequence in *Bird*, dir. Clint Eastwood, 1988.

(p. 89)   *Okey Dokie...* The spelling, which differs from that usually given, is found in an early review of the single (*Down Beat*, May 20, 1949) and may represent the artists' original intention, rather than what is shown on the actual record-label. The phrase was one of Charlie's favourite expressions, and is believed to derive from the Wolof and Mandingo languages (David Dalby, "The Etymology Of OK," *The Times*, January 14, 1971).

(p. 89)   *a song from the French Caribbean...* Ross interview by David Freeman, Jazz-fm, London, March 1996. In apparent confirmation of the song's derivation, the announcement by Chet Baker preceding his own 1954 version is worded as follows: "A little tune we picked up from Charlie Parker a couple of years ago just after...his return from Paris" (Pacific Jazz 31573).

(p. 89)   *his second biggest seller...* Bill Kirchner from research by Phil Schaap, notes to Verve 559 835-2.

(p. 90)   *"Bird was a flawless player...";* *"It just so happened..."* Baker, pp. 55–57.

(p. 90)   *"When you were in my office..."* Letter reproduced in Vail, p. 111.

(p. 90)   *"He was very drunk..."* Reisner, p. 192.

(p. 91)   *"jazz wars" were still very intense...* Charlie admired Hodges enormously, but might have been unsure of his approval at this stage. In an interview by Ira Gitler (NEA Jazz Oral History Project, November 23, 1982, reprinted in Woideck, *Companion*, pp. 151–61), Howard McGhee, who was briefly with the Ellington band in the early 1960s, said that Hodges had complained in the 1940s about Charlie's lack of tone. "When I worked with Duke, I asked Johnny... 'What do you think of Charlie Parker?' He said, 'Oh, he was beautiful.' I said, 'But Johnny, you told me he didn't have no sound.' He said, 'Well, I didn't know what I was talking about. He's one of the baddest.'"

(p. 91)   *Hodges, who plays first...* It seems clear, from the continuity of the rhythm-section's playing, that Charlie jumps in immediately at the end of Hodges' solo. However, the apparent entry of Carter right after Charlie is achieved by means of an obvious tape edit, which raises the question of whether Charlie played longer than the other two altoists and was then trimmed back.

(p. 91)   *"Charlie Parker came in one night..."* Diary entry in Dahl, p. 220.

(p. 91)   *wanting to learn golf...; horse-riding lessons...; painting lessons...* Reisner, pp. 218, 128 and 75.

(p. 92)   *"The communists paid better..."* Chan Richardson Parker, p. 33.

(p. 92)   *an attempt to combine both tapes...* The sterling work by engineer Doug Pomeroy is less than totally convincing because, even after speed correction, there are miniscule fluctuations of pitch – and therefore speed – between the two recorded sources. It is a pity the opportunity was not taken to include a mono version of the same performance on this near-complete reissue (Jazz Classics CD-JZCL-5014).

(p. 92)   *sessions organized by Joe Maini...* Miller, p. 28. This would have been before Maini and Knepper were imprisoned in July 1951 on drugs-related charges (see letter reproduced in Parker and Paudras, p. 208 and quoted in Vail, p. 118).

(p. 92)   *"a gift from an Englishman..."* Interview by Leonard Feather, broadcast, WABC, March 30, 1953.

(p. 92)   *"The manufacturer's representative..."* Interview by Bruce Lundvall, Elektra-Musician E1-60019, 1982. These English products were marketed in North America by the Gretsch company.

(p. 93)   *"No pawnbroker would offer him..."* Gelly's article notes that the Grafton was also favoured by John Dankworth in the early 1950s and by Ornette Coleman thereafter (*Jazz Magazine* [UK] no. 27, December 1994).

(p. 93)   *"My right to pursue..."* Letter dated February 17, 1953, quoted by Maxwell T. Cohen, *Down Beat*, March 11, 1965. Chan Richardson Parker's reference to this letter (p. 36) mentions a "lawyer who was trying to have that most unjust law repealed," but Cohen only become involved in this campaign later and states that he did not know Charlie personally.

(p. 93)   *"One day two detectives..."* Chan Richardson Parker, p. 36.

(p. 93)   *at least once sitting in...* Steve Lacy (*Down Beat*, July 2004) said that "Bird played with Ellington and the rhythm-section, and then the band started riffing behind him, and they played *Honeysuckle Rose*, *Tea For Two* and a blues. Just three tunes. It was unforgettable." The research of Ken Vail shows this Sunday afternoon to be almost certainly February 15, 1953, i.e. two days before Charlie's letter about his cabaret card.

(p. 93)   *"Charlie Parker left the Band Box..."* Down Beat, April 8, 1953.

(p. 93)   *"I need a good rhythm-section..."* Reisner, p. 89.

(p. 94)   *he'd already mentioned admiringly...* Levin and Wilson, op. cit.

(p. 94)   *"Now, I'd like to do..."* Interview by Nat Hentoff, broadcast, WMEX, c. December 1952, edited for publication in *Down Beat*, January 28, 1953.

(p. 94)   *a fourth score...* A copyist's score of the *Yesterdays* arrangement, probably a piano part or a conductor's part, was included in the materials auctioned by Christie's in September 1994.

(p. 95)   *Charlie also asked for and received...* Miller, p. 69.

(p. 95)   *Despite the overdubbed bass...* Miller (p. 82) also asserts that there are edits within at least one track (*Salt Peanuts*), which is untrue. There are late starts in switching on the tape for the opening number of each set, *Perdido* and *Wee*, and unlike all previous releases of the material the 1990 reissue (Mingus' *Complete Debut Recordings*) attempts to reconstitute these missing parts.

(p. 95)   *"In place of his normal..."* Davis, p. 151.

(p. 96)   *"What you hear depends..."* Interview by Nat Hentoff, op. cit.

(p. 96)   *"Most of the things..."* Interview by John McLellan, broadcast, WHDH, June 13, 1953.

(p. 96)   *was barred from the premises...* It is unclear exactly when this took place. Though there were no official Parker bookings between June 1953 and late August 1954, Frank Foster states very specifically that "The second and last time I heard him live, I played with him at Birdland. My first night in New York, 27th July 1953, the only date I can remember apart from my birthday" (Grime, p. 37).

(p. 96)   *"I know how unsettled you are..."* Letter (undated) reproduced in Parker and Paudras, p. 321.

(p. 97)   *"The woman who..."* Chan Richardson Parker, p. 36.

(p. 97)   *"Here! You feed them..."* Reisner, p. 25.

(p. 97)   *sold the Cadillac...; "Life with Bird..."; "Although Bird..."* Chan Richardson Parker, pp. 37, 40 and 51.

(p. 97)   *"I was not in good health..."* Chan Richardson Parker, p. 43.

(p. 97)   *the Shaw office was writing...* Letter dated October 7, 1953, reproduced in Vail, p. 136.

(p. 97)   *managed to get reported...; financial adjudication...* Correspondence in Parker and Paudras, pp. 326, 328 and 331 and Vail, pp. 136, 138–41 and 154.

(p. 98)   *"I'll never forget the energy…"* Wein, p. 106.

(p. 98)   *"We were all saying…"; "All of a sudden…"* Gitler, *Swing to Bop*, p. 296.

(p. 99)   *"This is one time…"* Letter reproduced in Vail, p. 147.

(p. 99)   *"In one Southern town…"* Reisner, p. 207.

(p. 99)   *"Thank you for making…"* Telegram dated February 24, 1954, reprinted in Vail, p. 151 and partially reproduced in Parker and Paudras, p. 306.

(p. 100)   *"taken to a Los Angeles Police Station…"* Letter to AFM, May 22, 1954, in Parker and Paudras, p. 347 and Vail, pp. 157–58.

(p. 100)   *"I could have nailed him…"* O'Grady, p. 51.

(p. 100)   *"My darling my daughter's death…"* Telegrams dated March 7, 1954, quoted by Maxwell T. Cohen, *Down Beat*, March 11, 1965.

(p. 100)   *because it paid so well…* Chan Richardson Parker, quoted in Hentoff, p. 190. Accounts from Gale Agency Inc. (reproduced without comment in Parker and Paudras, p. 350) show that the agency received $2804.29 for Charlie's appearance fees from January–March 1954 and deducted, in addition to Charlie's expenses, a total of $832.93 – i.e. more than 30 per cent – in commission.

(p. 100)   *claims against various promoters…* Correspondence reproduced in Vail, pp. 144–64.

(p. 100)   *the Tiffany Club's complaint…* Letter from AFM, October 26, 1954, in Parker and Paudras, p. 348 and Vail, p. 166.

(p. 101)   *"My darling I just wanted to let you know…"* Telegram reproduced in Parker and Paudras, p. 359. Close perusal reveals the date of "1954 MAY 18," visible at the head of the telegram, while the date lower down is altered by hand to read "1954 AUG 18." A different reproduction of the same document in Vail (p. 162), made when the original was offered for sale at auction, shows the print clearly (yet the sending of the telegram occurs in Vail's chronology on "August 18 1954"). See also the reference (p. 217) to a week at the Apollo Theatre.
   These emendations sufficiently confused the present author that, in the first edition of this book, the Apollo gig and Charlie's telegram were ascribed to April and May of *1953*! My misdating of the telegram is repeated in at least one other publication (see Miller, p. 69).

(p. 101)   *"Brewster is one of the most…"* Reisner, p. 219.

(p. 101)   *the fourth night of the engagement…* Reisner, p. 16.

(p. 101)   *Later he claimed…* Reisner, p. 71.

(p. 102)   *"He had conned…"* Chan Richardson Parker, p. 50.

(p. 102)   *"Bird played brilliantly…"* Gitler, *Swing to Bop*, p. 298.

(p. 102)   *paid his respects...* Reisner, p. 146.

(p. 102)   *"Charles Parker came walking..."* Reisner, p. 40.

(p. 103)   *"Pretty soon..."* Gitler, *Swing to Bop*, p. 297.

(p. 103)   *"That's when I knew..."* Interview by Julian Joseph, BBC Radio 3, June 12, 2004.

(p. 103)   *"cost him a couple..."* Reisner, p. 117.

(p. 103)   *"My watch doesn't work..."* Reisner, p. 71.

(p. 103)   *The Rubáiyát of Omar Kháyyám...* Reisner (p. 15) has an account where Reisner himself brings up the poem first. However, Charlie was already quoting it to interviewer Steve Race and French pianist Eddy Bernard at the Paris Jazz Fair in 1949 (see letter from Bernard in Vail, p. 93).

(p. 103)   *"Shortly before I left for Europe"* Down Beat, April 20, 1955.

(p. 104)   *"I don't want to see..."* Quoted by Joe Segal, *Down Beat*, March 11, 1965.

(p. 104)   *"Look, man, I goofed..."* Quoted by Guy Warren, unidentified clipping (possibly from *Melody Maker*).

(p. 104)   *"Man, I'm not long for this life..."* Reisner, p. 215. It's worth noting that Ira Gitler (*Jazz Masters*, p. 44, confirmed by e-mail to the author, December 19, 2004) believes this story to be apochryphal.

(p. 104)   *come-back-all-is-forgiven-one-more-once...* The last three words allude to a fameous spoken comment by Count Basie on his *April In Paris*, recorded in 1955 and first performed and popularized at Birdland. Basie's name, indeed, was to become more synonymous with the club than Parker's

(p. 104)   *"very much in charge..."* E-mail to the author, August 2, 2004.

(p. 104)   *the leader announced his name...* Gitler, *Jazz Masters*, p. 54.

(p. 104)   *"I"ve been dead for four years..."* Keepnews, pp. 96 and 98. Another quotation from the Baroness confirms Charlie's broad tastes: "I never heard him condemn any musician – even the lousiest. Hodges had been his god and he admired [Earl] Bostic... He loved Thelonious Monk's records – all of them; and at any time. And Billie Holiday. Especially *You're My Thrill*" (interview by Tony Brown, *Melody Maker*, February 16, 1957).

(p. 104)   *"They can get it out of your blood..."* Letter dated February 7, 1947, reproduced in Parker and Paudras, p. 72 and quoted in Russell, pp. 236–38.

7 the song is you

(p. 106)   *"What he did..."* Gillespie with Gene Lees, *Down Beat*, May 25, 1961 (in Woideck, *Companion*, pp. 161–67).

(p. 106) *"There are countless records…"* Reisner, p. 37.

(p. 106) *"If Charlie Parker wanted…"* Interview by Leonard Feather, *Down Beat*, May 18, 1951.

(p. 106) *"They don't know…"* Grime, p. 146.

(p. 106) *"I doubt, though…"* Gillespie with Gene Lees, op. cit.

(p. 107) *holes in Charlie's theoretical knowledge…* Woideck (*Music and Life*, p. 170) picks up on one of these in the informal lesson taped by Meldonian.

(p. 107) *"You didn't find…"* Gillespie with Gene Lees, op. cit.

(p. 107) *does not need a knowledge of theory…* In my experience, non-players are often more aware of the limitations of musical description and analysis, and therefore gain more from it, than musicians or would-be musicians. Those without an instrument at their fingertips can find a creative awareness of the Parker style by memorizing particular passages and either whistling along with the records or singing them in the bath. That's certainly how some of the author's non-musician friends first got into this music so, if chord-symbols or transcribed notes are not your thing, that doesn't bar you from understanding this chapter.

(p. 108) *"No wonder many who heard…"* Reisner, p. 139.

(p. 108) *"What a lot of people…"* Interview by the author, notes to Verve 539 757-2.

(p. 108) *"The sound has its double edge…"* Russell, p. 23.

(p. 109) *such a simple phrase…* So simple in fact that Martin Williams (p. 144) openly disapproved of its use by Charlie, while on the very next page stating that "The emotional basis of his work is the urban, Southwestern blues idiom that we also hear running through every performance by the Basie orchestra of the late 30s."
    Hootie Blues, like some later solos, is thus an example of Teddy Reig's comment that "He'll drop into an older groove for three or four bars and then leap right into the modern. Like shifting gears" (interview by Bob Porter, notes to Savoy S5J 5000).

(p. 109) *non-blues sequence…* This JATP *Lady Be Good* is an excellent example of "turning into a blues" a popular song that in its original form has little connection with the blues. Charlie's solo not only abounds in blues gestures, but it opens with a quotation from Lester Young's solo on the Basie blues *Pound Cake*.

(p. 110) *playfully varying its timing…* Perhaps for the sake of simplicity and legibility, Woideck (*Music and Life*, p. 114) writes the phrase in its conventional timing, whereas Charlie's first "downbeat" is half a beat late and that of bar 3 of the chorus is almost two beats late. A later use of this phrase at a faster tempo (the March 5 *Barbados*) has the entire phrase occurring exactly one beat later than it would be written.

(p. 110) *in the opening phrase...* The effect is exaggerated (and perhaps concealed) by an unintended reed-squeak, but it may be assumed that the other tonal variations are deliberate.

(p. 110) *later used by many others...* Both Woideck (*Music and Life*) and Koch note the use of this phrase in Wardell Gray's famous solo on *Twisted* (the one lyricized by Annie Ross and covered by Joni Mitchell *et al.*). Koch also observes that Charlie's own 1953 *Now's The Time* reprises this *Billie's Bounce* opening, as well as the blues phrase described in the previous two sentences.

(p. 111) *"Rhythmically, he was quite advanced..."* Gillespie, p. 177.

(p. 111) *comparatively "hard" approach...* That Charlie was aware of the difference is evident in a comment from Chan Richardson Parker (pp. 21–22). "Critics always said that Bird had been influenced by Lester Young. This annoyed him... Pres phrased behind the beat. How could they think Bird came out of Pres? Bird...said that he didn't dig rushing either, that he felt the placement of time right on."

(p. 111) *a sense of its own history...* To be fair, the sympathetic music critic Winthrop Sergeant drew attention to the polyrhythm described here in his *Jazz: Hot and Hybrid*, published back in 1938, but most jazz writers and musicians preferred anecdotal to analytical comment at this period.

(p. 112) *another quotation from the common stock...* The *Cool Blues* riff is described by Koch (p. 102) as being based on a phrase from Charlie's recorded solo on the issued version of *Yardbird Suite*, but in fact used to be a broadcast theme-song of the John Kirby group and derived ultimately from Ellington's *Blue Ramble* of 1932 (Stanley Crouch, Duke Ellington Study Conference, Copenhagen, May 29, 1992).

(p. 113) *can be played in Latin...* All of this has been tried in the intervening years, with *Billie's Bounce* tackled by Joseph and Byron Bowie's band Defunkt (Hannibal HNCD1301) and *Moose The Mooche* played in a half-time rock rhythm by Mel Lewis And Friends (A & M Horizon SP-716). The already Caribbean feel of *Barbados* has also been wedded to a more reggae-influenced beat by the UK-based Jazz Jamaica (Hannibal HNCD1397) while the Parker-associated Miles Davis tune *Donna Lee* was notably adapted by bassist Jaco Pastorius with the sole accompaniment of congas by Don Alias (Epic EK64977).

(p. 113) *from "swing" eighth notes into "even"...* Koch (p. xiii) notes that there are other instances "when the feeling goes from uneven to even," quite deliberately during Charlie's improvisations. His solo on Gillespie's 1945 *Hot House*, at bars 17–18, is an example among many.

(p. 114) *a soloist's line in isolation...* Obviously, this book is open to the same accusation. But the example has been set by Berliner (pp. 680–88 and 693–708) for presenting full transcriptions, in his case of Miles Davis and John Coltrane, where the rhythm-section's reactions and provocations are shown alongside the soloist.

(p. 114) *"He had a funny way..." Jazz Review*, February 1959.

(p. 114) *It has been said...* Williams, p. 138.

(p. 115) *"We would play a number..."* Dance, pp. 291–92. The printed version of the interview omits Johnson's presumed pause for breath between "just a half-step" and the words "to C." Running this together as one phrase makes no sense, hence my editorial parenthesis.

(p. 115) *"Bird had a way of starting..." Melody Maker*, May 28, 1955 (in Woideck, *Companion*, pp. 135–39). This has been frequently misquoted in a way that renders it nonsensical, for instance in Reisner, p. 188.

(p. 115) *"Bird got a lot of things..."* Taylor, p. 53.

(p. 115) *cycle-based chord-sequence...* As far as I can recall, it has not been pointed out that the A-section of *Confirmation* is another adaptation of a standard popular song, in this case the opening bars of *I'm Afraid The Masquerade Is Over* (published in 1939). As well as the related blues themes mentioned, Charlie also used these chords as substitutions on some live versions of *Cool Blues* from 1952–53 (e.g. the Rockland Palace performance).

(p. 116) *"He was twice as fast..."* Interview by Tony Williams for Russell, p. 138.

(p. 116) *"Where they would go..."* Gitler, *Swing to Bop*, p. 69.

(p. 116) *Parker's solo on* Shaw 'Nuff... The solo is transcribed in Martin (p. 52) with the relevant bar 3–4 and bar 11 phrase seen in the third and the ninth staves. What Martin hears as F and D, however, I hear as F-flat and D-flat – as with the phrase on *Thriving From A Riff* mentioned in the next sentence (see Martin, p. 61, tenth stave).

(p. 117) *dominant harmony of the previous bar...* This habit is one of Charlie's clearest derivations from the work of Coleman Hawkins, which contains numerous instances, for example in the famous 1939 *Body And Soul*. His re-entry after the bass solo on his 1943 *The Man I Love* is even more striking in delaying the harmony expected in the first bar of the chorus.

(p. 117) *observed by the rhythm-section...* In the second half of bar 24, the piano plays B9(13) as a flatted-5th substitute for F7 (while the E-flat and B from the bass fit perfectly), followed by their expected B-flat major7 at the start of bar 25. Parker, on the other hand, begins bar 25 by outlining the B9(13) arpeggio against the rhythm-section's B-flat major7, resulting in a considerable clash on paper but which is heard as merely playing with the time.

It should be noted that Martin's transcription (p. 81) has incorrect pitches in place of this arpeggio: in fact, B, D-sharp, F-sharp, A and C-sharp should precede the high A-flat (or G-sharp), and the next nine notes after that are all shown a semitone too high. It goes without saying that any theoretical conclusions based on inaccurate transcription are suspect.

(p. 117) *"I would say that..."* Interviews by Per Møller Hansen for Danmarks Radio (1970s), edited by Maxine Gordon and released on Blue Note BN34200.

(p. 117) *"The flat 5, the flat 9th"...* The theoretical background to all this – including the way in which flatted 9ths and raised 9ths are derived from the flatted-5th substitution of the root – is conveniently summarized by Koch (pp. 19–20).

(p. 117) *soloists such as Roy Eldridge...* Charlie's familiarity with Eldridge is demonstrated by the fact that his first-ever recording (c. 1940) contains a quotation from the classic Chu Berry–Roy Eldridge version of *Body And Soul*. His own use of raised and flatted 9ths may also be inferred from his *Yardbird Suite*, already in the repertoire of the McShann band and often said to be based on the chords of *Rosetta* – when recorded in 1946, its second bar is played over IVm–bVII7 but, if *Rosetta* was the chord-sequence, the melody would contain a raised 9th and flatted 9th.

(p. 117) *After You've Gone...* The relevant portion of the clarinet solo, closely coordinated with Wilson's backing, is transcribed (see bar 20) in the Goodman entry of the *New Grove Dictionary Of Jazz* (2001 edn, vol. 2, p. 62).

(p. 118) *might be construed as...* This is a more impressionistic manner of using unexpected intervals than that derived from the flatted-5th substitution, but it might well have been thought of by Parker as an example of the same phenomenon.

(p. 118) *a quotation from another song...* As first pointed out by Giddins (*Ridin' On A Blue Note*, New York: Oxford University Press, 1981), Parker's opening phrase mirrors Sam Coslow's *A Table In A Corner*, which must have lodged in the altoist's unconscious when it was new, again in the late 1930s.

(p. 118) *take A has been analysed...* Williams, p. 137; Tirro, p. 370 (beware some strangely inaccurate chord symbols with this version); Koch, pp. 339–42; Martin, pp. 71–82.

(p. 118) *a suitable case for analysis...* As in one of the fundamental debates concerning jazz education, scepticism is in order if writers (or teachers) select a topic to write about (or teach) simply because it's easy to write about (or teach).

(p. 118) *two of the slowest ballad performances...* Take A, taken at Parker's preferred tempo, needs 2mins:00secs to complete the 32 bars of his solo, compared to 1:54 for both Lester Young's 1945 *These Foolish Things* and Billie Holiday's 1944 version of *Embraceable You*. Since take A was deemed too long to print as a single release, take B begins at a slightly brighter tempo before gradually slowing to near the speed of take A.

Though take B was first to be released, Russell later found a way to get take A onto a single after all. Confusingly, he then put it out under the same catalogue number. (The same thing happened years later to John Coltrane's *Ascension*.)

(p. 118) *the original Gershwin song...* It is a pity some writers give the impression that Parker's solos are based on the same chord-sequence as published. A straight version would likely begin with F | Fo | C/E – Gm/D | C7 but Parker's amended chord-sequence (which lends great effectiveness to his prominent G in bar 2 of both takes) is F | Bø – E7 | Gm7 | C7. This amendment was possibly devised by Tadd Dameron, whereas Bud Powell used a further re-harmonization of bars 3–4.

(p. 119) *recorded only minutes later...* It would be fascinating to know if there was a playback of take A in the studio. My guess is not, since probably both artist and producer would not have wanted to break the spell after it became clear the first version was too long. (Russell's book makes no mention of the second take, and his amateurish musical description of take A is useless too.) If there was no playback, most of the resemblances between takes must arise from the melodic vocabulary Charlie found appropriate to this song – but see also the next three notes.

(p. 119) *interchangeable use of short motives...* Owens was probably inspired by the statement of Lennie Tristano (in Reisner, p. 224) likening the use of short phrases able to be "used in conjunction with any of the other phrases" to "a jig-saw puzzle which can be put together in hundreds of ways."

(p. 119) *one familiar formula...* Most interestingly, Woideck (*Music and Life*, p. 114) also finds this phrase in the 1943 tenor rendition of *Body And Soul*.

(p. 119) *would come out very differently...* The idea receives some indirect confirmation from Koch (p. 339), who observes that Charlie's various versions of *Out Of Nowhere* contain ornamentation that is hardly ever used on other songs.

(p. 119) *less convincing...* Even Martin (footnote 128, p. 147) uses these words about his analysis of Parker's first chorus, compared to the final chorus. Underlining the significance of rhythm, Tirro (p. 289) has a chart showing the huge variety of note values employed in Charlie's solo here, whereas Martin is only concerned to find a justification for the note choices.

(p. 119) *the "blue" inflection...* See various transcriptions. Woideck (*Music and Life*, pp. 237–39), drawing on his experience as a saxophonist, notates these blue 3rds with a C-sharp grace-note (A-sharp in alto key) whereas other transcribers imply only a manipulation of the embouchure.

(p. 121)   Confirmation *and* Quasimado... Perhaps the lyrical chord-sequences of these two (*Quasimado* is a written line on the harmonies of *Embraceable You*) inspired the creation of melodies more compelling than, say, *Charlie's Wig*, which is based on the relatively static *When I Grow Too Old To Dream* (and which is presumably so titled because of using the original title's initials as an acronym).

(p. 121)   *The former has been described...* Williams, p. 147.

(p. 121)   *various witnesses such as...* Reisner, p. 229. In an interview at present untraced (possibly in a French periodical), saxophonist Sam Rivers made a similar observation about Charlie's playing on his visits to Boston.

(p. 122)   *Gillespie apparently wrote...* Bill Kirchner (notes to Savoy 92911) quotes Joshua Berrett's suggestion that the intro "possibly is derived from the closing four bars of the Gershwin original ('Who could ask for anything more') with some possible rhythmic overlay from Khachaturian's *Sabre Dance*" – which sounds just too musicological for words.

(p. 122)   *alto-and-trumpet theme...* A combination of writers has pointed out that the *Hymn* theme (a) is identical to that used on the McShann group's Wichita session, eventually released as *Wichita Blues*, (b) is derived from the same source as the Ellington-Miley *Black And Tan Fantasy* theme, i.e. Stanley Adams's *The Holy City* and (c) is re-used by Miles Davis in his 1956 *Trane's Blues*. It might be worth adding that (d) it was also heard as a backing for Johnny Hodges in late-period versions of the Ellington-Hodges *Things Ain't What They Used To Be*.

(p. 122)   *of the kind Davis later undertook...* Such dialogues in later Davis records are heard in the 1956 versions of *The Theme* and *Salt Peanuts* and the 1961 quintet (with Hank Mobley) on versions of *No Blues/Pfrancing*.

(p. 122)   Another Hair-Do *also mixes...* Although under a different title, there is an interestingly loose version of this same idea by the Ornette Coleman associates Prince Lasha and Sonny Simmons (on *Red's Mood*, Contemporary OJCCD1945-2). The track, also a 12-bar blues but in the key of A, similarly mixes ensemble and solo statements, and interprets the timing of the closing phrase even more loosely than Parker on his master take.

(p. 123)   *a melodic relationship...* As well as the comparison offered here, there is the melodic similarity of bar 3 to bar 2 of the secondary theme of Ravel's *Boléro*, worth noting since at least twice Charlie included Ravel among his favourite composers.

(p. 123)   *a famous 1965 London concert...* The music was released on LP (Polydor 623246/623247) but is not yet reissued on CD. The audience member was saxophonist Harry Salisbury.

8 confirmation

(p. 125)   *"I thought it wasn't..."* Jazz Review, September–October 1960.

(p. 125)   *a fellow musician...* Both theories were mentioned in print for the first time by Woideck, *Music and Life*, p. 50.

(p. 126)   *"Later, I realized..."* Chan Richardson Parker, p. 53.

(p. 127)   *undergoing a course of treatment...* Nisenson, p. 68.

(p. 127)   *was being held temporarily...* Davis, p. 178.

(p. 127)   *only fifteen months after...* New York Times, June 25, 1956. Russell made his comment during a panel discussion at the International Association of Jazz Record Collectors conference, London, July 1994.

(p. 127)   *"just another broke..."* Davis, p. 78.

(p. 128)   *The fourth, unnamed writer...* Orrin Keepnews, e-mail to the author, August 7, 2004.

(p. 130)   *a would-be saxophonist...* An early c. 1958 recording by Lenny Bruce (*The Interview*, Fantasy FCD60-023) includes a hilarious impersonation of another fictional junkie revelling in misplaced idolatry, with the words "I got Bird's axe, you know. He was really tore up the last time I saw him."

(p. 131)   *other original 32-bar sequences...* One of these, *Jayne* (named after Ornette's then wife Jayne Cortez) is played, except for bars 3–4 and 19–20, over the chords of one of Charlie's favourite standards, *Out Of Nowhere*. Bars 25–28, however, have a melody implying chords similar to bars 29–32 in Sonny Rollins's *Airegin*, and pianist Walter Norris's failure to use that sequence makes Ornette's tune sound less harmonically-based (and more modal) than it was.

(p. 131)   *began reviving the repertoire...* Just so that nobody is tempted to ascribe this development to Wynton Marsalis, it's worth recalling he was eleven years old at the time.

(p. 132)   *he stood impassively still...* Many saxophonists who saw him play, or have seen the video evidence, have made the observation summarized by Chan Richardson Parker (p. 56), "He didn't waste time, space, and effort with his fingers. They hugged the keys. That gave him his rapid execution."

(p. 133)   *preserved in an attic...* Gary Giddins, notes to Stash ST-260.

(p. 133)   *incompletely documented, partially preserved...* Phil Schaap's contribution to the notes of Mosaic MD7-129 underlines the enormity of the problems he had to solve.

(p. 135)   *reflected her view of Charlie...* Stanley Crouch, one of the many African-American writers and musicians who criticized the movie's stance, put it more strongly. "All of the things that Chan knew little about, or preferred to ignore, remain outside the film" (*New Republic*, February 27, 1989, in Woideck, *Companion*, pp. 251–62).

(p. 135) *The portrayal of Parker...* The film's music director Lennie Niehaus noted that Eastwood's first edit was four hours long, which Warners required to be drastically shortened. "He says 'Well, I can't cut out this part, and I can't cut out that part.' But he got it down to two hours 40, and they accepted that" (interview by Nick St. George for Testbed/BBC Radio 2, recorded November 16, 2004).

(p. 135) *While possibly acceptable on paper...* Doris Parker is quoted (in Crouch, ibid.) as saying "Charlie didn't play by himself. When you take him away from his real musicians, you destroy what inspired him to play what he did." This collective mode of creation, though very present in all schools of jazz, is frequently ignored in enthusiasts' appreciation of the music, and indeed in most academic writing about it.

(p. 135) *airshot of the Jay McShann band...* One wonders seriously how long it can be before someone turns up a live recording of the 1943 Hines band or the 1944 Eckstine band.

(p. 135) *an annual Charlie Parker Jazz Festival...* In 2003 organization of this was taken over by New York's City Parks Foundation. The two free concerts of the 2004 event, one in Tompkins Square and one in Marcus Garvey Park in Harlem, included a new composition by Jimmy Heath entitled *Bird Is The Word* and commissioned by the Foundation.

(p. 136) *her archive of memorabilia...* Before the sale, some of the documents pictured in the book *To Bird With Love*, and several others that were not, were borrowed and copied (with permission) by Ken Vail for his 1996 publication *Bird's Diary 1945–1955*.

(p. 136) *jazz group led by Charlie Watts...* The group's two Parker-related albums were released in conjunction with the re-publication of Watts' tiny 1965 volume of drawings and ornithological captions entitled *Ode to a High-flying Bird* (Continuum, 1991).

(p. 136) *roughly equivalent to $185,000...* A little over ten years later on February 20, 2005, Charlie's King Super-20 realized $225,000, the top price at a sale of jazz memorabilia by the New York auction house Guernsey's.

(p. 136) *But in 50 or 75 years...* Interview by Nat Hentoff, op. cit.

(p. 138) *with Bird still outside...* The local Jazz Ambassadors organization still hopes to provide a new stone for the grave at Lincoln Cemetery.

bibliography

Baker, Chet. *As Though I Had Wings*. New York: St. Martin's Press, 1997.

Berliner, Paul. *Thinking in Jazz*. Chicago: University of Chicago Press, 1994.

Bjorn, Lars, and Jim Gallert. *Before Motown*. Ann Arbor: University of Michigan Press, 2002.

Chilton, John. *Who's Who of Jazz*. 4th ed. London: Macmillan, 1985.

Dahl, Linda. *Morning Glory: A Biography of Mary Lou Williams*. New York: Pantheon, 1999.

Dance, Stanley, *The World of Count Basie*. New York: Scribners, 1980.

Dankworth, John. *Jazz in Revolution*. London: Constable, 1998.

Davis, Miles, with Quincy Troupe. *Miles: The Autobiography*. New York: Simon and Schuster, 1989.

Ellington, Mercer, with Stanley Dance. *Duke Ellington in Person*. Boston: Crescendo, 1978.

Feather, Leonard. *Inside Jazz*. New York: Robbins, 1949.

Giddins, Gary. *Celebrating Bird*. New York: Beech Tree Books, 1987.

Gillespie, Dizzy, with Al Fraser. *Dizzy: To Be or Not to Bop*. Garden City, NY: Doubleday, 1979.

Gitler, Ira. *Jazz Masters of the Forties*. New York: Macmillan, 1966.

—*Swing to Bop*. New York: Oxford University Press, 1985.

Grime, Kitty, with Valerie Wilmer. *Jazz at Ronnie Scott's*. London: Robert Hale, 1979.

Harrison, Max. *Charlie Parker*. London: Cassell, 1960.

Haydon, Geoffrey. *Quintet of the Year*. London: Aurum, 2002.

Hentoff, Nat. *Jazz Is*. New York: Random House, 1976.

Hentoff, Nat, and Albert McCarthy, eds. *Jazz*. New York: Rinehart, 1959.

Hodeir, André. *Jazz: Its Evolution and Essence*. New York: Grove, 1956; first published in French as *Hommes et Problèmes de Jazz*. Paris: Au Portulan/Flammarion, 1954.

Jones, Max. *Talking Jazz*. Basingstoke: Macmillan, 1987.

Keepnews, Orrin. *The View from Within*. New York: Oxford University Press, 1988.

Koch, Lawrence O. *Yardbird Suite: A Compendium of the Music and Life of Charlie Parker*. Rev. ed. Boston: Northeastern University Press, 1999.

Lyons, Jimmy, with Ira Kamin. *Dizzy, Duke, the Count and Me*. San Francisco: California Living, 1978.

Martin, Henry. *Charlie Parker and Thematic Improvisation*. Lanham, MD: Scarecrow Press, 1996.

McCarthy, Albert. *Big Band Jazz*. London: Barrie & Jenkins, 1974.

Meehan, Norman. *Time Will Tell: Conversations with Paul Bley*. Berkeley: Berkeley Hills Books, 2003.

Miller, Mark. *Cool Blues*. London, Ontario: Nightwood Editions, 1989.

Morgenstern, Dan. *Living with Jazz*. New York: Pantheon, 2004.

Nisenson, Eric. *Open Sky: Sonny Rollins and His World of Improvisation*. New York: St. Martin's Press, 2000.

O'Grady, John. *O'Grady: The Life and Times of Hollywood's No.1 Private Eye*. Los Angeles: J.P. Tarcher, 1974.

Oliphant, Dave, ed. *The Bebop Revolution in Words and Music*. Austin, TX: Harry Ransom Humanities Research Center, University of Texas, 1994.

Owens, Thomas. *Bebop: The Music and its Players*. New York: Oxford University Press, 1995.

Parker, Chan Richardson. *My Life in E-flat*. Columbia, SC: University of South Carolina Press, 1999. First published in French translation as *Ma Vie En Mi Bémol*. Paris: Plon, 1993.

Parker, Chan Richardson, and Francis Paudras. *To Bird With Love*. Poitiers: Editions Wizlov, 1981.

Priestley, Brian. *Mingus: A Critical Biography*. London: Quartet, 1982.

Reisner, Robert. *Bird: The Legend of Charlie Parker*. New York: Citadel, 1962.

Russell, Ross. *Bird Lives!* New York: Charterhouse, 1973.

Schuller, Gunther. *The Swing Era*. New York: Oxford University Press, 1989.

Shapiro, Nat, and Nat Hentoff, eds. *Hear Me Talkin' to You*. New York: Rinehart, 1955.

Shipton, Alyn. *Groovin' High*. New York: Oxford University Press, 1999.

Sidran, Ben. *Talking Jazz*. San Francisco: Pomegranate, 1992.

Taylor, Art. *Notes and Tones*. New York: Perigee Books, 1982.

Tirro, Frank. *Jazz: A History*. 2nd ed. New York: W.W. Norton, 1993.

Vail, Ken. *Bird's Diary 1945–1955*. London: Castle Communications, 1996.

Wein, George, with Nate Chinen. *Myself Among Others*. Cambridge, MA: Da Capo, 2003.

Williams, Martin. *The Jazz Tradition*. Rev. ed. New York: Oxford University Press, 1983.

Woideck, Carl. *Charlie Parker: His Music and Life*. Ann Arbor: University of Michigan Press, 1996.

Woideck, Carl, ed. *The Charlie Parker Companion*. New York: Schirmer, 1998.

index